# What Your Colleagues Are Saying...

MW00772242

"This book brings together the best of Visible Learning and the teach[ing of]
learning intentions, success criteria, misconceptions, formative eval[uation is]
stunning. Rich in exemplars, grounded in research about practice, a[nd relating]
surface and deep learning in math, it's a great go-to book for all who tea[ch] [math]ematics."

—John Hattie, **Laureate Professor,**
**Deputy Dean of MGSE, Director of the Melbourne Education Research Institute,**
**Melbourne Graduate School of Education**

"This handbook supports teachers in moving from pacing to planning instruction by providing the tools needed to ensure that mathematics lessons work for every student. More important, it will engage teachers in the critical process of continual improvement. It is a must-have for teachers, leaders, and mathematics educators alike!"

—Matt Larson, **President,**
**National Council of Teachers of Mathematics**

"Often teachers entering the classroom have had little opportunity for extensive lesson planning in their preparation programs. Throughout the book, definitions and explanations are clear so that readers share a common understanding of the language. As a teacher reads, the vignettes encourage the reader to reflect on similar situations in their own classrooms. The well-written questions included in the text will help guide teachers to personal insights that ultimate lead to increased student learning."

—Connie S. Schrock, **Emporia State University,**
**National Council of Supervisors of Mathematics President, 2017–2019**

"We all know that good instruction is well-planned instruction. We also know that effective lesson planning is a complicated decision-making process. This incredibly practical book—filled with delightful vignettes and clarifying examples—provides powerful ideas and structures for simplifying the complexities of planning great K–2 mathematics lessons. This book is a wonderful resource for teachers, coaches, administrators, and teacher educators."

—Steve Leinwand,
**American Institutes for Research**

"Finally! *The Mathematics Lesson-Planning Handbook* offers that necessary blueprint for serious analysis of the planning process. Planning to teach mathematics is serious business, and this book goes way beyond thinking about the mathematics standard/objective for the next day's lesson, or jotting notes for a planning book. The *Handbook* will truly engage teachers and communities of learning in a carefully choreographed grade-level designated thread of mathematics tasks, which serve as anchors for developing understanding and use of each aspect of the planning process. This book is a treasure, and will be read, re-read, and referenced daily!"

—Francis (Skip) Fennell, **Professor of Education,**
**McDaniel College and Past-President of the National Council of**
**Teachers of Mathematics and the Association of Mathematics Teacher Educators**

"*The Mathematics Lesson-Planning Handbook* is a comprehensive and practical guide for coaches and teachers of mathematics in Grades K–2. It provides the background that teachers need before they even begin to write a lesson plan! It then incorporates the research on what teachers need to think about as they begin to lay out a plan for instruction that will meet the needs of all K–2 students and moves on to effective facilitation. This guide provides a roadmap to planning effective lessons that will provide the essential foundation to ensure that all primary level students begin their mathematics journey with high quality teaching and learning. This book is a must for every K–2 teacher, coach or school's professional library!"

—Linda M. Gojak, **Past President,**
**National Council of Teachers of Mathematics**

"One of the hallmarks of accomplished K–2 teachers of mathematics is the guidance they provide to help students *own* how to learn. In *The Mathematics Lesson-Planning Handbook: Your Blueprint for Building Cohesive Lessons*, authors Kobett, Miles, and Williams provide a clear, engaging, and masterful roadmap for helping each and every teacher *own* the lessons they design and use each and every day. The authors reveal the purposes, the success criteria, and the nature of the mathematical tasks and materials to be chosen. They describe in detail the student engagement necessary to design daily mathematics lessons that will significantly impact student learning. Reading, listening to, and using their wisdom and advice will result in an empowering impact on each and every teacher and teacher leader of K–2 mathematics."

—Timothy Kanold, **Educator and Author**

"This is what we've been waiting for: a go-to resource for planning and facilitating mathematics lessons in K–2! Teachers must consider the needs of their students, relevant mathematical content, and appropriate pedagogy when designing and implementing effective learning opportunities. Through authentic vignettes and examples, connections to relevant research, and guiding reflection questions, this *Handbook* guides readers through the process from beginning to end."

—Susie Katt, **K–2 Mathematics Coordinator, Lincoln Public Schools**

"Planning is so much more than identifying materials, making copies, or filling out a form. Many of us were not trained to identify purpose, think about our students, look for quality instructional tasks, consider representations, or anticipate what our students will do. Finally, this handbook is here! We have our blueprint. This tool is a must-have for anyone new to teaching mathematics or anyone else who supports those who teach mathematics."

—John SanGiovanni, **Coordinator, Elementary Mathematics,**
**Howard County Public School System, MD**

"Planning is one of the most important instructional activities that teachers undertake. But how many teachers know how to plan lessons that are purposeful, coherent, and rigorous that also take into account the rich perspectives of diverse classroom of students? This teacher resource makes explicit what it takes to plan lessons that truly support student learning while also speaking to principals, coaches, and preservice educators who support teacher learning. I will certainly be using this valuable resource in my own work with teachers."

—Linda Ruiz Davenport, **Director of K–12 Mathematics,**
**Office of Instructional Research and Development, Boston Public Schools**

"This book is a must-read for anyone who wants to challenge themselves to reexamine their math instruction. The interesting examples and challenging reflection questions make this book perfect for individual or group reading."

—Janel Frazier, **Classroom Teacher,**
**Montgomery County Public School System, Upper Marlboro, MD**

"This must-have book has well thought-out lesson plans that combine rich tasks with high quality questions. I am confident that every teacher, administrator, specialist, and math supervisor needs to have a copy of this book."

—Kathleen Williams Londeree, **Math Specialist/Coach,**
**Caroline County Schools, VA**

"The book is a step-by-step guide for building a cohesive lesson. It is research-based and relevant to what teachers are being asked to do."

—Ann Thomas Lewis, **Content Coach,**
**Stafford County Public Schools, Fredericksburg, VA**

"In the continuing quest for congruence between the written, taught, and assessed curricula, the weakest link is often the taught curriculum. *The Mathematics Lesson-Planning Handbook* will help all teachers strengthen the instructed curricula by developing lesson plans with coherence, purpose and rigor throughout. The *Handbook* is a must for teachers of all levels of experience."

—Deborah Kiger Bliss, **K–12 Mathematics Coordinator,**
**Virginia Department of Education, Retired**

"*The Mathematics Lesson-Planning Handbook* will make planning for any mathematics class more meaningful. Reading this book will truly enable any teacher to develop organized and well prepared plan and move from the written objective to quality instructional delivery. The many grade level examples and templates are a must-have for any classroom teacher. I highly recommend this user-friendly resource for ALL mathematics teachers, and it is greatly needed as education meets the many educational challenges ahead."

—Debbie Anderson, **Retired Administrator,**
**Washington County, VA**

"At a time when open educational resources are flooding our classrooms, *The Mathematics Lesson-Planning Handbook* helps bring focus and intentionality as to why we should choose one task over another. It thoughtfully lays out the smaller nuances that are most commonly overlooked and it helps bring clarity to the art of building coherence."

—Graham Fletcher, **Math Specialist, Atlanta, GA**

# *The Mathematics Lesson-Planning Handbook, Grades K–2*
# at a Glance

**A step-by-step guide to walk you through every facet of planning cohesive, standards-based mathematics lessons, including**

Asking yourself essential questions about your standards-based learning intentions, lesson purpose, tasks, materials, lesson format, and how to anticipate and assess student thinking

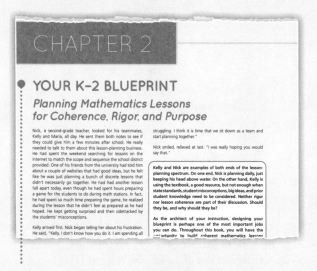

## CHAPTER 2

### YOUR K–2 BLUEPRINT
#### *Planning Mathematics Lessons for Coherence, Rigor, and Purpose*

Nick, a second-grade teacher, looked for his teammates, Kelly and Maria, all day. He sent them both notes to see if they could give him a few minutes after school. He really needed to talk to them about this lesson-planning business. He had spent the weekend searching for lessons on the Internet to match the scope and sequence the school district provided. One of his friends from the university had told him about a couple of websites that had good ideas, but he felt like he was just planning a bunch of discrete lessons that didn't necessarily go together. He had had another lesson fall apart today, even though he had spent hours preparing a game for the students to do during math stations. In fact, he had spent so much time preparing the game, he realized during the lesson that he didn't feel as prepared as he had hoped. He kept getting surprised and then sidetracked by the students' misconceptions.

Kelly arrived first. Nick began telling her about his frustration. He said, "Kelly, I don't know how you do it. I am spending all

struggling. I think it is time that we sit down as a team and start planning together."

Nick smiled, relieved at last. "I was really hoping you would say that."

Kelly and Nick are examples of both ends of the lesson-planning spectrum. On one end, Nick is planning daily, just keeping his head above water. On the other hand, Kelly is using the textbook, a good resource, but not enough when state standards, student misconceptions, big ideas, and prior student knowledge need to be considered. Neither rigor nor lesson coherence are part of their discussion. Should they be, and why should they be?

As the architect of your instruction, designing your blueprint is perhaps one of the most important jobs you can do. Throughout this book, you will have the opportunity to build coherent mathematics lessons

Using your curriculum to think about all of your lessons as a cohesive progression across units, throughout the year

## CHAPTER 3

### LAYING YOUR FOUNDATION
#### *It Starts With Big Ideas, Essential Questions, and Standards*

As required by a new district policy, two veteran second-grade teachers, Roberta and Manny, sat down with their school administrative leader to review their students' benchmark assessments. Roberta, who had not yet seen the results, had been nervous all day about this meeting. She knew that Leah, the school principal, supported their work, but the situation was still incredibly nerve-wracking.

Leah pulled up the screen with the results and displayed them. "Let's just take a few minutes to look at them before we dis...

At first, ...
looked ...
his face. ...

Leah sai...
the stud...
These sc...

Leah said, "I am so glad that all this effort paid off! Now, let's look at what we need to work on."

Roberta said, "My students were completely confused about the representations used for equations."

Manny exclaimed, "Mine were, too! Do you think it has anything to do with the new standards? We always taught equations, but we never used those balances that were on the test. We are going to need to review those new standards."

## CHAPTER 6

### CHOOSING TASKS
#### *The Heart of a Lesson*

Frustrated, Jessica stared at the mathematics standard and the lesson seed idea provided by her school district (Figure 6.1):

**Figure 6.1**

| Standard | Lesson Task |
| --- | --- |
| Add up to four two-digit numbers using place value models. | Jacob was on vacation at the beach with his family and found 23 seashells on the beach on Monday. On Tuesday, he found 13 more. On Wednesday, he found 34 seashells. How many seashells did Jacob find? |

**Figure 6.2**

This is a map of Dory's travels.

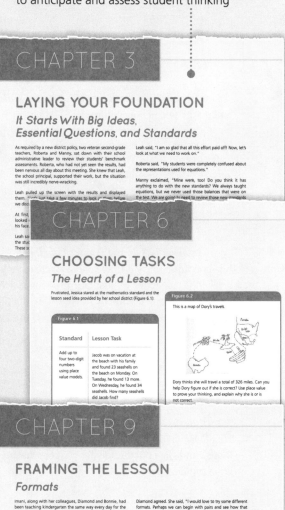

Dory thinks she will travel a total of 326 miles. Can you help Dory figure out if she is correct? Use place value to prove your thinking, and explain why she is or is not correct.

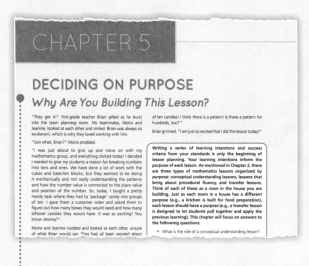

## CHAPTER 5

### DECIDING ON PURPOSE
#### *Why Are You Building This Lesson?*

"They got it!" first-grade teacher Brian yelled as he burst into the team planning room. His teammates, Moira and Jeanine, looked at each other and smiled. Brian was always so exuberant, which is why they loved working with him.

"Got what, Brian?" Moira prodded.

"I was just about to give up and move on with my mathematics group, and everything clicked today! I decided I needed to give my students a reason for breaking numbers into tens and ones. We have done a lot of work with the cubes and base-ten blocks, but they seemed to be doing it mechanically and not really understanding the patterns and how the number value is connected to the place value and position of the number. So, today, I taught a pretty meaty task where they had to 'package' candy into groups of ten. I gave them a customer order and asked them to figure out how many boxes they would need and how many leftover candies they would have. It was so exciting! You know Jeremy?"

Moira and Jeanine nodded and looked at each other, unsure of what Brian would say. They had all been worried about

of ten candies! I think there is a pattern! Is there a pattern for hundreds, too?"

Brian grinned. "I am just so excited that I did this lesson today!"

Writing a series of learning intentions and success criteria from your standards is only the beginning of lesson planning. Your learning intentions inform the *purpose* of each lesson. As mentioned in Chapter 2, there are three types of mathematics lessons organized by purpose: conceptual understanding lessons, lessons that bring about procedural fluency, and transfer lessons. Think of each of these as a room in the house you are building. Just as each room in a house has a different purpose (e.g., a kitchen is built for food preparation), each lesson should have a purpose (e.g., a transfer lesson is designed to let students pull together and apply the previous learning). This chapter will focus on answers to the following questions:

- What is the role of a conceptual understanding lesson?

Determining whether you're designing a lesson to focus on conceptual understanding, procedural fluency, or transfer of knowledge

## CHAPTER 9

### FRAMING THE LESSON
#### *Formats*

Imani, along with her colleagues, Diamond and Bonnie, had been teaching kindergarten the same way every day for the past five years. At this point, Imani really wanted to shake up the way they had been organizing the math class. She felt like it had not been meeting all of her students' needs, particularly the stragglers, who were not working unless she was constantly reminding them, and she wanted to try some new things to engage all of her students. They needed more opportunities to talk with one another and learn how to work together on problems. In order to facilitate this kind of shared experience, Imani knew that she would need to be available to monitor the students while they were working; she did not want to be tied up in an instructional group. She still believed in small-group instruction; she just felt that her students needed to be working together more often.

As Imani sat down with her team, she shared the following: "I think we really need to take a look at our lesson format. We have been using the same center/math rotations for years. I am not sure we are building enough opportunities for math

Diamond agreed. She said, "I would love to try some different formats. Perhaps we can begin with pairs and see how that goes. I think the students will be very excited about solving some problems together. We can also work on the social learning intentions at the same time!"

Bonnie was also on board. She said, "Let's do it! I suggest that we begin with the inventory task we did in the workshop last week. Let's plan this conceptual lesson first, try it out, and come back and share our thoughts."

**Lessons need structure. Lesson formats give you that structure. Lesson formats refer to how you organize your class for the lesson. Some lessons work better when students are in collaborative groups, and some are more effective when students move around to different centers. For instance, rotating stations may be a good decision for a procedural fluency lesson but not for the introductory lesson on a new concept. As you select a lesson format for a particular lesson, you should base**

# CHAPTER 11

## PLANNING TO
## LAUNCH THE LESSON

Amirah, a second-grade teacher, began her lesson by displaying the picture in Figure 11.1.

### Figure 11.1

Amirah asked, "What do you notice about the picture? Please let me know about something your Turn and Talk Buddy noticed."

Hands waved wildly in the air as students strained to share their partners' observations. Amirah wrote quickly to include what they saw. Then she asked her students to share their think and wonders (Figure 11.2).

### Figure 11.2

| See | Think and Wonder |
|---|---|
| It looks like a sandbox. | Will she fall? |
| The girl is jumping. | What team is she on? |
| The girl is in the air. | How high is she in the air? |
| The girl might fall. | How far can she jump? |
| There are numbers. | What are the numbers for? |

# CHAPTER 12

## PLANNING TO
## FACILITATE THE LESSON

Janey, a kindergarten teacher, had always imagined herself as an educator. As a child, she collected worksheets from her teachers and stored them in her basement, which she set up as a school. She cajoled neighborhood friends into playing school with her for hours on end.

By the time that Janey actually started teaching, she knew that the approach to education had shifted from her own days as a student. She recognized the need to encourage her students to construct meaning through carefully planned activities and to allow her students to talk to each other, explain their thinking, and even productively struggle, but she still felt conflicted with how to best support her students' communication skills. She hated to watch them struggle, even a little bit. She frequently found herself falling right into the trap of saving a student way too early instead of asking a question or providing a suggestion. Just the other day, one of her students, Jeremy, had asked for help, and she had picked up a pencil and started showing him what to do. She hadn't even realized it until she glanced at him and caught him grinning from ear to ear.

very fashionable principal. For this lesson, the students traced their principal on paper, measured, and designed clothes for her paper cutout to wear. The project concluded with a fashion show of all the paper principal cutouts and clothing designs, complete with measurements. Both Janey and David had been amazed at how well the kindergartners had worked on the project, particularly as they had negotiated decisions about who would measure Mrs. Palmer. Janey and David had spent all of their time supporting the students and questioning them as they worked.

As the teachers discussed this lesson with their math coach, David asked, "So how can we capture that kind of energy and student-centered learning every day?"

**Witnessing those moments when students are engaged productively in mathematical thinking, reasoning, and communication is so exciting to see. Sometimes they**

# CHAPTER 13

## PLANNING TO
## CLOSE THE LESSON

The second-grade team members at Hollins Elementary School were discussing some of their closure experiences.

"Closure?" questioned Abe, a third-year teacher. "I hardly ever get a chance for closure. My lessons always go to the last minute and sometimes even run over into recess."

"I have that problem sometimes," chimed in Jane, the veteran teacher in the group. "I am getting better, but last week my class had to remind me to stop because it was time for lunch! My goal for this year is to improve my closure. I'm working on it."

Cilia, a second-year teacher, spoke up. "I went to a workshop this summer and they talked about how important closure is to determine how students are grasping a lesson. I have been trying some of the suggestions. I like using exit slips, and my kids seem to like them. I let them write me notes at the end of the lesson to tell me if there was anything they didn't understand. I have been using those notes to help me launch my next lesson."

Jane said, "It's funny that you mentioned a workshop. I went to a workshop about closure two years ago. We discussed how closure is about reflection. And we used exit slips too, but we learned that there are other things you can do, like pair sharing. Another option is to do a more in-depth exit task, like we learned in the formative assessment workshop."

"Stop keeping all these ideas a secret!" Abe said. Then he smiled and added, "You two need to do a closure workshop for me!"

**If you have ever looked at the clock and realized that you not only lack time for closure but also have run overtime, you are not alone. Abe, Jane, and Celia have been working on closure for a few years and continue to struggle to fit it all in. Planning for closure is the first step in using it your classroom. This chapter will discuss closure and several different closure formats while answering the following questions:**

Illustrative vignettes at the start of each chapter focus on a specific part of the lesson-planning process

# In every chapter you will find

Standards
LI and SC
Purpose
Tasks
Materials
Student Thinking
Lesson Structures
Form. Assess.
Lesson Launch
Lesson Facilitation
Closure

Based on these characteristics, it is important to point out that all worthwhile tasks are problems, but not all problems are worthwhile tasks.

To determine if a task is worthwhile for you to use in a lesson, use the rubric shown in Figure 6.3. The first column identifies the characteristic, and the next three columns allow you to rate the degree to which you feel the task has met that characteristic by checking the box, with 1 being not acceptable and 3 being a good example of that characteristic. The final column is for any comments you would like to discuss with your colleagues.

### Figure 6.3

**Determining a Worthwhile Task Rubric**

| Characteristic | 1 | 2 | 3 | Notes |
|---|---|---|---|---|
| Uses significant mathematics for the grade level | | | | |
| Rich | | | | |
| Problem solving in nature | | | | |
| Authentic/interesting | | | | |
| Equitable | | | | |
| Active | | | | |
| Connects to Standards for Mathematical Practice or Process Standards | | | | |
| High cognitive demand | | | | |

This Determining a Worthwhile Task Rubric can be downloaded for your use at resources.corwin.com/mathlessonplanning/k-2

Thinking about Jennifer and Carlos and their tasks, rate the tasks using the checklist in Figure 6.3. Discuss your results with a colleague. Whose example is a worthwhile task and why? Note your thoughts below.

Opportunities to stop and reflect on your own instruction

Examples of each lesson feature from classrooms in Grades K–2

## WHAT IS THE ROLE OF REPRESENTATIONS IN MATHEMATICS LESSONS?

The Annenberg Learner Foundation (2003) offers this definition:

"Mathematical representation" refers to the wide variety of ways to capture an abstract mathematical concept or relationship. A mathematical representation may be visible, such as a number sentence, a display of manipulative materials, or a graph, but it may also be an internal way of seeing and thinking about a mathematical idea. Regardless of their form, representations can enhance students' communication, reasoning, and problem-solving abilities; help them make connections among ideas; and aid them in learning new concepts and procedures. (para. 2)

Since mathematical concepts are abstract, when teachers teach, they represent the concepts in a variety of ways. Representations can be thought of as a broad category of models. According to Van de Walle et al. (2016), there are seven ways to represent or model mathematical concepts:

1. Manipulatives
2. Pictures or drawings
3. Symbols
4. Language (written or spoken)
5. Real-world situations
6. Graphs
7. Tables

Selecting a representation is a vital part of your decision making while lesson planning. You must decide, "What representations will help achieve the learning intentions of today's lesson?" Here is an example of a teacher using a representation to help students make sense of rounding.

Example: Alvaro

When planning a lesson that involves rounding two-digit numbers, Alvaro, a second-grade teacher, decided to use a number line from 20 to 30. When he asked his students to place the number 23 on the number line, he asked, "Is 23 closer to 20 or 30?"

Alvaro used a number line as a representation to model the relationship of the numbers from 20 to 30 in order. By using this representation, students can easily see that 23 is closer to 20 than 30, working toward a conceptual understanding of rounding.

The charts in Figures 7.1, 7.2, and 7.3 show examples of representations that can be used with selected standards.

### Figure 7.1

**Kindergarten**

| Counting and Cardinality Standards | Representation |
|---|---|
| Know number names and the count sequence. | |
| • Count to 100 by ones and by tens. | |

*(Continued)*

**Building Unit Coherence**

Connecting lesson purposes across a unit develops coherence because you are strategically linking conceptual understanding, procedural fluency, and transfer lessons to build comprehensive understanding of the unit standards. As you develop your lesson, consider the purposes of the lessons that come before and after the lesson you are constructing. Over the course of one unit, you should develop and facilitate lessons with all three purposes, bearing in mind how and when the lesson purposes should be positioned within the unit. Some teachers map out their unit with lesson purposes in mind to ensure that they are developing coherence within lesson purpose (Figure 5.8).

**Figure 5.8**

Unit:

| Day 1 | Day 2 | Day 3 | Day 4 | Day 5 |
|---|---|---|---|---|
| Conceptual | Conceptual | Conceptual | Procedural Fluency | Procedural Fluency |
| Day 6 | Day 7 | Day 8 | Day 9 | Day 10 |
| Conceptual | Conceptual | Conceptual | Procedural Fluency | Transfer |

Now that you have been introduced to the three lesson purposes, reflect on the lessons in your curriculum guide, textbook, or supplemental materials. Can you categorize the lessons into these three categories? Do you notice one type being more prevalent than the others? Note any thoughts or concerns here.

_____

_____

_____

_____

_____

_____

_____

Chapter 5 ■ Deciding on Purpose **63**

Side tabs: Standards | LI and SC | Purpose | Tasks | Materials | Student Thinking | Lesson Structures | Form. Assess | Lesson Launch | Lesson Facilitation | Closure

---

How features of a lesson are interrelated to build cohesiveness across a unit

Bolded key terms that are defined in a glossary in Appendix D

---

# Appendix D

## Glossary

**academic language.** The vocabulary used in schools, textbooks, and other school resources.

**access to high-quality education.** Phrase refers to the National Council of Teachers of Mathematics (NCTM) position statement on equal opportunity to a quality K–12 education for all students. Related to the NCTM position on equitable learning opportunities.

**agency.** The power to act. Students exercise agency in mathematics when they initiate discussions and actively engage in high-level thinking tasks. When students exercise agency, they reason, critique the reasoning of others, and engage in productive struggle.

**algorithm.** In mathematics, it is a series of steps or procedures that, when followed accurately, will produce a correct answer.

**big ideas.** Statements that encompass main concepts in mathematics that cross grade levels, such as place value.

**classroom discourse.** Conversation that occurs in a classroom. Can be teacher to student(s), student(s) to teacher, or student(s) to student(s).

**closed-ended questions.** Questions with only one correct answer.

**closure.** The final activity in a lesson with two purposes: (1) helps the teacher determine what students have learned and gives direction to next steps and (2) provides students the opportunity to reorganize and summarize the information from a lesson in a meaningful way.

**coherence.** Logical sequencing of mathematical ideas. Can be vertical, as in across the grades (e.g., K–2), or can be horizontal, as in across a grade level (e.g., first-grade lessons from September through December).

**common errors.** Mistakes made by students that occur frequently; usually these mistakes are anticipated by the teacher due to their frequency.

**computation.** Using an operation such as addition, subtraction, multiplication, or division to find an answer.

**conceptual understanding.** Comprehension of mathematical concepts, operations, and relationships.

**content standards.** See **standards.**

**decompose.** To break a number down into addends. A number may be decomposed in more than one way (e.g., 12 can be decomposed as 10 + 2, 9 + 3, and 5 + 5 + 2).

**discourse.** See **classroom discourse.**

**distributed practice.** See **spaced practice.**

**district-wide curriculum.** A K–12 document outlining the curriculum for a school system.

**drill.** Repetitive exercises on a specific math skill or procedure.

**English Language Learner (ELL).** A person whose first language is not English but who is learning to speak English.

**essential question.** A question that unifies all of the lessons on a given topic to bring the coherence and purpose to a unit. ... fully linked to the big idea to frame student inquiry, promote critical thinking, and assist in ...

... nd of a lesson or group of lessons that provides a sampling of student performance. An exit task is ...

... lesson closure where students answer a question related to the main idea of the lesson on a slip of ... lips of paper.

Appendix D **199**

---

## HOW DO IDENTITY AND AGENCY INFLUENCE LESSON PLANNING?

**Identity** and **agency** are two concepts that help teachers understand the dynamics that take place in a classroom, which, in turn, helps teachers better understand their students and how best to meet their needs. Identity is how individuals know and see themselves (i.e., student, teacher, good at sports, like math) and how others know and see us (i.e., short, smart, African American). When defined broadly, identity is a concept that brings together all the interrelated elements that teachers and students bring to the classroom, including beliefs, attitudes, emotions, and cognitive capacity (Grootenboer, Lowrie, & Smith, 2006).

Agency is the power to act. Students develop their agency when they actively engage in the learning process (Wenmoth, 2014). Since student learning is greatest in classrooms where students are engaged in high-level thinking and reasoning (Boaler & Staples, 2008), teachers need to ensure that tasks they choose promote this engagement on a regular basis.

The types of lessons teachers design, the approach they take to teaching, the tasks they select, the types of questions they ask, the classroom climate, and social norms of the classroom all affect student engagement and are influenced by the teachers' identity. For example, in a classroom where the teacher sees his or her identity as the giver of knowledge, students are passive recipients of knowledge, working individually at their desks on assignments designed by the teacher. In this approach, there is no opportunity for students to exercise agency. In addition, student identities are lost as they are treated as a group with all the same learning needs rather than as individuals with unique learning needs.

If teachers think about teaching and learning as social activities (Vgotsky, 1962, 1978), then they must take the initiative to put structures into place in the classroom that support the social nature of learning. These

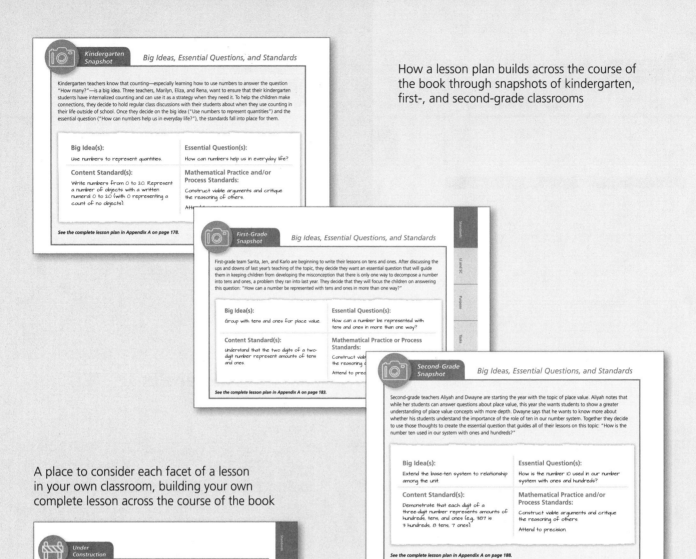

How a lesson plan builds across the course of the book through snapshots of kindergarten, first-, and second-grade classrooms

**Kindergarten Snapshot** — *Big Ideas, Essential Questions, and Standards*

Kindergarten teachers know that counting—especially learning how to use numbers to answer the question "How many?"—is a big idea. Three teachers, Marilyn, Eliza, and Rena, want to ensure that their kindergarten students have internalized counting and can use it as a strategy when they need it. To help the children make connections, they decide to hold regular class discussions with their students about when they use counting in their life outside of school. Once they decide on the big idea ("Use numbers to represent quantities") and the essential question ("How can numbers help us in everyday life?"), the standards fall into place for them.

**Big Idea(s):**
Use numbers to represent quantities.

**Essential Question(s):**
How can numbers help us in everyday life?

**Content Standard(s):**
Write numbers from 0 to 20. Represent a number of objects with a written numeral 0 to 20 (with 0 representing a count of no objects).

**Mathematical Practice and/or Process Standards:**
Construct viable arguments and critique the reasoning of others.

*See the complete lesson plan in Appendix A on page 178.*

**First-Grade Snapshot** — *Big Ideas, Essential Questions, and Standards*

First-grade team Sarita, Jen, and Karlo are beginning to write their lessons on tens and ones. After discussing the ups and downs of last year's teaching of the topic, they decide they want an essential question that will guide them in keeping children from developing the misconception that there is only one way to decompose a number into tens and ones, a problem they ran into last year. They decide that they will focus the children on answering this question: "How can a number be represented with tens and ones in more than one way?"

**Big Idea(s):**
Group with tens and ones for place value.

**Essential Question(s):**
How can a number be represented with tens and ones in more than one way?

**Content Standard(s):**
Understand that the two digits of a two-digit number represent amounts of tens and ones.

**Mathematical Practice or Process Standards:**
Construct viable arguments and critique the reasoning of others.

Attend to precision.

*See the complete lesson plan in Appendix A on page 183.*

**Second-Grade Snapshot** — *Big Ideas, Essential Questions, and Standards*

Second-grade teachers Aliyah and Dwayne are starting the year with the topic of place value. Aliyah notes that while her students can answer questions about place value, this year she wants students to show a greater understanding of place value concepts with more depth. Dwayne says that he wants to know more about whether his students understand the importance of the role of ten in our number system. Together they decide to use those thoughts to create the essential question that guides all of their lessons on this topic: "How is the number ten used in our system with ones and hundreds?"

**Big Idea(s):**
Extend the base-ten system to relationship among the unit.

**Essential Question(s):**
How is the number 10 used in our number system with ones and hundreds?

**Content Standard(s):**
Demonstrate that each digit of a three-digit number represents amounts of hundreds, tens, and ones (e.g., 387 is 3 hundreds, 8 tens, 7 ones).

**Mathematical Practice and/or Process Standards:**
Construct viable arguments and critique the reasoning of others.

Attend to precision.

*See the complete lesson plan in Appendix A on page 188.*

A place to consider each facet of a lesson in your own classroom, building your own complete lesson across the course of the book

**Under Construction**

Now it is your turn! You need to decide what big idea, essential question, and standards you want to build a lesson around. Start with your big idea and then identify the remaining elements.

**Big Idea(s):**

**Essential Question(s):**

**Content Standard(s):**

**Mathematical Practice and/or Process Standards:**

Download the full Lesson-Planning Template from resources.corwin.com/mathlessonplanning/k-2
Remember that you can use the online version of the lesson plan template to begin compiling each section into the full template as your lesson plan grows.

Appendix A shows how the complete lesson plan has come together for each grade

A blank lesson-planning template in Appendix B (also available for download at resources.corwin.com/mathlessonplanning/k-2) for your ongoing use

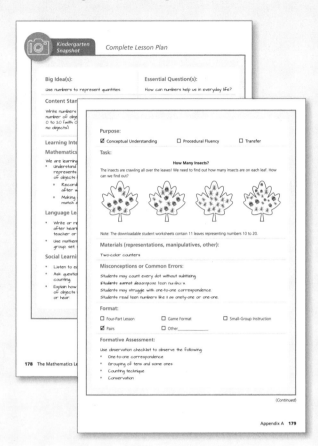

Additional key reading and online resources you may find useful in Appendix C

# The Mathematics Lesson-Planning Handbook

## Grades K–2

## Your Blueprint for Building Cohesive Lessons

**Beth McCord Kobett**

**Ruth Harbin Miles**

**Lois A. Williams**

Name: _____

Department: _____

Learning Team: _____

A JOINT PUBLICATION

NATIONAL COUNCIL OF
TEACHERS OF MATHEMATICS

CORWIN
A SAGE Publishing Company

FOR INFORMATION:

Corwin

A SAGE Company

2455 Teller Road

Thousand Oaks, California 91320

(800) 233-9936

www.corwin.com

SAGE Publications Ltd.

1 Oliver's Yard

55 City Road

London EC1Y 1SP

United Kingdom

SAGE Publications India Pvt. Ltd.

B 1/I 1 Mohan Cooperative Industrial Area

Mathura Road, New Delhi 110 044

India

SAGE Publications Asia-Pacific Pte. Ltd.

3 Church Street

#10-04 Samsung Hub

Singapore 049483

Program Manager, Mathematics: Erin Null

Developmental Editor: Renee Nicholls

Editorial Development Managers: Julie Nemer and Cynthia Gomez

Editorial Assistant: Jessica Vidal

Production Editor: Melanie Birdsall

Copy Editor: Gillian Dickens

Typesetter: Integra

Proofreader: Susan Schon

Indexer: Molly Hall

Cover Designer: Rose Storey

Interior Designer: Scott Van Atta

Marketing Manager: Margaret O'Connor

Copyright © 2018 by Corwin

See, Think, and Wonder task in Chapter 11 submitted by Amirah Russell. Used with permission.

Original drawing in Chapter 6 submitted by Jessica Steinbacher. Used with permission.

*Library of Congress Cataloging-in-Publication Data*

Names: Kobett, Beth McCord, author. | Miles, Ruth Harbin, author. | Williams, Lois A., author.

Title: The mathematics lesson-planning handbook, grades K–2 : your blueprint for building cohesive lessons / Beth McCord Kobett, Ruth Harbin Miles, Lois A. Williams.

Other titles: Mathematics lesson planning handbook, grades K–2

Description: Thousand Oaks, California: Corwin, [2018] | Includes bibliographical references and index.

Identifiers: LCCN 2017050410 | ISBN 9781506387819 (spiral: alk. paper)

Subjects: LCSH: Mathematics—Study and teaching (Elementary) | Curriculum planning.

Classification: LCC QA11.2.K63 2018 | DDC 372.7/044—dc23

LC record available at https://lccn.loc.gov/2017050410

Printed in the United States of America

This book is printed on acid-free paper.

SUSTAINABLE FORESTRY INITIATIVE
Certified Chain of Custody
Promoting Sustainable Forestry
www.sfiprogram.org
SFI-01268
SFI label applies to text stock

18 19 20 21 22 10 9 8 7 6 5 4 3 2 1

# Contents

 Visit the companion website at
**resources.corwin.com/mathlessonplanning/k-2**
for downloadable resources.

# Acknowledgments

To Tim, Hannah, and Jenna for their continuing love, support, and patience. Thank you, Kitty, for always listening. Thank you to Skip and Jon for your warm friendship and our productive collaboration. I am also grateful to my Stevenson University family, David and Debby, for supporting my ideas and to my students (past and present) for inspiring me with your passion and commitment to teaching.

—Beth McCord Kobett

Thank you to all my teaching colleagues in Albemarle County, Virginia, who, over the years, have generously shared their wisdom about teaching and planning mathematics lessons. Some of that wisdom resulted directly from questions for which I had no answers. Additional wisdom resulted from coincidental meetings in the halls between classes when I needed a friendly comment or math joke. I am grateful for what you have taught me.

And to Mike, my husband, for always standing by me.

—Lois A. Williams

Special thanks are due to the very best teacher I have ever known, my incredible father, Dr. Calvin E. Harbin, who taught me to value my education and at the age of 101 is still modeling lifelong learning. Acknowledgment and thanks must also be given to my extraordinary mentors, Dr. Ramona Anshutz and Dr. Shirley A. Hill, who both inspired me to become a mathematics education leader. Their influence and guidance completely changed my life's work. Words could never express the thanks and credit I owe to my incredible writing partners Dr. Ted H. Hull, Dr. Don S. Balka, Linda Gojak, Dr. Lois A. Williams, Dr. Beth Kobett, Dr. Jean Morrow, and Dr. Sandi Cooper who over the years helped me coauthor 37 published books. Most important, I thank my loving husband, Sam Miles, for *always* supporting me.

—Ruth Harbin Miles

We would also like to thank Erin Null for her enduring support for our work on this book, incredible creativity, and commitment to this project. Her insightful perspective, vision for the project, and ability to ask just the right question at just the right time is appreciated and valued.

—Beth, Ruth, and Lois

## Publisher's Acknowledgments

Corwin gratefully acknowledges the contributions of the following reviewers:

Janel Frazier
Classroom Teacher
Montgomery County Public School System
Upper Marlboro, MD

Cathy Martin
Director, Mathematics
Denver Public Schools Denver, CO

Sara Delano Moore
Mathematics Education Consultant
SDM Learning
Kent, OH

John SanGiovanni
Elementary Mathematics Supervisor
Howard County Public School System
Ellicott City, MD

Kathleen Williams Londeree
Math Specialist
Caroline County Schools
Milford, VA

# Letter to K–2 Teachers

Dear K–2 Teachers,

As a teacher, you make hundreds of decisions every day! Many of these decisions fall into the categories of classroom management or paperwork, such as selecting which student gets to be line leader or determining if you need to call that parent tonight or tomorrow. Some decisions are crucial to the classroom climate and environment and set the stage for how students learn. Among the hundreds of decisions you make, the most important decisions influence student learning. Designing, planning, and facilitating lessons reflect critical teacher decision-making opportunities that affect student learning. Oftentimes, these decisions get relegated to a few moments of planning time.

In this book, *The Mathematics Lesson-Planning Handbook: Your Blueprint for Building Cohesive Lessons*, you will experience the decision-making processes that are involved in planning lessons, and you will get to build a lesson of your own using a specially designed format just for you. Your decisions will revolve around creating mathematics lessons with purpose, rigor, and coherence. In addition, we will help you address the decisions involved in selecting your resources (e.g., "How do I make the best use of my textbook or state/district instructional materials?"), your classroom structure (e.g., "Do I use small group or a large group?"), your worthwhile tasks (e.g., "How do I know one when I see it?"), your learning intentions (e.g., "What are my objectives?"), and your success criteria (e.g., "How will I know my students have learned?"). We will show you the importance of identifying big ideas, anticipating student misconceptions, implementing formative assessment, facilitating a lesson with questioning, and closing a lesson with reflection techniques.

Each chapter includes a vignette, examples for each grade level (K–2), an opportunity to reflect on the ideas presented, suggestions for building a unit from your lesson, and an Under Construction section to help you build a lesson on the content of your choice. A glossary in Appendix D provides definitions for words highlighted in each chapter.

Keep in mind that the goal of teaching is student learning. The best lessons that students can experience always begin with a prepared teacher.

Sincerely,

Beth McCord Kobett
Ruth Harbin Miles
Lois A. Williams

# Letter to Elementary Principals

Dear Elementary Principals,

Some teachers *implement lesson plans* written by textbook publishers or by other professional curriculum writers. We argue that this is not enough. To positively affect the learning of their students, teachers need professional decision-making opportunities.

In this book, *The Mathematics Lesson-Planning Handbook: Your Blueprint for Building Cohesive Lessons*, your teachers will experience the decision-making processes that are involved in planning lessons for purpose, rigor, and coherence, and they will build a lesson of their own using a format created for them. In addition, we will help them address the decisions involved in selecting resources (e.g., "How can teachers make the best use of their textbook or state/district instructional materials?"), classroom structure (e.g., "Should there be small-group or large-group instruction?"), worthwhile tasks (e.g., "How do they recognize them?"), lesson intentions (e.g., "What are the objectives?"), and success criteria (e.g., "How will the teachers know their students have learned?"). We will help them examine the importance of identifying big ideas, anticipating student misconceptions, implementing formative assessment, facilitating a lesson with questioning, and closing a lesson with reflection techniques.

Your faculty of individual classroom and special education teachers all bring different knowledge, unique skills, and distinct ideas to the lesson-planning process. As a leader, you may wish to supply every teacher with a personal copy of the book for use as a schoolwide initiative or book study. Providing the opportunity for teachers to engage and use the book in grade-level planning with colleagues will allow teachers to dig deeply into their standards and collaborate to leverage each other's knowledge and experience. Be sure to invite teachers to bring this resource to all planning and professional development sessions. You may even want teachers to start or end a meeting by sharing a lesson they have planned based on the suggestions and strategies found in this book. As part of a faculty book study, this book will influence professional practice in lesson planning that promotes student achievement. After all, your best-prepared teachers are the most effective players on your team!

Sincerely,

Beth McCord Kobett
Ruth Harbin Miles
Lois A. Williams

# Letter to Mathematics Coaches

Dear Mathematics Coaches,

Your work with teachers must, undoubtedly, encompass a great deal of time and effort planning mathematics lessons. This guide is designed to unpack the lesson-planning process to help teachers understand the importance of teacher decision making as they plan effective mathematics lessons to support student growth. Currently, some teachers simply *implement lesson plans* written by textbook publishers or by other professional curriculum writers. We argue that this is not enough. To positively affect the learning of their students, teachers need professional decision-making opportunities.

As you know, collaborative planning can be particularly powerful for teams of teachers. You may find that a three-step process, incorporating a planning, trying, and reflective cycle, will be most helpful for your teachers. Consider beginning small, tackling the content by chapter, to increase successful implementation.

In this book, *The Mathematics Lesson-Planning Handbook: Your Blueprint for Building Cohesive Lessons*, your teachers will experience the decision-making processes that are involved in planning lessons for purpose, rigor, and coherence, and they will build a lesson of their own using our format. In addition, we will help them address the decisions involved in selecting resources (e.g., "How can teachers make the best use of their textbook or state/district instructional materials?"), classroom structure (e.g., "Should there be small-group or large-group instruction?"), worthwhile tasks (e.g., "How do they recognize them?"), lesson intentions (e.g., "What are the standards and objectives?"), and success criteria (e.g., "How will the teachers know their students have learned?"). We look at the importance of identifying big ideas, anticipating student misconceptions, implementing formative assessment, facilitating a lesson with questioning, and closing a lesson with reflection techniques.

Your faculty of individual classroom and special education teachers all bring different knowledge, skills, and distinct ideas to the lesson-planning process. Providing the opportunity for teachers to engage and use the book in grade-level planning with colleagues will allow teachers to dig deeply into their standards and collaborate to leverage each other's knowledge and experience. Be sure to invite teachers to bring this resource to all planning and professional development sessions. You may even want teachers to start or end a meeting by sharing a lesson they have planned based on the suggestions and strategies found in this book. As part of a faculty book study, this book will influence professional practice in lesson planning that promotes student achievement. After all, your best-prepared teachers are the most effective players on your team!

Sincerely,

Beth McCord Kobett
Ruth Harbin Miles
Lois A. Williams

# Letter to Preservice College and University Instructors

Dear Preservice College and University Instructors,

K–2 preservice teachers must learn how to develop lesson plans to professionally prepare for teaching their students. One of the critical goals of a methods class is to guide preservice teachers and help them learn to create effective, well-crafted, and engaging mathematics lesson plans.

A recent study published in the *American Educational Research Journal* states that elementary preservice teachers remember and use what they learned in teacher-prep programs about writing lesson plans for mathematics (Morris & Hiebert, 2017). You have a major role to play, and this book can help you unpack the lesson-planning process.

*The Mathematics Lesson-Planning Handbook: Your Blueprint for Building Cohesive Lessons* helps your preservice teachers experience the decision-making processes involved in planning lessons for purpose, rigor, and coherence, and it guides them through the steps of building a lesson of their own using a format created for them. In addition, we help them address the decisions involved in selecting resources (e.g., "How can teachers make the best use of their textbook or state/district instructional materials?"), classroom structure (e.g., "Should there be small-group or large-group instruction?"), worthwhile tasks (e.g., "How do they recognize them?"), lesson intentions (e.g., "What are the objectives?"), and success criteria (e.g., "How will the teachers know their students have learned?"). We look at the importance of identifying big ideas, anticipating student misconceptions, implementing formative assessment, facilitating a lesson with questioning, and closing a lesson with reflection techniques.

The handbook includes 14 chapters that may easily be incorporated into a 14-, 15-, or 16-week methods course. The resource provides the opportunity for preservice teachers to engage and study the content chapter by chapter. As a result of their learning, this book will influence professional practice in lesson planning. After all, the preservice teachers' knowledge influences how they plan for instruction throughout their career.

Sincerely,

Beth McCord Kobett
Ruth Harbin Miles
Lois A. Williams

# How to Use This Book

In the words of Benjamin Franklin, "Failing to plan is planning to fail." The best lessons students can experience always begin with a prepared teacher who considers student learning the primary goal of instruction.

Searching the Internet for lesson plans to use or adapt may seem to be an efficient way to plan. However, you will likely spend hours searching for the perfect lesson only to find that what you needed/wanted was not quite what you found. In contrast, planning your own lessons is a special skill that has invaluable rewards both for you and for your students. This guide will help you plan lessons that are strategically designed with YOUR students in mind.

When you are able to build your own mathematics lessons, you have the power to make decisions about all aspects of your students' learning, including how to make the content meet your students' individual needs. This approach may seem overwhelming in the beginning, because creating an effective lesson plan requires thinking and practice to consider all the factors you need. The good news is that after a bit of practice, it will become second nature.

Part I of this book begins with the premise that good instruction should be planned with purpose, coherence, and rigor in mind. It includes a chapter emphasizing that children all have different needs and that, as a teacher, you need to plan lessons in accordance with those needs. At the beginning of Part II, you will find the lesson-planning template that reflects all of the decisions a teacher makes when planning and facilitating a lesson. It may seem overwhelming at first glance. However, with practice, you will find that these decisions become second nature to your planning process. The template can also be found in Appendix B and is available to download online at resources.corwin.com/mathlessonplanning/k-2.

Part II comprises a series of chapters for each component of the template. Each chapter includes the following:

- A real-world scenario of K–2 teachers who are wrestling with the decision-making part of the component
- Ideas and information to help with your decision-making process
- Snapshots that model the construction of a K, 1, and 2 lesson plan chapter by chapter
- A section highlighting the importance of coherence for future lessons in a unit
- Questions for reflection
- An Under Construction section for you to begin planning your own lesson

Part III helps you put it all together with suggestions for planning to launch, facilitate, and close your lesson.

Throughout the book, you will find words that appear in bold type. You can find their meanings in the glossary in Appendix D.

You may wish to begin the planning process by tackling one chapter at a time. You can read about an approach, try it out, and then, after completing the next chapter, integrate additional new concepts into your planning process. Take it slow, reflect along the way, and, before you know it, you will be planning robust mathematics lessons! Let's begin!

# PART I

# YOU ARE THE ARCHITECT OF YOUR CLASSROOM

# CHAPTER 1

# SURVEYING YOUR SITE
## *Knowing Your Students*

On the first day of school, Lizette looked at the expectant faces of 23 first graders. She swallowed nervously.

As she scanned the room, she recognized Alvaro, a new English Language Learner (ELL) student whose family had just moved here from Nicaragua. He was grinning broadly and nodding his head at a classmate named Sue, who was animatedly telling him a story.

Lizette had met Alvaro's mother, Mrs. Ramos, at the open house, along with another family member who had helped to interpret. Lizette wanted to make sure that she continued to motivate Alvaro and support his use of new English words. She knew that ELL children needed many opportunities to work with other children in the classroom.

"Mrs. Martin?" called a young woman from the doorway. Lizette turned toward the door to see a mother holding the hand of a crying little boy, whom she recognized as Matty.

"Oh dear," she thought. Parents weren't supposed to get past the Kiss and Hug zone at the front of the building.

"He doesn't want me to go." Matty's mother sniffed, clearly holding back her own tears.

Lizette responded directly to Matty."Isn't it great to have a mommy who is so wonderful you don't want to leave her? How about if you pick out a book from my book corner for her to read to you? At the end of the book, she will kiss you goodbye so you can meet all your new friends in our classroom."

Matty agreed, and his mother smiled and looked relieved.

"MRS. MARTIN!" The screeching voice belonged to a little girl named Penny, who was standing near a corner of the classroom.

"Yes, Penny?" Lizette called.

"I NEED TO GO TO THE BATHROOM!"

As Lizette rushed over to Penny to suggest that she lower her voice, she caught sight of the little girl's hearing aid. She recalled from meetings with the kindergarten teacher that Penny had suffered extreme hearing loss about a year ago and was still struggling to moderate her own voice. The kindergarten teacher had recommended a successful strategy that involved using five fingers to cue Penny about her voice level. One finger meant that Penny should talk softly (Level 1), and five fingers meant that Penny should talk at the top of her voice (Level 5). Lizette leaned down to Penny and said, "Miss Hammond told me about your cool five-finger voice idea. Could we use that idea in our classroom, too?"

Penny nodded seriously and replied, "Do you need me to teach you how to do it?"

"Yes, that would be wonderful, Penny," Lizette responded.

---

**How would you describe your students? Every classroom is distinctive. The students you teach are uniquely yours, and they enter your classroom with a vast array of learning needs, interests, hopes, and even dreams about how they will spend their time with you. The focus of this chapter is to encourage you to think about the many needs of your learners and connect it to your preparation for planning. We will explore the following questions:**

- Why is it so important to know your students?
- What do access and equity really mean?
- What is prior knowledge in mathematics?
- What do culturally and linguistically diverse students need?
- What do students living in poverty need?
- What are the common themes?

# WHY IS IT SO IMPORTANT TO KNOW YOUR STUDENTS?

As a teacher, you surely appreciate the value of knowing the children in your classroom because you recognize how this intricately connects your teaching to your students' learning. Consider a time when you looked at a lesson plan constructed by someone else and thought, "This will never work with my kids." You know your students, and you were able to imagine how they would respond to the particular activities, content, or facilitation in the lesson plan.

As Bransford, Brown, and Cocking (1999) note, your knowledge of students is critical because students "come to formal education with a range of prior knowledge, skills, beliefs, and concepts that significantly influence what they notice about the environment and how they organize and interpret it. This, in turn, affects their abilities to remember, reason, solve problems, and acquire new knowledge" (p. 10). While it is vitally important to understand the mathematics content you teach, it is equally important to know and understand everything you can about the students you teach.

The children in your classroom have unique backgrounds that influence the ways in which they respond to you. At the same time, the ways you respond to your students may be influenced by your own cultural and language preferences and beliefs. All this information can help you plan lessons and design learning activities that both capitalize on students' cognitive, behavioral, and social-emotional strengths and **scaffold** their learning challenges.

As you work your way through this book, you will be constructing a mathematics lesson on the topic of your choice for your grade level. While this book is about lesson planning, it is essential for you to begin the lesson-planning process with a focus on your own learners' needs. As you read the brief discussion about different learning needs, consider how the descriptions apply to your own group of students.

**Think about a situation when knowing about a student's needs in your class helped you plan an instructional activity that supported mathematical learning. Briefly describe the details here.**

As a teacher of young children, you know firsthand that students walk into your classroom with a wide array of backgrounds and experiences. **Prior knowledge** refers to the mathematics knowledge or content that students know as they enter your classroom. If you do not help students engage their prior knowledge, they may not be able to integrate new knowledge meaningfully. Accessing and connecting prior knowledge to new learning can affect students' motivation to learn and how much they will learn (Dolezal, Welsh, Pressley, & Vincent, 2003).

How students experience mathematics at home is one influence on their mathematics learning in the classroom. For example, if your students count regularly at home or shop with their parents at the grocery store, you can connect these experiences to your instructional activities. If students do not regularly have access to these kinds of opportunities, you will need to create instructional activities that help your students construct foundational knowledge for standards you will be teaching in the future. One way you can do this is by integrating routines like counting jars and number talks into your overall instructional plan.

Example: Maria

Maria, a first-grade teacher, begins each week of the first month of school with a counting jar routine. She fills four large jars (one for each group of students) with items for the week, such as marbles, shells, buttons, and wooden apples, and asks students to estimate and count the items in the jar that is assigned to their group (Figure 1.1).

### Figure 1.1

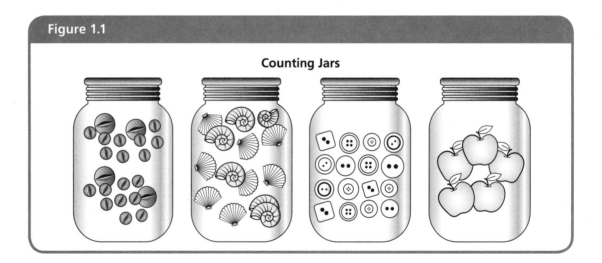

**Counting Jars**

Each day, Maria rotates the jar to another group. She supplies students with empty egg cartons, bowls, empty ten frames, and **hundred charts** to help them organize their counting. Students record their counts on sticky notes and post them each day on a special board for classmates to see. At the end of the day, she asks students to share counting strategies. While all students may not need the development of prior knowledge, Maria knows that all students will benefit from the exploration and conversation that the counting jars naturally elicit.

**What do you know about your students' prior knowledge? Make a list and share it with another teacher who knows your students.**

_____

_____

_____

_____

_____

## WHAT DO ACCESS AND EQUITY REALLY MEAN?

Knowing your students is the first step in providing equitable learning opportunities and **access** to high-quality mathematics instruction. The National Council of Teachers of Mathematics' (2014a) Access and Equity Position Statement states the following:

> Creating, supporting, and sustaining a culture of access and equity require being responsive to students' backgrounds, experiences, cultural perspectives, traditions, and knowledge when designing and implementing a mathematics program and assessing its effectiveness. Acknowledging and addressing factors that contribute to differential outcomes among groups of students are critical to ensuring that all students routinely have opportunities to experience high-quality mathematics instruction, learn challenging mathematics content, and receive the support necessary to be successful. Addressing equity and access includes both ensuring that all students attain mathematics proficiency and increasing the numbers of students from all racial, ethnic, linguistic, gender, and socioeconomic groups who attain the highest levels of mathematics achievement.

Without equal access, students' opportunities to learn are reduced. Students' knowledge gaps are often the result of instructional gaps, which happen when students are not appropriately challenged because beliefs about what they learn and how they can learn are reflected in the types of instruction they receive. Equitable instruction is a key factor in supporting students' opportunities for access to high-quality mathematics instruction. Knowledge of your students should inform and support high expectations and beliefs about what your students can learn and do in your mathematics classroom. Later in this book, you will have an opportunity to apply what you know about your students to your own lesson-planning process.

**How do you ensure that *all* your students have access to high-quality mathematics instruction? Record your response here.**

_____

_____

_____

_____

## HOW DO IDENTITY AND AGENCY INFLUENCE LESSON PLANNING?

**Identity** and **agency** are two concepts that help teachers understand the dynamics that take place in a classroom, which, in turn, helps teachers better understand their students and how best to meet their needs. Identity is how individuals know and see themselves (i.e., student, teacher, good at sports, like math) and how others know and see us (i.e., short, smart, African American). When defined broadly, identity is a concept that brings together all the interrelated elements that teachers and students bring to the classroom, including beliefs, attitudes, emotions, and cognitive capacity (Grootenboer, Lowrie, & Smith, 2006).

Agency is the power to act. Students develop their agency when they actively engage in the learning process (Wenmoth, 2014). Since student learning is greatest in classrooms where students are engaged in high-level thinking and reasoning (Boaler & Staples, 2008), teachers need to ensure that tasks they choose promote this engagement on a regular basis.

The types of lessons teachers design, the approach they take to teaching, the tasks they select, the types of questions they ask, the classroom climate, and social norms of the classroom all affect student engagement and are influenced by the teachers' identity. For example, in a classroom where the teacher sees his or her identity as the giver of knowledge, students are passive recipients of knowledge, working individually at their desks on assignments designed by the teacher. In this approach, there is no opportunity for students to exercise agency. In addition, student identities are lost as they are treated as a group with all the same learning needs rather than as individuals with unique learning needs.

If teachers think about teaching and learning as social activities (Vgotsky, 1962, 1978), then they must take the initiative to put structures into place in the classroom that support the social nature of learning. These include creating a classroom climate in which students feel safe to test hypotheses and ask questions. In this environment, teachers present tasks that afford students the opportunity to act, to explore, to move, and to exercise some choice. They set social norms in the classroom that encourage students to work together on challenging tasks and engage in productive struggle. They not only encourage student-to-student discourse, but they intentionally plan for it. Students hypothesize, listen to one another, critique ideas, and formulate questions. They exercise their agency. In this student-centered approach, students become "authors" of mathematical ideas and texts and not "overhearers" (Larson, 2002).

Let's look at an example in which students from racial groups often challenged to find voice and agency in classrooms were engaged in a task that allowed them to exercise their agency. Arthur Powell (2004), a researcher from Rutgers University, captured African American and Latinx students exercising their agency during a study under a grant from the National Science Foundation (REC-0309062). In this study, Powell describes how students who had never before used Cuisenaire Rods were given a set to help them investigate fractions. Cuisenaire Rods are proportional rods of ten different colors, each color corresponding to a different length as pictured in Figure 1.2.

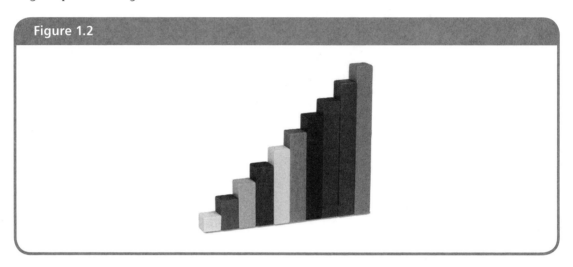

**Figure 1.2**

Powell (2004) describes,

> Students were invited to work on the question, "If the blue rod is 1, what is yellow?" Many students manipulated the rods to observe how many white rods they needed to place end-to-end to construct a length equivalent to the blue rod. Malika lists how many white rods make up each of the other rods. She calls the yellow rod 5, and later she and Lorrin say that yellow is five-ninths. Building a model of a blue rod alongside a train of one yellow and four white rods, with a purple rod beneath the white rods, Lorrin and Malika show that the purple rod is four ninths. The students at their table determine number names for all the rods, except that they are uncertain about what to call the orange rod. Eventually, this group of students resolves what number name to give to the orange rod. One student remarks that ten-ninths is an improper fraction. A male colleague [student] … says assertively, "It's still ten-ninths. That ain't gonna change it because it's an improper fraction. That makes it even more right." (p. 46)

In this example, the teacher did not overtly give students a set procedure to follow to work out the name for the yellow rod. The teacher did, however, establish the social norms of the classroom so that students knew what was expected of them. Malika manipulated the materials to name all of the rods. Student-to-student discussion provided the opportunity to use reasoning to name the orange rod, a question that was not asked by the investigator. Students were posing their own questions at this point in the investigation. Powell reports that the students held a misconception about fractions when the investigation began—the numerator cannot be larger than the denominator—but, through their own exploration, had convinced themselves by the end of the session that the belief was incorrect. The students had agency in this example because of the task they engaged in and the social norms in place to help them. The teacher expected students to move around, manipulate objects, engage in the task by talking with one another, and challenge each other's ideas.

In this book, you will read more about tasks, misconceptions, and discourse to support students in exercising their agency.

## WHAT DO CULTURALLY AND LINGUISTICALLY DIVERSE STUDENTS NEED?

If you are lucky enough to teach culturally and linguistically diverse students, then you know of the rich experiences these students bring to your classroom. An **English Language Learner (ELL)** is defined as "an active learner of the English language who may benefit from various types of language support programs" (National Council of Teachers of English, 2008, p. 2). While these students may share some common needs because they are learning English and mathematics as well as other subjects, they also can, and often do, have very different learning needs. You can gather information about these students by asking them to show you what they know, observing them as they interact with other students, speaking to them often, using visual cues to communicate, and encouraging them to draw pictures. The National Council of Supervisors of Mathematics' (2009) position paper, titled "Improving Student Achievement in Mathematics by Addressing the Needs of English Language Learners," recommends that mathematics educators do the following:

- Realize that mathematics is neither value free nor culture free but instead is a product of human activity. Thus, race, class, culture, and language play key roles in its teaching and learning.

- Understand that language is not only a tool for communicating but also a tool for thinking. Every mathematics teacher is a language teacher—particularly the **academic language** used to formulate and communicate mathematics learning (Lager, 2006).

- Realize that regular and active classroom participation— in the form of discussing, explaining, writing, and presenting—is crucial to ELLs' success in mathematics and that ELLs can produce explanations, participate in presentations, and engage in discussions as they are learning English.

- Recognize that ELLs, like English-speaking students, require consistent access to high cognitive demand tasks in mathematics.

- Learn to see the evidence of ELLs' mathematical thinking, hear how ELLs use language to communicate about mathematics, understand the competence that ELLs bring, build on this competence, and provide access to opportunities for advancing their learning.

- Value the home language of each ELL student and find ways to promote its use whenever possible.

- Provide and participate in ongoing professional development to help mathematics teachers shape instructional practices to foster success of ELLs in mathematics, including the development of language-rich classrooms for the benefit of all students.

- Establish district-wide and schoolwide structures that promote collaboration among teachers of mathematics, specialists in English as a second language, bilingual teachers, and language arts teachers to meld skills and knowledge in the service of ELLs' learning of mathematics.

Culturally and linguistically diverse students also benefit from particular strategies that invite them to regularly engage in mathematical discourse (Banse, Palacios, Merritt, & Rimm-Kaufman, 2016). This discourse is critical because ELL students need to have opportunities to talk as well as to listen. Banse et al. (2016) recommend that ELL teachers should proceed as follows:

1. Ask **open-ended questions** that invite student thinking and explanation and support students' development of conceptual understanding (Figure 1.3).

### Figure 1.3

| Example | Nonexample |
| --- | --- |
| How could you group or sort your shapes? | Count to find the number of objects. |

**2.** As needed, follow open-ended questions with **closed-ended questions** that are scaffolded to help the ELLs focus on one or two options (Figure 1.4).

**Figure 1.4**

| Example | Nonexample |
|---|---|
| How are these two shapes alike [pointing to a square and rectangle]? | Which one is a square? |

**3.** Scaffold students' responses by repeating, extending, and rephrasing so ELLs can benefit from having additional conversations about their explanations and solutions, which can be extended by peers and/or the teacher (Figure 1.5).

**Figure 1.5**

| Example | Nonexample |
|---|---|
| You counted four sides on the square and rectangle and said that they are the same. We see that both shapes have the same number of sides. What is one thing that is different? | Yes. Each shape has four sides. Notice that the square's sides are equal. Do you see that not all of the sides of the rectangle are equal? |

**4.** Model mathematical vocabulary in context, always using correct vocabulary and applying it in context so that ELLs can make connections about meaning (Figure 1.6).

**Figure 1.6**

| Example | Nonexample |
|---|---|
| A square has four sides and four angles. | A circle is like a ball … |

5. Strive to include ELLs in mathematical discourse each day; ideally, both teachers and students should engage in mathematical discourse with ELL students (Figure 1.7).

**Figure 1.7**

| Example | Nonexample |
|---|---|
| ELL students and non-ELL students work in pairs and participate in flexible grouping. | ELL students are isolated in their own group. |

Review the five recommendations for teachers of ELL students. Which ones do you already use in your planning? Which ones would you like to integrate more? How might you do that? Briefly list the details here.

_____

_____

_____

_____

## WHAT DO STUDENTS LIVING IN POVERTY NEED?

About 21% of the children living in the United States live below the poverty threshold. Another 22% live in low-income homes, comprising 43%, or 30.6 million, of all the children in the United States (National Center for Children in Poverty, 2017). Given this statistic, it is quite likely that you are teaching at least one child living in poverty.

While it is important to not overgeneralize or make assumptions about children living in poverty, research suggests that some children in this situation may experience prolonged stress that may influence the ways in which they respond to the classroom environment and that may negatively affect school performance (Harvard Center for the Developing Child, 2007). Students may have difficulty concentrating or attending to tasks (Erickson, Drevets, & Schulkin, 2003), reduced ability to navigate in social situations (National Institute of Child Health and Human Development Early Child Care Research Network, 2005), and impaired memory, critical thinking, and creativity (Farah et al., 2006; Lupien, King, Meaney, & McEwen, 2001). While many strategies can support your students who are living in poverty, the following three strategies may support your instructional decision making about lesson planning.

1. **Build upon the students' strengths.** Students in poverty need educators to recognize the strengths that they bring to school. Ensure that you are focusing on and building up students' specific strengths by first determining those strengths and then highlighting them during lessons.

2. **Consistently work toward building relationships with your students.** Intentionally pursue relationships with your students. Ensure that you use their names in positive ways, and provide opportunities for students to build relationships with each other. Consider using the students' names and interests in word problems and contexts for lessons.

3. **Seek to understand your students' responses to stressful situations.** Consider why students might be responding to classroom situations in particular ways by observing and noting potential triggers. As you plan your lessons, partner students to increase access to tasks. Think about how your task contexts might engage or alienate students who are living in poverty. For example, tasks that focus on acquisition or buying items may create unintentional consequences.

Lindsay, a first-grade teacher, used all three of these strategies to attend to one of her first grader's needs. She had noticed that Michael usually entered the classroom in the morning very agitated and had trouble settling into the routine. The student had developed a pattern of entering the room, slamming his books down, and then engaging in conflict with another student. To counteract this pattern, Lindsay decided to greet Michael at the classroom door to have a positive conversation about how he was doing. Lindsay enlisted the boy's help by asking Michael to help her take photographs for a lesson launch. After about a week of making this effort, Lindsay noticed that Michael was much calmer, focused, and ready to learn at the start of each day. He seemed to look forward to their daily chats and was often ready to tell her a story.

**How do you use students' strengths to design instructional activities? Briefly note the details here.**

_____

_____

_____

_____

_____

_____

_____

_____

_____

## WHAT ARE LEARNING NEEDS?

Every student you teach is distinct, possessing specific learning strengths and learning challenges. Students with explicit learning disabilities typically possess a significant learning challenge in one or more of the following areas: memory, self-regulation, visual processing, language processing (separate from ELL), academic skills, and motor skills. The Individuals With Disabilities Education Act (IDEA) requires public schools to provide the least restrictive environment to children with identified disabilities. Students' **Individualized Education Plan (IEP)** must reflect the individual needs of the students.

As you consider the learning needs of your students, you will need to study their IEPs carefully to determine how you can meet their needs in your instructional planning. You may want to develop learning profiles of your students' mathematics strengths and needs to inform your instructional decision making. You might complete a learning profile for each student with the IEP accommodations at the beginning of the year, and then add to it as you learn new information throughout the year.

Example: Lizette

Figure 1.8 shows a completed learning profile that Lizette, the teacher in our vignette, created after getting to know Penny. In the form, she noted Penny's strengths in self-regulating her behavior and her advanced fine motor skills. After just one day, Lizette was beginning to gather some excellent evidence about Penny's strengths.

## Figure 1.8

### Learner Profile for Mathematics Teaching and Learning

**Name:** Penny

| Memory and Retention | Self-Regulation | Visual Processing | Language Processing | Academic Skills | Motor Skills |
|---|---|---|---|---|---|
| Strengths | Strengths<br><br>Monitors behavior and reminds me about techniques to help her moderate her voice | Strengths | Strengths | Strengths | Strengths<br><br>Advanced fine motor skills |
| Challenges | Challenges | Challenges | Challenges<br><br>Hearing impaired | Challenges | Challenges |

IEP Accommodations:

Seat the student near the teacher in whole- and small-group instruction

Access to teacher to repeat directions as needed

Speech and language - twice a week

 This tool can be downloaded from resources.corwin.com/mathlessonplanning/k-2

By providing students with opportunities to see and use multiple representations in learning activities, from concrete to abstract, you can support their mathematical understanding. This concrete-to-abstract sequence is described in two ways—Concrete-Representation-Abstract (CRA) and Concrete–Semi-Concrete–Abstract (CSA)—and it supports students with disabilities' conceptual understanding (Sealander, Johnson, Lockwood, & Medina, 2012). This teaching sequence is very familiar to early educators because it begins with concrete experiences using manipulatives, moves to a representational stage where students draw pictures and use visuals to show their thinking, and then provides opportunities for students to apply their learning using abstract symbols. As you make instructional decisions for your students with learning needs, you will want to consider giving ample time for students to use manipulatives before moving to the representation stage. They may also need opportunities to move back and forth between the stages of the CRA/CSA sequence to continue to build fluency (Van de Walle, Karp, & Bay-Williams, 2016). For instance, Figure 1.9 shows the many ways you might ask your students to represent the number 24.

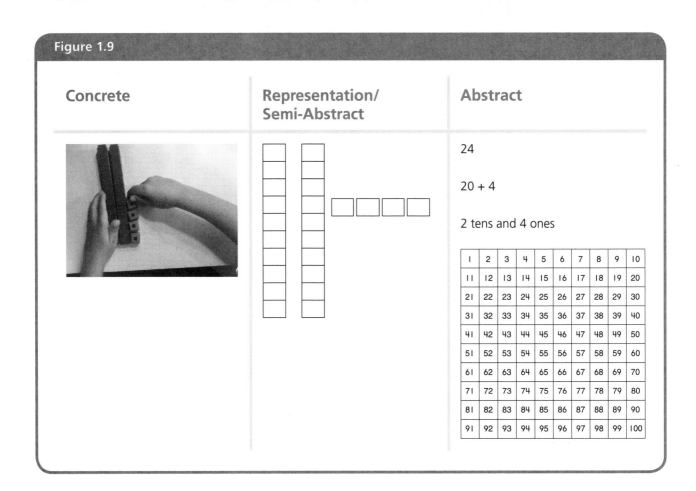

Figure 1.9

| Concrete | Representation/ Semi-Abstract | Abstract |
|---|---|---|

Abstract column content:

24

20 + 4

2 tens and 4 ones

| 1 | 2 | 3 | 4 | 5 | 6 | 7 | 8 | 9 | 10 |
|---|---|---|---|---|---|---|---|---|---|
| 11 | 12 | 13 | 14 | 15 | 16 | 17 | 18 | 19 | 20 |
| 21 | 22 | 23 | 24 | 25 | 26 | 27 | 28 | 29 | 30 |
| 31 | 32 | 33 | 34 | 35 | 36 | 37 | 38 | 39 | 40 |
| 41 | 42 | 43 | 44 | 45 | 46 | 47 | 48 | 49 | 50 |
| 51 | 52 | 53 | 54 | 55 | 56 | 57 | 58 | 59 | 60 |
| 61 | 62 | 63 | 64 | 65 | 66 | 67 | 68 | 69 | 70 |
| 71 | 72 | 73 | 74 | 75 | 76 | 77 | 78 | 79 | 80 |
| 81 | 82 | 83 | 84 | 85 | 86 | 87 | 88 | 89 | 90 |
| 91 | 92 | 93 | 94 | 95 | 96 | 97 | 98 | 99 | 100 |

How do you integrate your students' learning needs into your instructional planning? Briefly note the details here.

_____

_____

_____

_____

_____

_____

## WHAT ARE THE COMMON THEMES?

As you were reading this chapter, you may have thought that many of the suggested strategies could be applied to all of your learners. Instructional decision making begins with building relationships with students by getting to know them. This newfound knowledge helps you to create positive connections and build a learning community that fosters a rich learning environment. When you know your students, you can make the very best instructional decisions that will best meet their academic and social-emotional needs. Knowledge and awareness of each student's learning needs makes for purposeful lesson planning.

Consider all of the learning needs discussed in this chapter. Make a list of your own students' learning needs using the categories listed in this chapter. What do you notice? What will you need to keep in mind as you plan your lessons? Record your thoughts and concerns below.

Notes

# CHAPTER 2

# YOUR K-2 BLUEPRINT

## Planning Mathematics Lessons for Coherence, Rigor, and Purpose

Nick, a second-grade teacher, looked for his teammates, Kelly and Maria, all day. He sent them both notes to see if they could give him a few minutes after school. He really needed to talk to them about this lesson-planning business. He had spent the weekend searching for lessons on the Internet to match the scope and sequence the school district provided. One of his friends from the university had told him about a couple of websites that had good ideas, but he felt like he was just planning a bunch of discrete lessons that didn't necessarily go together. He had had another lesson fall apart today, even though he had spent hours preparing a game for the students to do during math stations. In fact, he had spent so much time preparing the game, he realized during the lesson that he didn't feel as prepared as he had hoped. He kept getting surprised and then sidetracked by the students' misconceptions.

Kelly arrived first. Nick began telling her about his frustration. He said, "Kelly, I don't know how you do it. I am spending all of my weekends and evenings planning lessons for the next day. What is your secret?"

Kelly replied, "I follow the textbook."

Nick said, "Oh, I didn't think we were supposed to do that. I thought the textbook was just a resource."

Just then Maria walked in, and Nick shared his concerns with lesson-planning issues.

Maria, a 20-year veteran, said, "Nick, you are absolutely right. Just picking lessons off the Internet, no matter how cute or enticing they are, can really mess with the coherence we are trying to create for students. I feel badly that you have been struggling. I think it is time that we sit down as a team and start planning together."

Nick smiled, relieved at last. "I was really hoping you would say that."

---

**Kelly and Nick are examples of both ends of the lesson-planning spectrum. On one end, Nick is planning daily, just keeping his head above water. On the other hand, Kelly is using the textbook, a good resource, but not enough when state standards, student misconceptions, big ideas, and prior student knowledge need to be considered. Neither rigor nor lesson coherence are part of their discussion. Should they be, and why should they be?**

**As the architect of your instruction, designing your blueprint is perhaps one of the most important jobs you can do. Throughout this book, you will have the opportunity to build coherent mathematics lessons for your grade level by following the many examples presented. Together, we will explore the answers to questions such as these:**

- What is coherence?

- What is rigor?

- What is the purpose of a lesson?

- How can you ensure that you plan lessons for coherence, rigor, and purpose?

**Let's begin by looking at foundational planning principles of coherence and rigor, which Nick and Kelly need to know. As you read, reflect upon how you currently think about your own lesson planning.**

# WHAT IS COHERENCE?

**Coherence** is probably the most crucial step in providing a quality mathematics education to students (Schmidt, Wang, & McKnight, 2005). Coherence is a logical sequencing of mathematical ideas. When lessons are coherent, they have a logical flow and are well organized to promote sense making. Lesson coherence should be both vertical and horizontal. For **vertical coherence,** you can look at the standards at the grade level before and after yours. How does your content fit in with what your students have already been taught, and how can you bridge that knowledge to what they will be learning next year? You need to consider what prior knowledge students are likely to have and where they'll be going next so that you can ensure a vertical coherence—planning lessons logically, allowing students to make sense of the mathematics across the grades. For example, Figure 2.1 shows a vertical articulation of selected K–2 standards.

## Figure 2.1

| Kindergarten | First Grade | Second Grade |
| --- | --- | --- |
| Count to 100 by ones and tens. | Relate counting to addition and subtraction (e.g., by counting on 2 to add 2). | Explain why addition and subtraction strategies work, using place value and the properties of operations. |
| | Add and subtract within 20, demonstrating fluency for addition and subtraction within 10. Use strategies such as counting on, making ten (e.g., $8 + 6 = 8 + 2 + 4 = 10 + 4 = 14$), decomposing a number leading to a ten (e.g., $13 - 4 = 13 - 3 - 1 = 10 - 1 = 9$), using the relationship between addition and subtraction (e.g., knowing that $8 + 4 = 12$, one knows $12 - 8 = 4$), and creating equivalent but easier or known sums (e.g., adding $6 + 7$ by creating the known equivalent $6 + 6 + 1 = 12 + 1 = 13$). | |

**Horizontal coherence** refers to daily lesson planning. Do your daily lessons follow a logical order, a gradual building up of a concept and/or skill over time? For example, in kindergarten, counting to 10 is a significant skill that needs to be mastered before introducing counting forward from a given number 1 through 10. Daily lesson plans that allow children to practice counting every day, with the reinforcement of counting the number of children in line at lunch and recess, make sense. Teaching counting on Mondays, addition on Tuesdays, and shapes on Wednesdays is not a logical, coherent sequence.

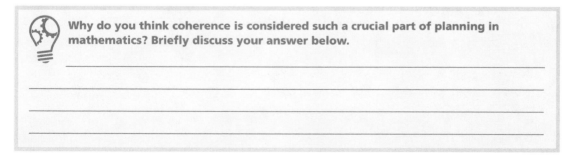

**Why do you think coherence is considered such a crucial part of planning in mathematics? Briefly discuss your answer below.**

Some teachers believe planning for **rigor** means providing more difficult material or asking students to complete more problems. This is not correct. Some even say that rigor means mathematical content is accelerated. However, as Hull, Harbin Miles, and Balka (2014) explain, mathematical rigor within a classroom is actually

> a direct result of active participation in deep mathematical thinking and intensive reasoning. There are dual meanings for rigor when planning great lessons. First, *content rigor* is the depth of interconnection concepts and the breadth of supporting skills students are expected to know and understand. Next, *instructional rigor* is the ongoing interaction between teacher instruction and students reasoning and thinking about concepts, skills, and challenging tasks that result in a conscious, connected, and transferable body of valuable knowledge for every student. (p. 22)

Since rigor results from active student participation and deep mathematical thinking and reasoning, let's compare two kindergarten examples of what it is and what it is not.

Shania and Anna are teaching **one-to-one correspondence**, which is embedded in their standard on comparing numbers. The standard states,

> Identify whether the number of objects in one group is greater than, less than, or equal to the number of objects in another group, e.g., by using matching and counting strategies.

Example: Shania

Shania passes out a worksheet and crayons (Figure 2.2) to her students and explains, "Class, I want everyone to take a crayon and draw a line to connect the pictures that match. Remember; connect only one shoe with one sock."

Figure 2.2

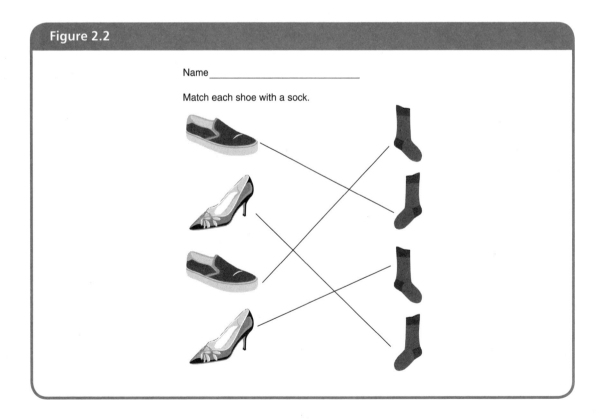

Name_____

Match each shoe with a sock.

Example: Anna

Like Shania, Anna is teaching one-to-one correspondence. She passes out the sheet in Figure 2.3 to students and asks, "Do we have enough buttons on this page for everyone in class to have one button?" Students then pair up and work together, trying different strategies to answer the question. Some students want to cut apart the buttons on the page, while others want to get buttons from the class button jar to model a solution. After the students arrive at their answers, Anna brings the class together for a discussion where students share the results of their investigation. After the class discussion of the task, Anna asks additional questions to see if the students can generalize the task and their strategies to other situations. She asks, "If I had fifteen pennies, would I have enough for everyone in the class? If I had twenty seashells, would I have enough? How would we know?"

**Figure 2.3**

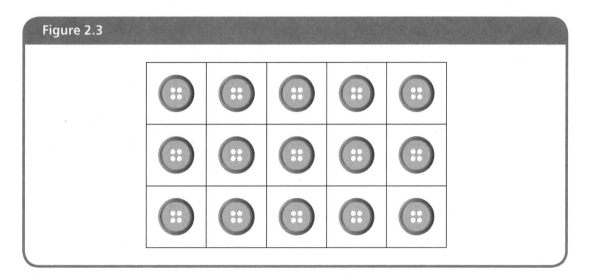

Both of these teachers are working with one-to-one correspondence. However, Anna's lesson is more rigorous. Students in Anna's class are encouraged to think and use reasoning. They are being asked to carefully apply what they know about one-to-one correspondence in a real-world setting. They may or may not have a clear understanding of one-to-one correspondence, but through the task, they have the opportunity to actively build new knowledge from a shared experience. Students may use buttons from a button jar in the classroom, use colorful cubes to represent the buttons, or cut apart the buttons on the page and discuss how they are going to approach the task. The follow-up questions encourage students to extend the current task to other similar situations.

On the other hand, Shania's task does not require any reasoning. Students are simply matching, a lower-level skill that will not extend beyond the task as written. While matching is stated in the standard, Shania narrowly interprets the standard as drawing lines to match objects one-to-one. Should teachers expect students to be able to just draw lines and match objects to compare amounts? Or should teachers want students to understand that the idea of "matching" goes beyond drawing lines? Shania's task does not encourage students to reason, use representations, or have a shared real-world experience. Her task is not rigorous.

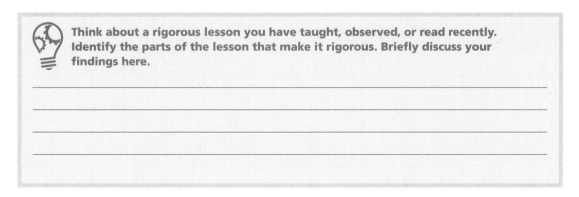

**Think about a rigorous lesson you have taught, observed, or read recently. Identify the parts of the lesson that make it rigorous. Briefly discuss your findings here.**

## WHAT IS THE PURPOSE OF A LESSON?

We can trace the purposes of mathematics lessons back to the National Research Council's (2001) conclusions in *Adding It Up: Helping Children Learn Mathematics*. The authors cite **conceptual understanding** and **procedural fluency** as two major strands that must be integrated into the teaching and learning of mathematics. It is important to note that not all mathematics lessons have the same purpose.

### What Is Conceptual Understanding?

Conceptual understanding means comprehension of mathematical concepts, operations, and relations. It involves knowing that mathematics is more than a set of rules or procedures and really understanding what is happening in different mathematical concepts. For example, students can recognize, interpret, and generate examples of concepts and identify and apply principles, facts, definitions, and so forth. The different approaches of two more teachers, Jose and Richard, show what a conceptual lesson looks like and what it does not.

Example: Jose

Jose introduces the "How Many Dots?" task (Figure 2.4) to his class.

---

**Figure 2.4**

**How Many Dots?**

Jose baked cupcakes and covered them with candy dots! How many dots are on Jose's cupcake?

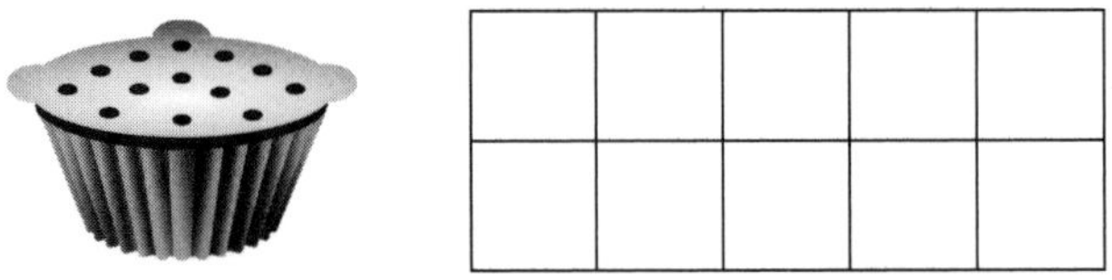

Ten frame

---

His students work in pairs and use ten frames to decompose the number of dots on the cupcake (pairs receive different amounts). They write the number of ten ones and some more ones. Student pairs then share how they counted, decomposed, and used the blank ten frame to find out how many dots are on the cupcake.

Example: Richard

Richard asks his students to complete the worksheet in Figure 2.5.

---

**Figure 2.5**

Name _____

How many tens and how many ones?

17 _____ tens _____ ones

19 _____ tens _____ ones

23 _____ tens _____ ones

28 _____ tens _____ ones

31 _____ tens _____ ones

---

Both teachers have first-grade lessons on tens and ones. However, when you compare the lessons to the criteria of conceptual understanding—which involves students recognizing, interpreting, and generating examples of concepts, as well as identifying and applying principles, facts, and definitions—you see that only Jose's lesson fits the criteria. His lesson requires students to identify what the number is and interpret the number of dots as tens and ones. Then they must apply this knowledge to a different representation, the ten frame.

On the other hand, Richard's worksheet, which covers the same content, can be completed by students without any understanding of tens and ones. Simply, for each row, the first digit goes on the first blank line, and the second digit goes on the second blank line. Once the students notice this pattern, they can follow it to complete the worksheet without giving the problems further thought. They do not need to know what tens and ones are to complete the worksheet.

A more in-depth discussion of conceptual understanding lessons appears in Chapter 5.

## What Is Procedural Fluency?

Procedural fluency describes the ability to use procedures accurately, efficiently, and flexibly. Students demonstrate procedural fluency when they refer to knowledge of procedures and have skill in performing them. They transfer procedures to different problems and contexts, and they know when a strategy or procedure is more appropriate to apply to a particular situation.

A lesson that develops procedural fluency is one in which students leverage their conceptual understanding and flexibly use various strategies that they find work best for the types of problems they are solving. **Distributed practice** over time helps students become proficient with the procedures so that they are more able to understand and manipulate more complex concepts in future learning.

When you start with lessons for conceptual understanding, you use representations to help students see the meaning behind the mathematical concept. Because children do not think abstractly, they support their thinking through the use of representations. A representation that helps students understand a concept can be a reliable tool that helps them understand procedures and thus develop procedural fluency.

Example: Kimi

Kimi is working on having her children understand addition to ten. Before any class activities to learn the basic facts that make ten, Kimi engages students in a conceptual understanding lesson. Each student receives a plastic bag with 10 black dots and the outline of a ladybug on a sheet of paper (Figure 2.6).

**Figure 2.6**

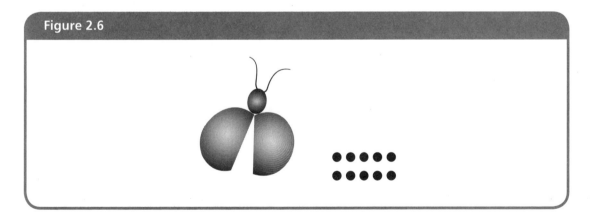

Kimi tells the students that the ladybug has lost her ten spots and they have to put them back on her wings. They can put them back in any combination on the wings as they wish.

Once the students have completed the task, Kimi displays all of the ladybugs and engages the students in a discussion of how they helped the ladybug, focusing on how many different ways they used to place the spots on the wings. She asks questions such as these:

Are any two combinations of spots the same?

How many different ways did we find to place ten spots on a ladybug?

What are these ways? How can we list them?

With this rich lesson, students are thinking about ten and how there are many different ways to combine spots to make ten. On another day, Kimi may follow this up with different representations such as ten frames, ten dots on butterfly wings, or a task that involves drawing pictures of ten pieces of candy separated different ways into two bags.

Once students have the concept that ten can be made with different combinations, Kimi can move these representations into procedural fluency lessons that deliberately link the basic facts that make ten back to the different arrangements of spots on a ladybug.

Procedural fluency lessons are discussed in more detail in Chapter 5.

## What Is Transfer?

A third purpose of a lesson in mathematics is **transfer.** A transfer lesson is a lesson in which students demonstrate transfer of learning; that is, they show that they are able to effectively use content knowledge and skill in a problem situation. According to Hattie and colleagues (2016), a transfer task should encourage connections. It is a task that can be open-ended with multiple entry points. Hattie and colleagues (2016) also point out that transfer, as a goal, "means that teachers want students to begin to take the reins of their own learning, think metacognitively, and apply what they know to a variety of real-world contexts" (p. 175).

In a lesson designed for transfer, students make sense of a problematic situation, think about how they can apply their skills and foundational understandings to solve the problem, and reflect on their own **problem-solving** process.

> Example: Sarah
>
> To create a transfer lesson, Sarah begins with the following first-grade **computation** standard.
>
> > Solve **word problems** that call for addition of three whole numbers whose sum is less than or equal to 20, e.g., by using objects, drawings, and equations with a symbol for the unknown number to represent the problem.
>
> From this standard, she decides to create a transfer lesson that asks students to demonstrate their understanding of word problems by posing the following task.
>
> > Jimmy solved a word problem and wrote 5 + 7 + 5 = 17. After school, his dog ate part of the paper, and Jimmy lost the word problem that went with the equation. Help Jimmy get a new word problem that works with his equation. Write a word problem that goes with Jimmy's equation.

For this transfer lesson, students are creating new and original content. There are **multiple entry points** for this task as well as an endless number of correct responses. Students need to relate their content knowledge about the addition equation to their conceptual understanding of addition in order to create a word problem. This is a **metacognitive** thought process because the students must reflect on everything they have learned and pull it all together to create a word problem.

Tasks in a transfer lesson may be similar to or even the same as those in a conceptual understanding lesson. The difference is in the learning intention of the lesson. When a task is used to develop conceptual understanding, students do not have a set of efficient strategies to solve the problem. They explore, use their background knowledge, and try to figure out how to solve the problem. They may unearth new ideas and test them. When the task is used to determine if students have mastered a concept and skill at the end of a unit, students bring the conceptual understandings and skills learned in the unit and use them efficiently and effectively to solve the problem.

Transfer lessons are discussed in more detail in Chapter 5.

> **Do you think teachers plan more conceptual, procedural, or transfer lessons? Why?**
>
> _____
>
> _____
>
> _____
>
> _____

## HOW CAN YOU ENSURE THAT YOU PLAN LESSONS FOR COHERENCE, RIGOR, AND PURPOSE?

Faced with so many decisions, teachers may feel forced to make daily planning decisions that individually work but, when examined together, do not promote coherence, rigor, and an overall purpose.

Lessons on a given mathematics topic need to be connected to enhance learning. They must involve a mix of conceptual understanding, procedural fluency, and transfer. When several coherent lessons on a topic come together as a whole, it is called a **unit plan.**

Second-grade teacher Matty was planning a measurement unit. She was short on time and gathered resources from several sources to cover the fifteen lessons she would need for the unit, as directed by the district's pacing guide. She found two fun activities from last year that involved using a ruler for measuring with inches and with centimeters. Then she found three measurement lessons on Pinterest that she knew her students would love doing and two more lessons in her textbook that asked children to color a picture of a balance. Her teaching partners gave her six more lessons on using a balance for mass, so she assembled a total of thirteen lessons. She left two lessons open for review.

After teaching the unit, Matty reviewed the collection of lessons and reflected on the instruction. She asked herself these questions:

- Did these lessons bring rigor to the study of measurement?
- Did the lessons meet/match grade-level standards?
- Did the lessons sequentially build students' mathematical understanding?
- Did the lessons connect the big ideas of measurement concepts?

While Matty felt that she did teach some successful lessons, she found that when she reviewed them as a unit, her lessons did not connect to enhance the students' learning. There was no coherence. Lessons did not build on one another. She decided that for next year, she will ensure that her teaching of measurement is rigorous, coherent, and purposeful by redesigning the entire unit with those goals in mind.

The lesson template in this book was designed to help you plan individual lessons. As you use this template to create successive lessons, be sure to keep big ideas and standards in mind. These steps will help you ensure that you create a coherent unit plan. Each chapter in Part II of this book will have a discussion on unit coherence.

**Big Idea(s):**

**Essential Question(s):**

**Content Standard(s):**

**Mathematical Practice or Process Standards:**

**Learning Intention(s) (mathematical/language/social):**

**Success Criteria (written in student voice):**

**Purpose:**

☐ Conceptual Understanding      ☐ Procedural Fluency      ☐ Transfer

**Task:**

**Materials (representations, manipulatives, other):**




---

**Misconceptions or Common Errors:**




---

**Format:**

☐ Four-Part Lesson        ☐ Game Format        ☐ Small-Group Instruction

☐ Pairs        ☐ Other_____

---

**Formative Assessment:**




---

**Launch:**




---

**Facilitate:**




---

**Closure:**

# PART II

# DRAFTING YOUR K–2 BLUEPRINT

# CHAPTER 3

# LAYING YOUR FOUNDATION

## *It Starts With Big Ideas, Essential Questions, and Standards*

As required by a new district policy, two veteran second-grade teachers, Roberta and Manny, sat down with their school administrative leader to review their students' benchmark assessments. Roberta, who had not yet seen the results, had been nervous all day about this meeting. She knew that Leah, the school principal, supported their work, but the situation was still incredibly nerve-wracking.

Leah pulled up the screen with the results and displayed them. "Let's just take a few minutes to look at them before we discuss."

At first, Roberta's heart sang, but then it plummeted. She looked over at Manny and noticed a confused expression on his face.

Leah said, "Let's begin with the successes. I am noticing that the students performed beautifully on place value concepts. These scores are way up from last year."

Roberta commented, "We really hit the place value hard this year. In fact, I was truly amazed with their conceptual understanding."

Manny added, "Yes, we integrated place value the entire year so the students would continue to build on their understanding. We also integrated it into our number routines and small groups."

Leah said, "I am so glad that all this effort paid off! Now, let's look at what we need to work on."

Roberta said, "My students were completely confused about the representations used for equations."

Manny exclaimed, "Mine were, too! Do you think it has anything to do with the new standards? We always taught equations, but we never used those balances that were on the test. We are going to need to review those new standards more carefully for next year."

Leah replied, "I think you are on to something, Manny. How could we strategically plan for the new standards so that we can create the same kind of success you had with place value concepts?"

> **Roberta and Manny's surprise about the assessment results may mirror the feelings of many teachers after states and districts implement new standards. In this chapter, we will focus on big ideas, essential questions, and standards as the building blocks of a lesson taught at the K–2 grade levels. We will also address the following questions.**
>
> - What are state standards for mathematics?
> - What are essential questions?
> - What are process standards?

# WHAT ARE STATE STANDARDS FOR MATHEMATICS?

For many years, research studies of mathematics education concluded that to improve mathematics achievement in the United States, standards needed to become more focused and coherent. The development of common mathematics **standards** began with research-affirmed **learning progressions** highlighting what is known about how students develop mathematical knowledge, skills, and understanding. The resulting document became known as the *Common Core State Standards for Mathematics* (CCSS-M) (National Governors Association and Council of Chief State School Officers, 2010). The landmark document was intended to be a set of shared goals and expectations for the knowledge and skills students need in mathematics at each grade level. The overall goal was college and career readiness.

Currently, the majority of states have adopted the *Common Core State Standards for Mathematics* as their own state standards. However, it is important to note that while many states adopted the *CCSS-M*, others have updated, clarified, or otherwise modified them, adopting the updated set as their new state standards. A few states have written their own standards.

Most standards documents are composed of **content standards** and **process standards** of some kind. It is important to recognize that no state standards describe or recommend what works for all students. Classroom teachers, not the standards, are the key to improving student learning in mathematics. The success of standards depends on teachers knowing how to expertly implement them. It is important as a teacher to be very knowledgeable about your own state standards and what they mean, not only at your grade level but also at the one above and below the one you teach. They are at the heart of planning lessons that are engaging, purposeful, coherent, and rigorous.

Regardless of whether your state has adopted *CCSS-M*, has modified the standards, or has written their own, the **big ideas** of K–2 mathematics are universal. Big ideas are statements that describe concepts that transcend grade levels. Big ideas provide focus on specific content. Here are the big ideas for K–2.

## Kindergarten

In kindergarten, students use numbers to represent quantities and to solve quantitative problems, such as counting objects in a set, counting out a given number of objects, comparing sets or numerals, and modeling joining and separating situations with sets of objects and simple equations such as $4 + 3 = 7$ and $7 - 4 = 3$. They study geometric ideas such as shape, orientation, and spatial relations. Kindergartners use basic shapes and spatial reasoning to model objects in their environment. At this grade, students work with measurement to compare measurable attributes and data to classify data and count the number of objects in each category.

## First Grade

First graders focus on developing understanding of addition, subtraction, and strategies for addition and subtraction within 20. They study place value, including grouping in tens and ones, and they work with linear measurement to measure lengths as iterating length units. Students at this level learn to tell and write time and represent and interpret data with graphs. In geometry, students compose and decompose shapes.

## Second Grade

Second-grade students extend understanding of the base-ten system, including counting in fives, tens, and multiples of hundreds, tens, and ones, as well as number relationships involving these units, including comparing. At this level, students use their understanding of addition to develop fluency with addition and subtraction within 100. They solve problems within 1,000 by applying their understanding of models for addition and subtraction. Second graders work with standard units of measure (centimeter and inch) and with time and money. They represent and interpret data. In geometry, students describe and analyze shapes by examining sides and angles, and they build, draw, and analyze two- and three-dimensional shapes to develop a foundation for understanding area, volume, congruence, similarity, and symmetry in later grades.

Standards

LI and SC

Purpose

Tasks

Materials

Student Thinking

Lesson Structures

Form. Assess.

Lesson Launch

Lesson Facilitation

Closure

## WHAT ARE ESSENTIAL QUESTIONS?

It is estimated that over the course of a career, a teacher can ask more than two million questions (Vogler, 2008). If teachers are already asking so many questions, why should they need to consider essential questions? An **essential question** is a building block for designing a good lesson. It is the thread that unifies all of the lessons on a given topic to bring the coherence and purpose discussed previously. Essential questions are purposefully linked to the big idea to frame student inquiry, promote critical thinking, and assist in learning transfer. (See Chapter 5 for more information on essential questions in transfer lessons.) As a teacher, you will want to revisit your essential question(s) throughout your unit.

Essential questions include some of these characteristics:

- *Open-ended.* These questions usually have multiple acceptable responses.

- *Engaging.* These questions ignite lively discussion and debate and may raise additional questions.

- *High cognitive demand.* These questions require students to infer, evaluate, defend, justify, and/or predict.

- *Recurring.* These questions are revisited throughout the unit, school year, other disciplines, and/or a person's lifetime.

- *Foundational.* These questions can serve as the heart of the content, such a basic question that is required to understand content to follow.

Not all essential questions need to have all of the characteristics. Here are some examples of essential questions that follow from big ideas for K–2.

- When and why do people estimate?

- Outside of school, when do we need to count?

- What patterns do you see when we look at place value?

- Why do we need standard units to measure?

- How many different ways can you represent 345?

- What would life be like if there were no numbers?

- What do mathematicians do when they get stuck on a problem?

- Where can we find two- and three-dimensional shapes in our world?

## WHAT ARE PROCESS STANDARDS?

Up to this point, we have been discussing content standards. However, every state also has a set of standards that define the **habits of mind** students should develop through mathematics. In 1989, the National Council of Teachers of Mathematics (NCTM) introduced these standards as process standards, stating that "what we teach [in mathematics] is as important as how we teach it" (NCTM, 1991), encouraging us to teach mathematics through these processes. Those standards are as follows:

- Communication
- Problem solving
- Reasoning and proof
- Connections
- Representations

The Common Core State Standards include the eight **Standards for Mathematical Practice** (SMPs), which also describe the habits of mind students should develop as they do mathematics (National Governors Association and Council of Chief State School Officers, 2010). The following SMPs are the same across all grade levels.

1. **Make sense of problems and persevere in solving them.** Students learn to understand the information given in a problem and the question that is asked. They use a strategy to find a solution and check to make sure their answer makes sense. If students reach a point where they are "stuck," they should not give up but relook and rethink about the problem in a different way, continuing to solve the problem.

2. **Reason abstractly and quantitatively.** K–2 students make sense of quantities and their relationships in problem situations. They develop operational sense by associating contexts to numbers, such as thinking about 4 + 3 as having four items and adding on three more items to find the total number of items.

3. **Construct viable arguments and critique the reasoning of others.** Students at this level begin to develop mathematical vocabulary and use it to explain their thinking and discuss their ideas. They listen to others and find how their own strategies are similar or different and why they work and/or make sense.

4. **Model with mathematics.** At the primary level, students use representations, models, and symbols to connect conceptual understanding to skills and applications. They may also represent or connect what they are learning to real-world problems.

5. **Use appropriate tools strategically.** K–2 students use a variety of concrete materials and tools, such as counters, tiles, straws, rubber bands, and physical number lines, to represent their thinking when solving problems.

6. **Attend to precision.** Students learn to communicate precisely with each other and explain their thinking using appropriate mathematical vocabulary. K–2 students expand their knowledge of mathematical symbols, which should explicitly connect to vocabulary development.

7. **Look for and make use of structure.** At this level, students discover patterns and structure in their mathematics work. Emphasis is placed on looking for structure through the use of physical models rather than algorithms.

8. **Look for and express regularity in repeated reasoning.** K–2 learners notice repeated calculations and begin to make generalizations. For example, they recognize that ten ones bundled together now represents a new unit, a ten. This helps students extend the understanding to bundling ten tens to make a new unit, a hundred.

The SMPs are not intended to be taught in isolation. Instead, you should integrate them into daily lessons because they are fundamental to thinking and developing mathematical understanding. As you plan lessons, determine how students use the practices in learning and doing mathematics.

Both sets of standards overlap in the habits of mind that mathematics educators need to develop in their students. These processes describe practices that are important when learning mathematics. Not every practice is evident in every lesson. Some lessons/topics lend themselves to certain practices better than others. For instance, you might use **classroom discourse** to teach a content standard through important mathematical practices.

Example: Michael

Michael, a first-grade teacher, uses the content of measurement to have his students engage in constructing viable arguments and critiquing the reasoning of the others.

Michael: What do you think is the best tool to measure the length of your math book?

Billy: I think I would use my yardstick.

Michael: Why did you choose the yardstick?

Billy: Because it has inches on it.

Michael: What does anyone think about measuring your math book with a yardstick? Do you agree that it is the best tool for the job?

LaRhonda: Yardstick is way too long. I think the ruler is better because it is shorter.

Michael: What about Billy's reason that a yardstick is good because it has inches?

Francis: But a ruler has inches, too, and it is shorter.

Through classroom discourse, Michael asked carefully selected questions about measurement to have his students engage in constructing viable arguments and critiquing the reasoning of the others. This is an example of how a content standard can be taught through important mathematical practices.

> **Think about the process standards/mathematical practices included in your state standards. Select one and reflect on how you weave it into your lessons.**
>
> _____
> _____
> _____
> _____
> _____
> _____
> _____
> _____
> _____
> _____
> _____
> _____
> _____
> _____

It is important to note that the decision to start with a big idea, essential question, or standard is up to you. Some districts have **pacing guides,** which dictate the order in which the standards must be taught. In that case, you need to do the following:

- Look at your standards and decide which big ideas it covers.

- Identify the common thread or essential question you want to weave through your lessons on this big idea.

If your district does not have a pacing guide, you may first want to select a big idea to teach and then select the state standards you will cover in the lessons.

## Building Unit Coherence

One of the best ways to build coherence between and among lessons within your unit is through the big ideas, essential questions, and standards. Keep in mind that connecting individual lessons through these three main elements promotes in-depth conceptual understanding, supports coherence, and unifies individual lessons. In fact, your lessons will share big ideas, essential questions, and shared standards within one unit. A big part of creating a coherent unit is strategically deciding how these three elements will be connected across the unit. Consider mapping the three components for the entire unit as you develop the lesson plan (Figure 3.1).

### Figure 3.1

**Unit-Planning Template**

**Unit Topic:**

| Unit Standards | Unit Big Ideas | Unit Essential Questions |
|---|---|---|
|  |  |  |

online resources — Download the Unit-Planning Template from resources.corwin.com/mathlessonplanning/k-2

Standards · LI and SC · Purpose · Tasks · Materials · Student Thinking · Lesson Structures · Form. Assess. · Lesson Launch · Lesson Facilitation · Closure

Kindergarten teachers know that counting—especially learning how to use numbers to answer the question "How many?"—is a big idea. Three teachers, Marilyn, Eliza, and Rena, want to ensure that their kindergarten students have internalized counting and can use it as a strategy when they need it. To help the children make connections, they decide to hold regular class discussions with their students about when they use counting in their life outside of school. Once they decide on the big idea ("Use numbers to represent quantities") and the essential question ("How can numbers help us in everyday life?"), the standards fall into place for them.

**Big Idea(s):**

Use numbers to represent quantities.

**Essential Question(s):**

How can numbers help us in everyday life?

**Content Standard(s):**

Write numbers from 0 to 20. Represent a number of objects with a written numeral 0 to 20 (with 0 representing a count of no objects).

**Mathematical Practice and/or Process Standards:**

Construct viable arguments and critique the reasoning of others.

Attend to precision.

*See the complete lesson plan in Appendix A on page 178.*

**What kinds of essential questions can you ask that encompass big ideas in your class? Record some of your responses below.**

_____

_____

_____

_____

_____

_____

_____

_____

_____

_____

_____

_____

_____

### Big Ideas, Essential Questions, and Standards

First-grade team Sarita, Jen, and Karlo are beginning to write their lessons on tens and ones. After discussing the ups and downs of last year's teaching of the topic, they decide they want an essential question that will guide them in keeping children from developing the misconception that there is only one way to decompose a number into tens and ones, a problem they ran into last year. They decide that they will focus the children on answering this question: "How can a number be represented with tens and ones in more than one way?"

**Big Idea(s):**

Group with tens and ones for place value.

**Essential Question(s):**

How can a number be represented with tens and ones in more than one way?

**Content Standard(s):**

Understand that the two digits of a two-digit number represent amounts of tens and ones.

**Mathematical Practice or Process Standards:**

Construct viable arguments and critique the reasoning of others.

Attend to precision.

*See the complete lesson plan in Appendix A on page 183.*

**What kinds of essential questions can you ask that encompass big ideas in your class? Record some of your responses below.**

Standards

LI and SC

Purpose

Tasks

Materials

Student Thinking

Lesson Structures

Form. Assess.

Lesson Launch

Lesson Facilitation

Closure

Second-grade teachers Aliyah and Dwayne are starting the year with the topic of place value. Aliyah notes that while her students can answer questions about place value, this year she wants students to show a greater understanding of place value concepts with more depth. Dwayne says that he wants to know more about whether his students understand the importance of the role of ten in our number system. Together they decide to use those thoughts to create the essential question that guides all of their lessons on this topic: "How is the number ten used in our system with ones and hundreds?"

### Big Idea(s):

Extend the base-ten system to relationship among the unit.

### Content Standard(s):

Demonstrate that each digit of a three-digit number represents amounts of hundreds, tens, and ones (e.g., 387 is 3 hundreds, 8 tens, 7 ones).

### Essential Question(s):

How is the number 10 used in our number system with ones and hundreds?

### Mathematical Practice and/or Process Standards:

Construct viable arguments and critique the reasoning of others.

Attend to precision.

*See the complete lesson plan in Appendix A on page 188.*

**Are there other topics in your grade level that could be guided by an essential question? Give some examples below.**

_____

_____

_____

_____

_____

_____

_____

_____

_____

_____

_____

_____

_____

**Under Construction**

Now it is your turn! You need to decide what big idea, essential question, and standards you want to build a lesson around. Start with your big idea and then identify the remaining elements.

**Big Idea(s):**

**Essential Question(s):**

**Content Standard(s):**

**Mathematical Practice and/or Process Standards:**

 Download the full Lesson-Planning Template from resources.corwin.com/mathlessonplanning/k-2
Remember that you can use the online version of the lesson plan template to begin compiling each section into the full template as your lesson plan grows.

Standards

LI and SC

Purpose

Tasks

Materials

Student Thinking

Lesson Structures

Form. Assess.

Lesson Launch

Lesson Facilitation

Closure

# CHAPTER 4

# REINFORCING YOUR PLAN
## Learning Intentions and Success Criteria

Leah, a first-grade teacher, felt her throat clench as she stood up to share her opinion. The entire staff at Robertson Primary had gathered together to brainstorm and decide upon goals for the following school year. Teachers had worked all morning deciding upon the language arts goals, and they were starting to get tired. She had been thinking about her idea for a schoolwide mathematics focus since a very awkward moment occurred in her classroom over two months ago. She just didn't know if she had the guts to tell the entire school. She looked at the expectant faces, took a deep breath, and began.

> I know that we have been posting objectives for years. I know that most of us also have the kids repeat or read the objective, too. Two months ago, I posted a measurement standard and read it to the students at the beginning of the lesson. Usually, they just stare at me and we move on. The standard said something like "describe measurable attributes." On this day, Kiley raised her hand and said, "What does that mean?" At first I said, "Well, you will find out when we do the lesson." But you know Kiley; she wasn't satisfied with that answer. I ended up launching into this whole explanation about how they would compare objects to find out which ones were long and short or heavy and light. Kiley raised her hand again and said, "Why can't you just say that?"

The teachers erupted in laughter, agreeing that primary students have a special way of making an obvious point for adults. Leah continued,

> About a week later, I ran across a blog about John Hattie's work, specifically regarding the importance of developing learning intentions and success criteria that students can understand. I think this is something we should explore. It just doesn't make sense to me that we are using learning objectives that our kiddos don't understand. Hattie's point is that students need to know what they are going to do and what success

looks like. I was thinking about it with our staff meeting today. Right at the start, Julia [the principal] told us what she wanted us to do and what we needed to accomplish before we left. Imagine if we didn't know the purpose of the meeting or what she needed from us before we left. We would be all over the place!

Again, the teachers laughed. One of Leah's colleagues, Jason, said,

> This seems so obvious! Let's think about how we can rewrite our objectives in kid-friendly language, and let's be sure to share them more deliberately in every lesson.

**Just as builders decide on the impact of structural changes, upgrades, and the timeline for completion, they must also envision how each of these decisions will affect the completed house. Just as builders need short- and long-term goals, teachers and students need specific learning intentions, or learning goals, that describe what you want the students to know, understand, and be able to do as a result of the learning experiences (Hattie et al., 2016). This chapter will explore the following questions:**

- What are learning intentions?
- What are mathematics learning intentions?
- What are language and social learning intentions?
- How do you communicate learning intentions with students?
- What are success criteria?
- How do learning intentions connect to the success criteria?
- When should learning intentions and success criteria be shared with students?

## WHAT ARE LEARNING INTENTIONS?

You begin the lesson-planning process by identifying the **learning intention.** The learning intention is "a statement of what students are expected to learn from the lesson" (Hattie et al., 2016, p. 41). The learning intention serves two purposes. First, it informs your design of the learning experience by focusing you and the students on deep learning rather than on completing activities. Second, it provides clarity to your students about their goal for the lesson. When students know the learning intention, they are more likely to focus on the lesson and take ownership for learning (Hattie et al., 2016). To ensure that the learning is rich and purposeful, students need to be active participants in discussing and understanding how the mathematics task or activity connects to the learning intention. Teachers design mathematics, language, and social learning intentions.

## WHAT ARE MATHEMATICS LEARNING INTENTIONS?

Mathematics learning intentions are aligned to the content standards. They focus on mathematics knowledge, skills, and/or concepts. NCTM's (2014b) *Principles to Actions: Ensuring Mathematical Success for All* identifies the importance of mathematics learning intentions in the first Exemplary Teaching Practice:

> Establish mathematics goals to focus learning. Effective teaching of mathematics establishes clear goals for the mathematics that students are learning, situates goals within learning progressions, and uses the goals to guide instructional decisions. (p. 10)

The mathematics learning intention is not a restatement of the standard. Rather, it is a scaffolded, student-friendly statement that reflects the part of the standard you are currently teaching. To design a mathematics learning intention, first begin with the standard and then construct one or more learning intentions using student-friendly language written from the students' point of view (see Figure 4.1).

---

**Figure 4.1**

| Standard | Mathematics Learning Intentions |
| --- | --- |
| Understand that the three digits of a three-digit number represent amounts of hundreds, tens, and ones. | I understand that each digit in a three-digit number represents a different value.<br><br>I understand that the position of the digit in a three-digit number identifies a specific value. |

---

You can also connect prior knowledge to mathematics learning intentions as you prompt students to share and talk about what they have already learned and how this connects to what they will be learning next. Some early childhood teachers prompt students to ask questions and pose "wonders" about what they will be learning on a Wonder Wall (Figure 4.2), activating students' prior knowledge and creating curiosity about new learning.

Standards

LI and SC

Purpose

Tasks

Materials

Student Thinking

Lesson Structures

Form. Assess.

Lesson Launch

Lesson Facilitation

Closure

**I Wonder...**

How high I can count?

If I can hold twenty things in my hand?

If my daddy can skip count by twos?

If there are 100 people in this school?

## WHAT ARE LANGUAGE AND SOCIAL LEARNING INTENTIONS?

### Language Learning Intentions

Language learning intentions connect to the Standards for Mathematical Practice (National Governors Association and Council of Chief State School Officers, 2010), state process standards, and mathematical vocabulary. Students are expected to develop and defend mathematical arguments, understand and explain their reasoning, and critique each other's reasoning.

When you create language learning intentions in addition to the mathematics content learning intentions, you help your students develop and use rich mathematics vocabulary (Hattie et al., 2016). Young children need to use new mathematics vocabulary often so it can be learned, integrated, and applied. Furthermore, English Language Learners are better supported with additional opportunities to speak about mathematics.

One way you can prompt language opportunities is to encourage your students to explain and justify their thinking. By providing specific language intentions, you create expectations for all of your students for using mathematical language in your classroom. You can develop the language learning intentions for the unit and then revisit them daily as they align to the mathematics learning intentions (Figure 4.3).

Figure 4.3

| Standard | Mathematics Learning Intentions | Language Learning Intentions |
|---|---|---|
| Understand that the three digits of a three-digit number represent amounts of hundreds, tens, and ones. | We are learning that<br><br>• each digit in a three-digit number represents a different value<br><br>• the position of the digit in a three-digit number identifies a specific value | We are learning to<br><br>• explain the value of each digit using place value vocabulary<br><br>• use mathematical words like *ones*, *tens*, *hundreds*, *place value*, and *digit* |

## Social Learning Intentions

Social learning intentions also connect to the Standards for Mathematical Practice (National Governors Association and Council of Chief State School Officers, 2010) and state process standards. Social learning intentions focus on particular social skills that students need to exhibit as they work together to collaboratively solve problems and communicate their thinking. Young children naturally construct learning through play, collaboration, and problem solving in formal and informal settings. Since learning is socially constructed through communication and collaboration with others (Vygotsky, 1978), you can tailor these social learning intentions to reflect what your students need. For instance, you can construct your social learning intentions to highlight the social skills your students need so they can work together to solve problems (Hattie et al., 2016). As with the language learning intentions, you can develop social learning intentions for the unit and specify the particular intentions you want students to work toward.

Example: Beatrice

Beatrice, a first-grade teacher, has been steadily working on helping her first graders solve problems in pairs. She decides to include four social learning intentions (Hattie et al., 2016) to target her first graders' listening skills (see Figure 4.4).

### Figure 4.4

**Learning Intentions for Partner Problem Solving**

We are learning to

- Listen when others are speaking
- Look at our partners when they are speaking
- Ask a question about what our partner shared with us
- Summarize what we heard our partner say

Example: Michelle

Michelle is one of many teachers charged with integrating the Standards for Mathematical Practice (National Governors Association and Council of Chief State School Officers, 2010) and other state process standards that ask students to "construct viable arguments and critique the reasoning of others" (para. 3). To address this charge, she regularly arranges her second graders in pairs to help solve a "debate" between two fictitious students who cannot agree on a mathematical solution (Figure 4.5).

### Figure 4.5

**Who wins the debate?**

Arnold and Arlette both have 105 buttons, but each person says the other one is describing the buttons incorrectly. Arnold says that he has ten groups of ten buttons and one group of five buttons. Arlette says that she has one group of one hundred buttons and a group of five buttons. Explain Arnold's and Arlette's reasoning. Be prepared to present your thinking to another pair of students.

Michelle's students must work together to understand the reasoning presented by the students in the example, explain their own reasoning to each other, come to an agreed-upon decision, and present their solution to another pair of students. Without such clear social and language learning intentions, the students might become confused about Michelle's expectation for this learning activity and miss out on important learning.

## HOW DO YOU COMMUNICATE LEARNING INTENTIONS WITH STUDENTS?

As you think about how to share learning intentions with your students, consider that the way in which you communicate the learning intentions reflects your beliefs about your students. By using positive and accessible language to frame what the students will learn, you can use learning intentions "as a means for building positive relationships with students" (Hattie et al., 2016, p. 48).

Consider two ways in which you might discuss the following place value standard and learning intentions.

**Standard:** Understand that the three digits of a three-digit number represent amounts of hundreds, tens, and ones; e.g., 706 equals 7 hundreds, 0 tens, and 6 ones. Understand the following as special cases: 100 can be thought of as a bundle of ten tens.

**Learning Intentions:** We are learning to

- Represent numbers using place value models

- Explain the value of any digit in a three-digit number

- Decide which numbers are greater or less by using what I know about place value

Now look at Figure 4.6. Which dialogue would you use to convey the intentions to students?

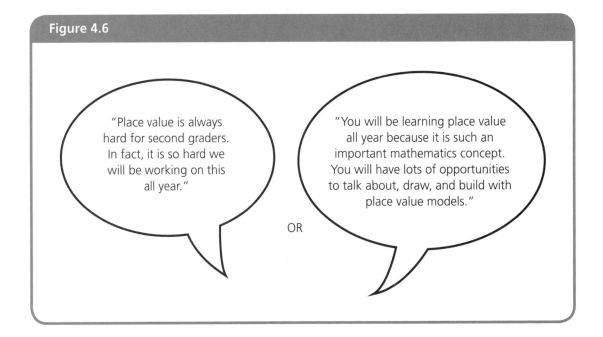

**Figure 4.6**

"Place value is always hard for second graders. In fact, it is so hard we will be working on this all year."

OR

"You will be learning place value all year because it is such an important mathematics concept. You will have lots of opportunities to talk about, draw, and build with place value models."

You can develop and post the language and social learning intentions for a series of lessons or the unit. Some teachers like to post the language and social learning intentions as they introduce the unit to the students. It can be particularly beneficial to focus on these learning intentions at the beginning of the year as you develop students' collaborative problem-solving and communication skills.

Standards

LI and SC

Purpose

Tasks

Materials

Student Thinking

Lesson Structures

Form. Assess.

Lesson Launch

Lesson Facilitation

Closure

> How does the way in which you communicate learning intentions support a positive environment for learning mathematics? Are there particular topics in your grade level that invite more positive discussions with students? Record some of your thoughts on this topic below.

## WHAT ARE SUCCESS CRITERIA?

Students also need to know how to tell when they have learned the mathematics. While learning intentions provide the purpose of the learning, the **success criteria** describe what the learning looks like when students understand and can do the mathematics they are learning. Clear success criteria can increase learner motivation because students know when they have learned and do not need to rely on a sticker, smiley face, or checkmark. Success criteria also prompt deeper, more meaningful learning because teachers can make sure that the success criteria mirror the learning intention and their students' learning needs. While all students are guided by the same learning intention, you can differentiate the success criteria to match your learners (Wiliam, 2011).

## HOW DO LEARNING INTENTIONS CONNECT TO THE SUCCESS CRITERIA?

It is also critical for you to include the students in understanding, monitoring, and celebrating achievement of the success criteria. Hattie and Yates (2013) identify five learning components that are valuable to determining learning intentions and success criteria. These include the following:

1. *Challenge.* Teachers must construct learning experiences that appropriately mix what students know with what they do not know.

2. *Commitment.* Teachers should also develop lessons that engage students' commitment to the learning.

3. *Confidence.* Students and teachers need to have confidence that the students will be able to learn the material. Confidence can be generated from the students' prior learning experiences, the teacher's skill in listening and providing targeted feedback, the selection of appropriate lesson tasks, and appropriate peer feedback.

4. *High expectations.* Teachers need to have high expectations for all students and believe that they can and will learn.

5. *Conceptual understanding.* Students need to be able to develop rich understanding of mathematics content.

As you write success criteria, be sure to use student-friendly language that focuses specifically on indicators of success.

Example: Bea

When Bea writes success criteria for her kindergarteners, she uses the same success criteria stem ("I know I am successful when …") to purposely trigger students' ownership. She then revisits the success criteria in individual progress conferences with students. During these conferences, she first focuses the students on the successes they have achieved. Then she identifies one or two criteria they have not yet achieved. Bea emphasizes the word *yet* to help her students understand that they are on their way. Together, Bea and her students determine strategies for improvement.

## WHEN SHOULD LEARNING INTENTIONS AND SUCCESS CRITERIA BE SHARED WITH STUDENTS?

Your decisions about when to share the learning intentions and success criteria with your students should depend solely on the purpose of your lesson. If you are presenting a problem or task for students to investigate because you want them to explore mathematics concepts first, then you should withhold the mathematics learning intention until later in the lesson. Once the mathematics learning intention is revealed, you can and should refer to the learning intention throughout the lesson.

Example: Emilio

Emilio, a first-grade teacher, posts the mathematics learning intention for problem-solving lessons but keeps it covered up until the point in the lesson when students begin to develop conceptual understanding and make connections. When his students see that a new learning intention has been posted and covered up, they get very excited because they know they will be exploring and problem solving. In a very strategic way, Emilio is communicating to the students that they are expected to solve the problem using multiple solutions, representations, and explanations.

How can you communicate success criteria with your students? Record a few of your ideas below.

## Building Unit Coherence

The focus on learning intentions and success criteria provides another good way to construct coherence across your lesson plans. Many of your learning intentions, particularly the language and social learning intentions, will be reflected over a longer time period, making this an ideal way to support coherence across your unit plan. As you design your lesson, keep a running list of those learning intentions and success criteria that students accomplish throughout the unit. Many teachers post the success criteria for the entire unit to help students see and understand what they are working toward.

Example: Tijuana

Tijuana, a first-grade teacher, uses a system of stars to signal to her students what they have achieved and an arrow to indicate the current success criteria that they are working on (Figure 4.7). This approach creates a coherent vision for both the teacher and her students.

### Figure 4.7

**Unit: Represent and interpret data**

**Success Criteria:**

★ I can collect, organize, and sort objects into groups.

★ I can show what I have sorted on a graph.

★ I can put labels and title on my graph.

⟶ I can talk about the information on a graph using math words.

Notes

Standards

LI and SC

Purpose

Tasks

Materials

Student Thinking

Lesson Structures

Form. Assess.

Lesson Launch

Lesson Facilitation

Closure

Kindergarten teachers Eliza, Marilyn, and Rena enjoy thinking about the learning intentions and success criteria for their students. They consider what great mathematics lessons would look like, particularly what they would do and what the students would do in the classroom to work through the set of standards they're planning to teach. In considering how to share the learning intentions and success criteria with their students, they decide to develop mathematics, language, and social learning intentions. Take a look at their decisions for just one important kindergarten standard.

## Learning Intention(s):

### Mathematics Learning Intentions

We are learning to
- Understand that a written number represents how many are in a group of objects by
  - Recording or writing numbers after we count groups of objects
  - Making a group of objects to match a number we see

### Language Learning Intentions

- Write or record numbers 0-20 after hearing the number called by our teacher or classmate.
- Use mathematical words like *subitize, group, set, match,* and *record.*

### Social Learning Intentions

- Listen to each other count.
- Ask questions about each other's counting.
- Explain how we know that a group of objects matches a number we see or hear.

## Success Criteria (written in student voice):

I know that I am successful when I can:
- Write a number I hear (even when not counted in order).
- Count a group of objects and record or write the number I counted.
- Write the number 0 for when there is no group of objects.
- Match a collection of objects with a subitized set.
- See a number and make a group of objects that matches that number.
- Match a group of objects to a number.

### Standards for Mathematical Practice Success Criteria:

- Stick with a problem even when I am not sure at first how to solve it.
- Listen to my classmates' explanations about place value and ask questions that show I understand place value.

*See the complete lesson plan in Appendix A on page 178.*

 **How could you communicate learning intentions and success criteria with your students? Record some of your ideas below.**

_____

_____

_____

_____

# Learning Intentions and Success Criteria

First-grade teachers Sarita, Jen, and Karlo are so excited to develop the learning intentions and success criteria that they create a "unit conference" for the students to help them understand what they will be learning and know when they are successful learning. During the conference time, teachers and students meet to talk about what the students will be learning and look at the manipulatives or tools that they plan to use. In addition, teachers send a copy of the learning intentions and success criteria home to families.

## Learning Intention(s):

### Mathematics Learning Intention

We are learning to
- Understand that a written number represents how many are in a group of objects by
  - Recording or writing numbers after we count groups of objects
  - Making a group of objects to match a number we see

### Language Learning Intentions

- Write or record numbers 0-20 after hearing the number called by our teacher or classmate.
- Use mathematical words like subitize, group, set, match, and record.

### Social Learning Intentions

- Listen to each other count.
- Ask questions about each other's counting.
- Work with a partner to count out how many tens and ones are in a group of objects.
- Explain how we know that a group of objects matches a number we see or hear.

## Success Criteria (written in student voice):

- Write a number I hear (even when not counted in order).
- Count a group of objects and record or write the number I counted.
- Write the number 0 for when there is no group of objects.
- Match a collection of objects with a subitized set.
- See a number and make a group of objects that matches that number.
- Match a group of objects to a number.

**See the complete lesson plan in Appendix A on page 183.**

 **How could you communicate learning intentions and success criteria with your families? Briefly write some ideas below.**

_____

_____

_____

_____

Second-grade teachers Dwayne, Aliyah, and Wilma decide to add some learning intentions that include the Standards for Mathematical Practices (National Governors Association and Council of Chief State School Officers, 2010) they want students to exhibit while learning mathematics. They note that thinking about the success criteria for the Standards for Mathematical Practice really helps them think about how they will frame their **instructional decisions** to align with these learning intentions and success criteria. Take a look at this team's work for this specific content standard.

## Learning Intention(s):
### Mathematics Learning Intentions

We are learning to

- Show three-digit numbers using base-ten blocks or other materials.
- Break apart three-digit numbers into the place values of hundreds, tens, and ones using manipulatives and drawings.
- Represent three-digit numbers using base-ten materials and pictures.

### Language Learning Intentions

- Explain our reasoning about place value to our classmates.
- Ask and answer questions about our place value understanding to our classmates.

### Social Learning Intentions

- Make sense of base-ten problems in collaboration with others.
- Productively struggle while solving them.

## Success Criteria
## (written in student voice):

- Explain the place value and value of each number in a one-, two-, and three-digit number.
- Explain and construct the place value and value of numbers when presented in varying orders (e.g., 3 tens, 4 hundreds, and 5 ones).
- Show the place value of three-digit numbers using base-ten blocks or pictures when presented with the number.
- Stick with a problem even when I am not sure at first how to solve it.
- Listen to my classmates' explanations about place value and ask questions that show I understand place value.

*See the complete lesson plan in Appendix A on page 188.*

 **Consider the process standards that you are required to use. How could you communicate the success criteria to your students? Write some of your ideas below.**

_____

_____

_____

_____

_____

_____

**Under Construction**

Your turn! Construct learning intentions and success criteria for the standard you previously identified.

**Learning Intentions (mathematical/language/social):**

**Success Criteria (written in student voice):**

 Download the full Lesson-Planning Template from resources.corwin.com/mathlessonplanning/k-2
Remember that you can use the online version of the lesson plan template to begin compiling each section into the full template as your lesson plan grows.

Standards

LI and SC

Purpose

Tasks

Materials

Student Thinking

Lesson Structures

Form. Assess.

Lesson Launch

Lesson Facilitation

Closure

# CHAPTER 5

# DECIDING ON PURPOSE

## *Why Are You Building This Lesson?*

"They got it!" first-grade teacher Brian yelled as he burst into the team planning room. His teammates, Moira and Jeanine, looked at each other and smiled. Brian was always so exuberant, which is why they loved working with him.

"Got what, Brian?" Moira prodded.

"I was just about to give up and move on with my mathematics group, and everything clicked today! I decided I needed to give my students a reason for breaking numbers into tens and ones. We have done a lot of work with the cubes and base-ten blocks, but they seemed to be doing it mechanically and not really understanding the patterns and how the number value is connected to the place value and position of the number. So, today, I taught a pretty meaty task where they had to 'package' candy into groups of ten. I gave them a customer order and asked them to figure out how many boxes they would need and how many leftover candies they would have. It was so exciting! You know Jeremy?"

Moira and Jeanine nodded and looked at each other, unsure of what Brian would say. They had all been worried about Jeremy because he was so reserved and seemed to consistently struggle with conceptual understanding. Brian spent a fair amount of time working with him individually.

"Well, first, he was engaged the whole time! Then at the end of the lesson, Jeremy said, 'I just noticed that in the number 24, the two means there are two tens so that would be two boxes

of ten candies! I think there is a pattern! Is there a pattern for hundreds, too?'"

Brian grinned. "I am just so excited that I did this lesson today!"

> **Writing a series of learning intentions and success criteria from your standards is only the beginning of lesson planning. Your learning intentions inform the *purpose* of each lesson. As mentioned in Chapter 2, there are three types of mathematics lessons organized by purpose: conceptual understanding lessons, lessons that bring about procedural fluency, and transfer lessons. Think of each of these as a room in the house you are building. Just as each room in a house has a different purpose (e.g., a kitchen is built for food preparation), each lesson should have a purpose (e.g., a transfer lesson is designed to let students pull together and apply the previous learning). This chapter will focus on answers to the following questions:**
>
> - What is the role of a conceptual understanding lesson?
> - What is procedural fluency and how does it build from a conceptual understanding lesson?
> - How do you know if you need a conceptual understanding or procedural fluency lesson?
> - How do you create a transfer lesson?

The National Research Council (2001) recommends five strands of proficiency that should be integrated into the teaching and learning of mathematics. These include the following:

*Conceptual understanding.* Comprehension of mathematical concepts, operations, and relationships.

*Procedural fluency.* The skill in carrying out procedures flexibly, accurately, efficiently, and appropriately.

*Strategic competence.* The ability to formulate, represent, and solve mathematical problems.

*Adaptive reasoning.* The ability to think logically, reflect, explain, and provide justification.

*Productive disposition.* The inclination to see mathematics as sensible, useful, and worthwhile, coupled with a belief in diligence and one's own efficacy.

These five stands of proficiency underlie the three types of mathematics lessons: conceptual understanding, procedural fluency, and transfer.

## WHAT IS THE ROLE OF A CONCEPTUAL UNDERSTANDING LESSON?

As described in Chapter 2, conceptual understanding involves comprehension of mathematical concepts, operations, and relations. In our scenario, Brian was very concerned that his students were not getting that depth of understanding about tens and ones. The National Assessment of Educational Progress's definition of conceptual understanding includes students demonstrating that they can recognize and generate examples of concepts using multiple representations (Braswell, Dion, Daane, & Jin, 2005). In addition, students compare and contrast concepts, operations, and relations.

Conceptual understanding lessons focus on providing opportunities for students to make sense of the mathematics they are learning. Students need an abundance of time and contexts to develop conceptual understanding. Therefore, your lessons need to provide time for students to build ideas through concrete experiences, engage in discourse about the mathematics they are learning, represent their thinking in multiple ways, and connect the concrete and pictorial **representations** to abstract ideas.

Your learning intentions, which come from your standards, help you decide if you need a conceptual lesson. For example, learning intentions that include verbs such as *understand, explain, relate, compose/decompose, represent,* and so forth imply that you want your students to show evidence that they can recognize, label, and generate examples of concepts. Your learning intentions that indicate you want a conceptual lesson involve students' reasoning in settings where they must make sense of concepts, relations, or representations. What follows are examples of learning intentions for K–2 that call for a conceptual lesson along with a conceptual task that will form the heart of a lesson.

*Kindergarten standard:* Work with numbers 11 to 19 to gain foundations for place value. Compose and **decompose** numbers from 11 to 19 into ten ones and some further ones, such as by using objects or drawings, and record each composition or decomposition by a drawing or equation (such as $18 = 10 + 8$); understand that these numbers are composed of ten ones and one, two, three, four, five, six, seven, eight, or nine ones.

Standards

LI and SC

Purpose

Tasks

Materials

Student Thinking

Lesson Structures

Form. Assess.

Lesson Launch

Lesson Facilitation

Closure

Figure 5.1

| Learning Intention | Conceptual Task |
|---|---|
| Students compose and decompose numbers from 11 to 19 into ten ones and leftover ones using manipulatives. | **How Many Can We Spin?**<br>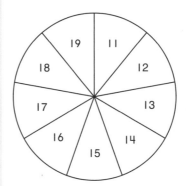<br>Students spin the spinner to find a number and then use blank ten frames to find ten ones and some more. Students record their spins. |
| Students represent numbers from 11 to 19 into ten ones and some more ones by drawing. | **How Many Can We Draw?**<br>Students receive digit cards for the numbers 11 to 19, drawing cards, and blank ten frames. Drawing cards have pictures for students to draw (e.g., circles, smiley faces, lines). |

| Ten Frame | More Ones | Number |
|---|---|---|
|  |  |  |
|  |  |  |

Have student pairs place the digit cards face down.

1. Taking turns, partners turn over a number card and a drawing card.

2. Each partner then draws the number of items to fill up the ten frame and the "extras" in the "more ones" section.

3. Partners then compare. Ask, "Do you have the same amount of ones or more ones?"

Figure 5.1 *(Continued)*

| Learning Intention | Conceptual Task |
|---|---|
| Students represent a number from 11 to 19 by using number bonds. | **Some More?**<br><br>Using ten-frame cards, students record a teen number as a ten and some ones using number bonds. Students begin with a filled-in ten frame:<br><br>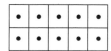<br><br>Then they draw another ten frame with "more ones" represented in the ten frame.<br><br>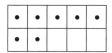<br><br>Students then create a number bond to represent that number.<br><br>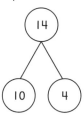 |
| Students represent a number from 11 to 19 by writing equations (e.g., 12 is $10 + 2 = 12$). | **Cut It!**<br><br>Give students strips of paper with dots, representing values of teen numbers.<br><br><br><br>Ask students to count ten and then cut the strip.<br><br>Finally, ask the students to record the ten and some more ones.<br><br>$10 + 5 = 15$<br><br>Students should do this for each teen number. |

Standards

LI and SC

Purpose

Tasks

Materials

Student Thinking

Lesson Structures

Form. Assess.

Lesson Launch

Lesson Facilitation

Closure

*First-Grade Standard:* Understand that the two digits of a two-digit number represent amounts of tens and ones. Understand the following as special cases:

- 10 can be thought of as a bundle of ten ones (called a "ten").
- The numbers from 11 to 19 are composed of a ten and one, two, three, four, five, six, seven, eight, or nine ones.
- The numbers 10, 20, 30, 40, 50, 60, 70, 80, and 90 refer to one, two, three, four, five, six, seven, eight, or nine tens (and 0 ones).

---

### Figure 5.2

| Learning Intentions | Conceptual Tasks |
|---|---|
| Students compose and decompose numbers from 11 to 19 into ten ones and leftover ones using manipulatives, representations, and writing. | **Birthday Candles!**<br><br>*Alanna, Nico, Marvin, Ronaldo, and Marjorie are celebrating their birthdays on the same day.*<br><br>*Alanna is 17, Nico is 16, Marvin is 15, Ronaldo is 13, and Marjorie is 11. They need your help arranging birthday candle sets of ten with the leftover ones.*<br><br>*Find out how many sets of ten and leftovers each birthday cake will have.*<br><br>Student pairs may draw or use objects to represent the tens and ones on the birthday cakes. Have student pairs order the cakes and explain how they determined the tens and ones.<br><br> |
| Students represent two-digit numbers using base-ten manipulatives, pictures, symbols, and/or objects. | **Spin It!**<br><br>Students use spinners to generate numbers to represent on a recording sheet using manipulatives, pictures, and symbols.<br><br> and |

---

**Figure 5.2 *(Continued)***

## Learning Intentions

## Conceptual Tasks

| Tens | Ones | Picture | Number |
|------|------|---------|--------|
|      |      |         |        |
|      |      |         |        |

Students identify, name, and explain the value of a group of ten within a number.

### How Many Tens?

Each student or pair of students places two sets of digit cards face down. Students draw a card from each set and form a number. Students then name the number and explain the value of the digit in the tens place. Students may also record the numbers.

| 0 | 1 | 2 | 3 | 4 |    | 0 | 1 | 2 | 3 | 4 |
|---|---|---|---|---|----|---|---|---|---|---|
| 5 | 6 | 7 | 8 | 9 |    | 5 | 6 | 7 | 8 | 9 |

| Number | Tens | Ones | Value of the Tens |
|--------|------|------|-------------------|
| 45     | 4    | 5    | 40                |
|        |      |      |                   |

Students identify and represent 10, 20, 30, 40, 50, 60, 70, 80, and 90 by the number of tens.

### Hundred Charts Tens Pattern

Distribute hundred charts to each group of students, and ask students to notice patterns in the multiples of tens column. Elicit from the students that the numbers are increasing by ten, that they are decreasing by ten, and that the digit in the tens place increases or decreases depending on the direction the students are viewing the hundreds chart. Ask students to represent 10, 20, 30, 40, 50, 60, 70, 80, and 90 using base-ten materials and record the number of tens.

*(Continued)*

Figure 5.2 (*Continued*)

| Learning Intentions | Conceptual Tasks |
|---|---|

| 1 | 2 | 3 | 4 | 5 | 6 | 7 | 8 | 9 | 10 |
|---|---|---|---|---|---|---|---|---|---|
| 11 | 12 | 13 | 14 | 15 | 16 | 17 | 18 | 19 | 20 |
| 21 | 22 | 23 | 24 | 25 | 26 | 27 | 28 | 29 | 30 |
| 31 | 32 | 33 | 34 | 35 | 36 | 37 | 38 | 39 | 40 |
| 41 | 42 | 43 | 44 | 45 | 46 | 47 | 48 | 49 | 50 |
| 51 | 52 | 53 | 54 | 55 | 56 | 57 | 58 | 59 | 60 |
| 61 | 62 | 63 | 64 | 65 | 66 | 67 | 68 | 69 | 70 |
| 71 | 72 | 73 | 74 | 75 | 76 | 77 | 78 | 79 | 80 |
| 81 | 82 | 83 | 84 | 85 | 86 | 87 | 88 | 89 | 90 |
| 91 | 92 | 93 | 94 | 95 | 96 | 97 | 98 | 99 | 100 |

*Second-Grade Standard:* Understand that the three digits of a three-digit number represent amounts of hundreds, tens, and ones (e.g., 706 equals 7 hundreds, 0 tens, and 6 ones). Understand the following as special cases:

- 100 can be thought of as a bundle of 10 tens, which is called a "hundred."
- The numbers 100, 200, 300, 400, 500, 600, 700, 800, and 900 refer to one, two, three, four, five, six, seven, eight, or nine hundreds (and 0 tens and 0 ones).

## Figure 5.3

| Learning Intentions | Conceptual Tasks |
|---|---|
| Students compose and decompose three-digit numbers into hundreds, tens, and ones in a context and with manipulatives. | **Hot Diggity Dog**<br><br>*Hot dogs come in packs of ten. Ten hot dog packages can be packed in a cooler. Samantha needs to buy 424 hot dogs for the school picnic. How many hot dog packs does she need? How many coolers will she need? How can you find out?*<br><br>After discussing the problem, arrange the students in small groups and distribute chart paper, markers, and base-ten manipulatives for students. Encourage the students to explain their reasoning. |

Figure 5.3 *(Continued)*

| Learning Intentions | Conceptual Tasks |
|---|---|
| Students can represent a hundred as ten groups of ten. | **Ten Tens!**<br><br>1. Arrange the students in pairs. Students need base-ten materials, digit cards, and a number cube.<br><br>2. First students decide on a target number. They can choose from 100, 200, 300, 400, 500, 600, 700, 800, or 900.<br><br>3. Students toss the number cube and then take that number of tens. Students will keep tossing until they reach 10 tens, which they will exchange for a hundred.<br><br>4. Students continue tossing until they reach the target number.<br><br>5. Have students explain how they exchanged the place values and the meaning of those exchanges. |
| Students can represent and explain the value of each digit in three-digit numbers. | **Spin and Talk**<br><br>Students need base-ten materials, spinners, and recording sheets. Students use spinners to generate numbers to represent on a recording sheet using base-ten manipulatives, pictures, and symbols.<br><br>Each partner spins, constructs the number, and records the number on the recording sheet. Partners describe their numbers using hundreds, tens, and ones vocabulary.<br><br>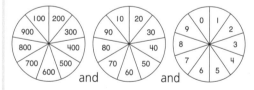 |

Hundreds, Tens, Ones, Picture, Number recording sheet:

| Hundreds | Tens | Ones | Picture | Number |
|---|---|---|---|---|
|  |  |  |  |  |
|  |  |  |  |  |

*(Continued)*

Standards

LI and SC

Purpose

Tasks

Materials

Student Thinking

Lesson Structures

Form. Assess.

Lesson Launch

Lesson Facilitation

Closure

**Figure 5.3 (*Continued*)**

| Learning Intentions | Conceptual Tasks |
|---|---|
| Students can explain the value of a zero in a three-digit number. | **Zoom in on Zero**<br><br>Students explore how a zero changes the value of the number.<br><br>Have the students place digit cards face down. Each student draws two cards. Then the students place the digit cards on the recording sheet, one row per person. Note that each row has a zero in a predetermined location. Students must place the digits cards in the remaining two locations. Then students draw pictures and record the numbers.<br><br><br>Ask students, "What do you notice about the number value when zero is in the hundreds place? Tens place? Ones place? If I have a 5, 8, and 0 digit card, what is the largest number I can make? Smallest number? What does a zero do to the value of the number?" |
| Students identify, name, and explain the value of a digit within a number by determining the position of the digit within a number. | **Switcheroo**<br><br>*What happens to the value of a number when we switch positions?*<br><br>Students will need digit cards or spinners from previous activities to create a number. After creating a number generated from the digit cards or the spinner, students will record the number in the recording sheet and use base-ten materials to represent the number. |

Recording sheet within "Zoom in on Zero":

| Hundreds | Tens | Ones | Picture | Number |
|---|---|---|---|---|
| 0 | | | | |
| 0 | | | | |
| | 0 | | | |
| | 0 | | | |
| | | 0 | | |
| | | 0 | | |

**Figure 5.3** *(Continued)*

| Learning Intentions | Conceptual Tasks |
|---|---|
| | 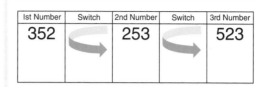 |
| | Ask students to explain what happens to the value of the number when the position of the digit is changed. |
| Students identify and represent 100, 200, 300, 400, 500, 600, 700, 800, and 900 by the number of hundreds. | **Rolling Hundreds**<br>Students will need a number cube or 0 to 9 spinner. Students toss a number cube or spin the spinner to determine the number of hundreds, draw a picture, and record the final value on the chart. |

## WHAT IS PROCEDURAL FLUENCY, AND HOW DOES IT BUILD FROM A CONCEPTUAL UNDERSTANDING LESSON?

While conceptual knowledge is an essential foundation, procedural fluency has its own prominent place in the mathematics curriculum. For years, there was debate in the mathematics education community over which is more important, conceptual understanding or procedural fluency. Procedural fluency involves more than simply memorizing basic facts and performing steps to an algorithm; conceptual understanding and procedural fluency have a balanced role to play in a student's mathematics education. All students need to be flexible in their thinking and know more than one way to perform a procedure. In addition, they should be able to select the most appropriate procedure for the situation (National Research Council, 2001). Here is an example where Juan, a first grader, is able to select the most appropriate strategy for a given question.

Teacher: What is seventeen minus four?

Juan: Thirteen.

Teacher: How did you do that so fast?

Juan: I counted. I say seventeen then sixteen, fifteen, fourteen, thirteen.

Teacher: What is fifteen minus twelve?

Juan: Three.

Teacher: And how did you do that?

Juan: I counted up! [Using his fingers] Thirteen, fourteen, fifteen. That's a three.

Juan demonstrated that he knew two different ways to subtract. In each situation, he used the procedure that was more efficient. In the first example, he counted down from 17. In the second example, he counted up to 15 from 12 and kept track of how many counts he used.

In their 2014 position statement on procedural fluency, the National Council of Teachers of Mathematics (NCTM) defined procedural fluency as "the ability to apply procedures accurately, efficiently, and flexibly; to transfer procedures to different problems and contexts; to build or modify procedures from other procedures;

LI and SC

Purpose

Tasks

Materials

Student Thinking

Lesson Structures

Form. Assess.

Lesson Launch

Lesson Facilitation

Closure

and to recognize when one strategy or procedure is more appropriate to apply than another" (NCTM, 2014c, para. 1). This definition involves more than memorization and more than knowing when to apply a given algorithm in a particular situation. From this example, you can see that Juan was able to recognize when one strategy was more appropriate/efficient than another.

Consider another example. Conrad, a first grader, has the conceptual understanding that numbers can be composed and decomposed. He also knows his basic "make 10" facts. Examine the following conversation between Conrad and his first-grade teacher:

> Teacher: What is eight plus four?
>
> Conrad: Ummmm … twelve.
>
> Teacher: How did you know that so quickly?
>
> Conrad: Well, first I think that four is two and two. And eight and two make ten. So ten and two more is [counting] ten … eleven, twelve.

Conrad showed that he knew he could make 10 and combine that with what he knew about decomposing the number 4 into 2 and 2. He was able to think flexibly. He demonstrated procedural fluency.

Just as your learning intentions help you decide if you should teach a conceptual understanding lesson, learning intentions also help you decide when procedural lessons are needed. In the previous example with Conrad, the teacher's learning intention was this: *The student will add two one-digit numbers fluently.* This required the teacher to give an example that was within the child's conceptual experience for decomposing numbers: 4 is the same as 2 and 2.

To develop procedural fluency, students need to experience integrating concepts and procedures. According to the mathematical teaching practices listed in *Principles to Actions: Ensuring Mathematical Success for All* (NCTM, 2014b), procedural fluency builds from conceptual understanding:

> Effective teaching of mathematics builds fluency with procedures on a foundation of conceptual understanding so that students, over time, become skillful in using procedures flexibly as they solve contextual and mathematical problems.

Conrad may not have been able to put the basic facts together with decomposing numbers if he had not had lessons that integrated the two ideas. Conrad's learning experiences were rooted in conceptual understanding. He had already been introduced to the idea that numbers can be composed and decomposed before he began memorizing basic facts to ten. But then he had experience integrating the two. Research backs up this sequencing of lessons, suggesting that once students memorize and practice a particular procedure or **algorithm,** they have little interest in learning how the procedure ties back to any concepts (Hiebert, 1999). Conceptual understanding lessons provide the foundation for flexible thinking with procedures, as in the example with Conrad and his teacher. For this reason, conceptual understanding lessons precede procedural fluency lessons. However, it is possible that you will need to go back and forth between conceptual and procedural lessons to help students make the connections.

Effective procedural fluency lessons connect procedures with the related concepts. Representations and discourse are the mortar that binds the lessons together. For example, look at a procedure that students in Grade 2 would be familiar with: subtraction. One example of a procedural lesson for subtraction involves asking students to complete a worksheet of 20 two-digit subtraction equations. A different lesson might center on the task shown in Figure 5.4.

---

**Figure 5.4**

Herbie completed a subtraction equation. Here is his work:

$$\begin{array}{r} 27 \\ -19 \\ \hline 12 \end{array}$$

---

**Figure 5.4** *(Continued)*

Herbie made a mistake. Find the correct answer. Write Herbie a letter telling him what he did wrong and how to solve the equation correctly.

*Student response:*

Herbie,

You made a big mistake! What were you thinking? The answer cannot be 12. Think about it like this. 19 is almost 20 and 27 minus 20 is only 7. Add one back from when you made 19 a 20 and you see the answer is only 8. You tried to subtract 9 – 7. I don't know why you did that.

In the Herbie task, students use discourse to connect what they understand about subtraction with the algorithm for subtraction. Students explain what they know. At the same time, the teacher can be investigating any common misconceptions about subtraction she or he finds. Students have an opportunity to justify their procedures and practice at the same time. This practice is brief, engaging, and purposeful. **Discourse** (written or spoken) allows students to link their conceptual understanding to the procedure.

The other lesson, the worksheet of 20 equations, does not tie into students' conceptual understanding of subtraction. The lesson may be ineffective and lead to math anxiety as per the findings of Isaacs and Carroll (1999). Computational methods that are overpracticed without understanding are forgotten or remembered incorrectly. This leads to student **misconceptions** (see Chapter 8).

The 20-equation worksheet scenario is an example of a traditional drill. **Drill** and **practice** are assignments often given to students to develop their procedural fluency. Traditionally, the terms *drill* and *practice* have been used synonymously. However, there is a difference. Practice, as noted previously, should be brief, engaging, and purposeful. Practice involves spreading out tasks or experiences on the same basic idea over time. Practice allows students the opportunity to solidify the conceptual understanding as the foundation for the procedures. The Herbie problem is an example of practice; students are being asked to solidify their reasoning of the procedure for subtraction. There is only one problem as opposed to 10, 20, or more, which is characteristic of drill. Drill refers to repetitive exercises designed to improve skills or procedures already known. It is a myth that drill is a learning tool. Drill is intended to be repetitive practice of what a student already knows.

Traditional **timed tests** of basic facts are examples of anxiety-producing drills. Some people erroneously equate timed tests with fluency. However, fluency involves the flexible use and understanding of numbers and quantities. A timed test of basic facts is based on memorization. There is no flexibility in thinking required. Research suggests that timed tests can cause **math anxiety** in children of all ability levels as early as 5 years old. This math anxiety can be seen in changes in the structure and workings of the child's brain (Young, Wu, & Menon, 2012). The anxiety is not limited to low achievers. According to Boaler (2012), the highest achievers can have the greatest amount of anxiety, even though this anxiety is shared across all achievement levels.

Fluency is *not* something that happens all at once in a single grade. Instead, it requires teachers to pay attention to student understanding and help them develop fluency over time. In primary grades, students learn about addition and subtraction **strategies** used to perform the operations. They apply this understanding to make computation more efficient. They learn that the numbers they are trying to calculate help them determine what strategy would be most efficient.

 **Think of a computation lesson you have read in a textbook or other source. How does it fit (or not fit) this summary of primary mathematical fluency? Note your answer here.**

_____

_____

_____

## HOW DO YOU KNOW IF YOU NEED A CONCEPTUAL UNDERSTANDING OR PROCEDURAL FLUENCY LESSON?

Your standards and learning intentions give you direction as to whether a lesson should be for conceptual understanding or procedural fluency. Standards and learning intentions that focus on understanding mathematics call for a conceptual lesson. A few examples can be found in Figure 5.5.

### Figure 5.5

| Standard | Conceptual Understanding | Procedural Fluency |
|---|---|---|
| Write numbers from 1–20. | | ✓ |
| Understand that the last number word said when counting answers the question "How many?" | ✓ | |
| Understand subtraction as an unknown addend problem. | ✓ | |
| Add and subtract within 20. | | ✓ |

Notice that some standards easily point to a purpose because they use the words *understand* or *add*. However, other standards are not so obvious. Let's look at a standard that is not so clear.

Apply properties of operations as strategies to add and subtract.

For this standard, teachers need to look at learning intentions. This standard can be unpacked into several learning intentions:

- Understand the identity property of addition $(4 + 0 = 4)$.
- Understand the commutative property of addition $(5 + 9 = 14$ and $9 + 5 = 14$ so $5 + 9 = 9 + 5)$.
- Use the commutative property to find the answer to related addition facts (e.g., by knowing $7 + 6 = 13$, I can use that fact to find $6 + 7$).
- Use the identity property to find answers to unknown facts such as $45 + 0 = 45$.

These mathematical learning intentions indicate that for students to master the standard, they must engage in conceptual understanding *and* procedural fluency lessons.

> Look at the standards you are about to teach. Collaborate with a colleague and decide what the purpose of the lessons should be to meet those standards. Note the key points from your discussion here.
>
> _____
>
> _____
>
> _____
>
> _____

## How Do You Create a Transfer Lesson?

Transfer is the primary goal of all instruction: to ensure that students are able to use what they have learned in the real world. This goal informs the third type of lesson in mathematics: transfer. While there are many different interpretations of transfer, a transfer lesson is one in which students demonstrate a transfer of learning (their ability to effectively use conceptual knowledge and procedural fluency skills in a problem situation). Chapter 1 discussed Hattie et al.'s (2016) definition of a transfer task as one that should encourage connections and be open-ended with multiple entry points.

So the question you must ask yourself in planning for transfer is "What is the understanding that my students will need in the future when they are no longer in school?" This should remind you of the essential questions discussion in Chapter 3. While your conceptual understanding and procedural fluency lessons are based on your learning intentions, your transfer lessons are based on your essential questions. After all, if you don't design lessons for transfer, why design lessons at all? If people know how to use a hammer and nails, it does not mean they can build a house. Likewise, if students know how to add or subtract, it does not mean they can balance a checkbook.

To know if you have created a transfer lesson, use the checklist in Figure 5.6.

### Figure 5.6

**Rubric for Creating a Transfer Lesson**

| Does the lesson allow students to | Yes or No |
|---|---|
| • make sense of a real-world problem as opposed to a contrived word problem? | |
| • persevere in solving the problem? | |
| • apply mathematical reasoning? | |
| • reason abstractly and quantitatively? | |
| • use appropriate tools strategically? | |
| • work with content of the big ideas or essential questions of the topic taught? | |
| • construct viable arguments or critique the reasoning of others? | |

 You can locate this Rubric for Creating a Transfer Lesson at
resources.corwin.com/mathlessonplanning/k-2

Figure 5.7 shows examples of transfer tasks for K–2 based on essential questions.

Standards

LI and SC

Purpose

Tasks

Materials

Student Thinking

Lesson Structures

Form. Assess.

Lesson Launch

Lesson Facilitation

Closure

**Figure 5.7**

| Kindergarten Essential Question | Transfer Task |
|---|---|
| How can numbers help us in everyday life? | Here is a bag of candy. You want to share it with all of your classmates. Do you have enough pieces in the bag for everyone to have one piece? Your friend Mark says no. Explain to Mark if he is right or wrong and how you know. |

| First-Grade Essential Question | Transfer Task |
|---|---|
| How can a number be represented with tens and ones in more than one way? | You give the cafeteria worker 27 cents for a bag of chips. How many different ways can you make 27 cents using only dimes and pennies? |

| Second-Grade Essential Question | Transfer Task |
|---|---|
| How is the number 10 used in our number system with ones and hundreds? | You just learned that there are many boys and girls around the world who do not go to school and don't know about place value in numbers. Write a short book in English with pictures teaching them about place value. |

Go back to the essential question and transfer task for your grade level. Apply the checklist and reflect on how each item fits the task. Summarize your thoughts below.

_____

_____

_____

_____

_____

_____

_____

_____

_____

_____

_____

Standards

LI and SC

Purpose

Tasks

Materials

Student Thinking

Lesson Structures

Form. Assess.

Lesson Launch

Lesson Facilitation

Closure

## Building Unit Coherence

Connecting lesson purposes across a unit develops coherence because you are strategically linking conceptual understanding, procedural fluency, and transfer lessons to build comprehensive understanding of the unit standards. As you develop your lesson, consider the purposes of the lessons that come before and after the lesson you are constructing. Over the course of one unit, you should develop and facilitate lessons with all three purposes, bearing in mind how and when the lesson purposes should be positioned within the unit. Some teachers map out their unit with lesson purposes in mind to ensure that they are developing coherence within lesson purpose (Figure 5.8).

### Figure 5.8

Unit:

| Day 1 | Day 2 | Day 3 | Day 4 | Day 5 |
|---|---|---|---|---|
| Conceptual | Conceptual | Conceptual | Procedural Fluency | Procedural Fluency |
| Day 6 | Day 7 | Day 8 | Day 9 | Day 10 |
| Conceptual | Conceptual | Conceptual | Procedural Fluency | Transfer |

Now that you have been introduced to the three lesson purposes, reflect on the lessons in your curriculum guide, textbook, or supplemental materials. Can you categorize the lessons into these three categories? Do you notice one type being more prevalent than the others? Note any thoughts or concerns here.

_____
_____
_____
_____
_____
_____
_____
_____
_____
_____
_____

Kindergarten teacher Rena begins the professional learning community meeting (PLC) by sharing the following:

I know that we always focus on conceptual understanding with our students. I will be the first to admit that I can get sidetracked by cute ideas I see on Pinterest. Sometimes, I feel like we need to make sure that we are really, truly purposeful in our lesson planning. I just need to be reminded that the lesson purpose centers on these ideas about conceptual, procedural, and transfer learning instead of the activity.

Marilyn suggests that they should indicate the purpose of every lesson in their PLC planning. Eliza quickly agrees that this is a great idea. Using the suggested template, they check the conceptual understanding box after deciding in PLC that the first lesson will be focus on concepts.

## Purpose:

☑ Conceptual Understanding ☐ Procedural Fluency ☐ Transfer

*See the complete lesson plan in Appendix A on page 178.*

**How do you decide on the purpose for your lessons? Write your thoughts below.**

_____

_____

_____

_____

_____

_____

_____

_____

_____

_____

_____

_____

_____

_____

_____

_____

_____

_____

_____

Standards

LI and SC

Purpose

Tasks

Materials

Student Thinking

Lesson Structures

Form. Assess.

Lesson Launch

Lesson Facilitation

Closure

## First-Grade Snapshot

### Lesson Purpose

First-grade teachers Sarita, Jen, and Karlo look over their plans from the previous year. Karlo shares, "I would like to include more transfer lessons in our planning. I think the students need more experiences applying what they learn to new situations."

Sarita replies, "I love this idea, Karlo. I think this will be really motivating for our students." They check the transfer box on their lesson-planning template and move on to discuss the lesson.

**Purpose:**

☐ Conceptual Understanding          ☐ Procedural Fluency          ☑ Transfer

*See the complete lesson plan in Appendix A on page 183.*

**How do you decide on the purpose of your lessons? Write your thoughts below.**

_____

_____

_____

_____

_____

_____

_____

_____

_____

_____

_____

_____

_____

_____

_____

_____

_____

_____

Dwayne begins the second-grade planning day with this announcement:

I think we should discuss how we can make sure that we are developing conceptual, procedural, and transfer lessons so that all students have the chance to experience all of them. In the past, some of our students haven't gotten an opportunity to engage in transfer opportunities. Remember Alberto last year. We were always using that lesson time to pull him in for extra help and we never asked him to do the transfer tasks. As we design our conceptual lessons, can we plan out how we will begin and end?

His colleagues, Aliyah and Wilma, nod their heads in full agreement.

Aliyah says, "Let's make sure we begin with a strong conceptual lesson."

**Purpose:**

☑ Conceptual Understanding        ☐ Procedural Fluency        ☐ Transfer

*See the complete lesson plan in Appendix A on page 188.*

**This second-grade team begins with a conceptual lesson. Would there ever be a time when you might begin with a procedural fluency or transfer lesson? Why? Explain your thinking below.**

Standards

LI and SC

Purpose

Tasks

Materials

Student Thinking

Lesson Structures

Form. Assess.

Lesson Launch

Lesson Facilitation

Closure

## Under Construction

Using the lesson plan you are designing, decide on your purpose. Remember that your purpose comes from your standards and learning intentions.

**Purpose:**

☐ Conceptual Understanding     ☐ Procedural Fluency     ☐ Transfer

**online resources** Download the full Lesson-Planning Template from resources.corwin.com/mathlessonplanning/k-2 Remember that you can use the online version of the lesson plan template to begin compiling each section into the full template as your lesson plan grows.

Notes

# CHAPTER 6

# CHOOSING TASKS
## *The Heart of a Lesson*

Frustrated, Jessica stared at the mathematics standard and the lesson seed idea provided by her school district (Figure 6.1):

### Figure 6.1

| Standard | Lesson Task |
|---|---|
| Add up to four two-digit numbers using place value models. | Jacob was on vacation at the beach with his family and found 23 seashells on the beach on Monday. On Tuesday, he found 13 more. On Wednesday, he found 34 seashells. How many seashells did Jacob find? |

### Figure 6.2

This is a map of Dory's travels.

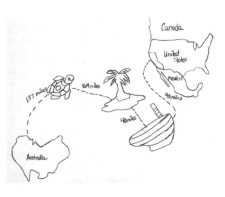

Dory thinks she will travel a total of 326 miles. Can you help Dory figure out if she is correct? Use place value to prove your thinking, and explain why she is or is not correct.

Source: Jessica Steinbacher, Stevenson University.

"This is just not going to work," she said to herself. Her students did not take beach vacations, and most of them had probably not held a seashell. She needed to make sure she used a task that reflected the students' interests and experiences. Lately, they had been completely obsessed with the *Finding Dory* movie. Even students who had not seen the movie seemed intrigued with the Dory stickers she had brought in to share with them. Jessica knew that this task needed to match the standard, be interesting to the students, be robust, and promote productive struggle. She also wanted the students to be able to create a mathematical argument. After several revisions, Jessica decided on the task shown in Figure 6.2.

Jessica decided to present the task and ask them to solve it in pairs and small groups. She was so excited to share this task with students, she could hardly wait!

A worthwhile task is the heart of a lesson. In fact, selecting the task is the most important decision teachers make that affects instruction (Lappan & Briars, 1995; Smith & Stein, 2011). This chapter will address the following questions:

- Why are tasks important?
- What is a worthwhile task?
- How do you adapt a task?
- What are some sources for worthwhile tasks?

## WHY ARE TASKS IMPORTANT?

Effective teachers understand that the **tasks** they choose influence how their students make sense of mathematics. Tasks should challenge students to explore mathematical concepts; they should not be designed simply to have children work to get the right answer. Getting students to use **higher-order thinking skills,** such as those from Bloom's Taxonomy (create, evaluate, apply, and so forth), is a hallmark of a worthwhile task. As you plan your lessons, be sure to select tasks to reach this goal. Consider the following two examples.

> Example 1: Jennifer
>
> Jennifer gives her first-grade students this challenge:
>
> > There are 7 candy bars on two tables. Draw a picture to show how the 7 candy bars can be arranged on the two tables. Can you find more than one way? How many ways do you think there are?
>
> Example 2: Carlos
>
> Carlos asks his first graders the following question:
>
> > John has 4 apples and Maria has 3 oranges. How many pieces of fruit do John and Maria have altogether?

These two examples illustrate the types of questions that teachers ask students all the time. However, only one is an example of a worthwhile task. The following section will identify the characteristics of a worthwhile task.

## WHAT IS A WORTHWHILE TASK?

There are eight characteristics of worthwhile tasks:

1. Uses significant mathematics for the grade level
2. Rich
3. Problem solving in nature
4. Authentic/interesting

5. Equitable
6. Active
7. Connects to the Process Standards
8. High cognitive demand

Take a look at each feature in more detail.

### Uses Significant Mathematics for the Grade Level

The big ideas, essential questions, and standards from your lesson should be your guiding light for finding a worthwhile task; these three elements keep your lesson plan coherent. Tasks based on significant mathematics focus on students' understandings and skills, and they stimulate students to make sense of the mathematics they are learning. A task should take into account students' prior knowledge and the understandings and skills already taught at this grade level or previous grades.

### Rich

Each task should be challenging, requiring students to use higher-order thinking skills. Smith and Stein (1998) refer to this kind of task as a *high cognitive demand task*. A **high cognitive demand** task encourages students to represent their thinking in multiple ways, explore various solution pathways, and connect procedures to mathematics. The task selected invites students to "do" the mathematics.

A rich task also has the potential for students to make connections and extend their thinking. Students must regulate their thinking and monitor their ideas and strategies to solve the problem.

As you evaluate the success of your tasks, keep this in mind: If students immediately know the answer, then the task was not challenging.

Standards
LI and SC
Purpose
Tasks
Materials
Student Thinking
Lesson Structures
Form. Assess.
Lesson Launch
Lesson Facilitation
Closure

## Problem Solving in Nature

When a task is problem solving in nature, students will not know how to immediately and routinely solve it. They will need to reason and develop a new strategy or try previously learned strategies to seek a solution. Simply applying an algorithm to arrive at the answer is not problem solving. **Productive struggle** is a hallmark of problem solving. This means that students wrestle with a solution strategy and must apply effort to make sense of the mathematics—to figure something out that is not obvious. The challenge may not come easy to them, but they persevere. Good problems have multiple entry points so that all students have an opportunity to learn.

## Authentic/Interesting

An authentic and interesting task is one that represents mathematics as a useful tool for navigating the real world. It captures students' curiosity and invites them to wonder and make conjectures. Authentic/interesting tasks prompt classroom discourse and pique student interest either through the topic or the method of engagement. This does not mean that the task must be real world. In fact, many young children are just as interested in fanciful stories that stimulate their curiosity.

## Equitable

When a task is equitable, it has multiple entry points and representations so that students of all levels, abilities, and skills can access the task. Nrich (2011) from the University of Cambridge describes these kinds of tasks as having a low threshold and high ceilings (LTHC), and Jo Boaler (2015) describes them as having low floors and high ceilings. Essentially, this means that when a task is equitable, "everyone in the group can begin and then work at their own level, yet the task also offers lots of possibilities for learners to do much more challenging mathematics, too" (Nrich, 2011, para. 6). The content can be fairly simple, but the processes and the thinking that students do are much more complex. Some students may solve a task using manipulatives while others apply symbols at a more abstract level. The task is also nonbiased, meaning it does not contain information that stereotypes individuals or groups of people, and it is culturally sensitive. The teacher honors and respects all students' ideas and solutions pathways.

## Active

With an active task, students are engaged in doing the mathematics. They are decision makers. An active task requires more than simply applying an algorithm. Students must develop reasons, offer explanations, and actively figure things out to make sense of the task and its solution.

## Connects to the Process Standards

The tasks you select should be designed to encourage students to exhibit process standards. Sometimes, teachers believe the way to challenge learners is by presenting them with higher-level content. However, this act alone does not necessarily support all students to reason, communicate mathematically, use and apply representations, see and use patterns, and recognize the underlying structure of the mathematics they are learning. By ensuring that a task incorporates opportunities for students to demonstrate the process standards, you support their learning.

## High Cognitive Demand

According to Van de Walle et al. (2016), "A high cognitive demand task is a task that requires students to engage in a productive struggle, that challenges them to make connections to concepts and to other relevant knowledge" (p. 37). These tasks always call for some degree of higher-level thinking, and students cannot routinely solve them. Students often use multiple representations such as manipulatives or diagrams to help develop the meaning of mathematical ideas and to work through the task to develop their understanding (Smith & Stein, 2011).

Based on these characteristics, it is important to point out that all worthwhile tasks are problems, but not all problems are worthwhile tasks.

To determine if a task is worthwhile for you to use in a lesson, use the rubric shown in Figure 6.3. The first column identifies the characteristic, and the next three columns allow you to rate the degree to which you feel the task has met that characteristic by checking the box, with 1 being not acceptable and 3 being a good example of that characteristic. The final column is for any comments you would like to discuss with your colleagues.

**Figure 6.3**

### Determining a Worthwhile Task Rubric

| Characteristic | 1 | 2 | 3 | Notes |
|---|---|---|---|---|
| Uses significant mathematics for the grade level | | | | |
| Rich | | | | |
| Problem solving in nature | | | | |
| Authentic/interesting | | | | |
| Equitable | | | | |
| Active | | | | |
| Connects to Standards for Mathematical Practice or Process Standards | | | | |
| High cognitive demand | | | | |

online resources — This Determining a Worthwhile Task Rubric can be downloaded for your use at
resources.corwin.com/mathlessonplanning/k-2

Thinking about Jennifer and Carlos and their tasks, rate the tasks using the checklist in Figure 6.3. Discuss your results with a colleague. Whose example is a worthwhile task and why? Note your thoughts below.

Standards
LI and SC
Purpose
Tasks
Materials
Student Thinking
Lesson Structures
Form. Assess.
Lesson Launch
Lesson Facilitation
Closure

## HOW DO YOU ADAPT TASKS?

In the vignette presented at the beginning of the chapter, Jessica wanted to develop a task that more closely aligned to her students' experiences and interests. You may also have experienced a time when you encountered a textbook or school district task that did not match the unique needs of your learners. Like Jessica, many teachers choose to adapt tasks to increase the cognitive demand (Smith & Stein, 2011) and to provide more entry points for students to reason mathematically. Here are a few examples.

Example: Michaela

Michaela, a second-grade teacher, found the task in Figure 6.4 in her textbook and adapted it to incorporate the process standards.

---

**Figure 6.4**

| Original Task | Adapted Task |
| --- | --- |
| Leo counted 32 books on the top shelf of his bookcase and 48 on the bottom shelf. How many books does he have on his bookcase? | Leo and Lettie are arguing about who has the most books on their bookshelves. Leo has two shelves with 32 books on one shelf and 48 on the other. Lettie has three shelves with 22, 18, 37 on each of her shelves. Who has the most books and how do you know? |

---

Example: Marty

Marty, a first-grade teacher, was given the task in Figure 6.5 by his school district. He wanted to design a low-floor high-ceiling task to provide more entry points for his students.

---

**Figure 6.5**

| Original Task | Adapted Task |
| --- | --- |
| Margot saw 2 dogs in the dog park. Each dog has 4 paws. How many paws did she see? | Margot saw 4 dogs in the dog park. How many paws did she see? How many ears? Did Margot see more ears or paws? |

---

Example: Andrea

Andrea, a second-grade teacher, found the task in Figure 6.6 after an Internet search.

**Figure 6.6**

| Original Task | Adapted Task |
|---|---|
| Decide if the statement is true or false.<br><br>$3 + 4 = 6 + 2$     $12 = 3 + 8$ | Some of these equations are true and some are false. Alex says that three are true and Mariana says that four are true. Explain who is correct.<br><br>$6 + 8 = 5 + 5$     $12 = 9 + 3$<br><br>$11 = 6 + 4$     $2 + 8 = 7 + 4$<br><br>$9 + 7 = 8 + 8$     $3 + 4 = 0 + 7$ |

**What do you notice about how each of the teachers enhanced the task? How might you "open" up your tasks to make them worthwhile? Jot a few notes below.**

_____

_____

_____

_____

## WHAT ARE SOME SOURCES FOR WORTHWHILE TASKS?

Tasks can be problems, short- or long-term projects, or games. In Chapter 5, we listed many tasks as they relate to K–2 learning intentions. You'll find some reliable sources for K–2 worthwhile tasks both online and in print form in Appendix C.

### Building Unit Coherence

Tasks are another great way to build coherence and ensure rigor throughout a unit. As you look across the unit, you can connect the tasks that you construct or select. Some primary teachers do this by linking the tasks across a theme. Others do this by extending tasks over two or three days so students have plenty of time to dive into the concept.

Example: Huan

Huan, a kindergarten teacher, designed a counting task that spanned three days for her students. Each day, the kindergartners counted and charted items in bags using different tools like ten frames, ice cube trays, bowls, and egg cartons to keep track of the amounts. At the conclusion of the three-day task, students shared their counting and recording techniques and decided which tool helped them accurately count.

Standards

LI and SC

Purpose

Tasks

Materials

Student Thinking

Lesson Structures

Form. Assess.

Lesson Launch

Lesson Facilitation

Closure

Three kindergarten teachers, Marilyn, Eliza, and Rena, are reviewing several tasks for the standard they selected on counting. They know they will need to teach several tasks for this lesson, and decide that they would like to have the students explore a counting task that aligns to their science unit on insects.

Rena shares, "Although we don't always have to match our tasks to other content areas, I find that some of the students retain more when we make cross-curricular connections."

Marilyn suggests, "We also need to be able to connect the task to the *counting, construct a mathematical argument,* and *use precise language learning intentions*. I would like to have them estimate first and then count."

## Task:

### How Many Insects?

The insects are crawling all over the leaves! We need to find out how many insects are on each leaf. How can we find out?

Note: The downloadable student worksheets contain 11 leaves representing numbers 10 to 20.

**See the complete lesson plan in Appendix A on page 178.**

 This task can be downloaded for your use at resources.corwin.com/mathlessonplanning/k-2

 **Why do you think this is a good kindergarten task? Use the task checklist to help you decide. Write any thoughts or concerns below.**

_____

_____

_____

_____

_____

_____

_____

_____

_____

_____

_____

Standards

LI and SC

Purpose

Tasks

Materials

Student Thinking

Lesson Structures

Form. Assess.

Lesson Launch

Lesson Facilitation

Closure

**First-Grade Snapshot**

*Task Selection*

Sarita hopes to convince her teammates to design a task that will match the conceptual purpose for developing place value. When she meets with Rena and Karlo, Rena shares how much the students enjoy hearing about the teachers' families. Karlo explains that his aunt is starting a cupcake business just down the road from the school. Together, they decide that this would be the perfect context for the place value task. Karlo will gather real pictures of his aunt's cupcake business! Sarita also reminds them that they need to make sure the task engages the students in problem solving and provides multiple entry points for students to reason.

## Task:

### Aunt Jasmine and Uncle Ronnie's Cupcakes

Aunt Jasmine has a new cupcake business. Uncle Ronnie is helping Aunt Jasmine keep track of how many she sells. He wants to know how many cupcakes she sold last week, but she doesn't know! She is so busy making cupcakes that she cannot keep track of her orders!

Aunt Jasmine needs your help sorting the cupcake orders. Uncle Ronnie needs to know how many groups of ten are in each order and how many leftovers are in each order. Can you help find the number of groups of tens and ones? You must be able to show and explain all of your thinking. The orders they received today are 47, 56, 39, 87, and 62.

| Aunt Jasmine's Cupcakes Order Form | Aunt Jasmine's Cupcakes Order Form | Aunt Jasmine's Cupcakes Order Form | Aunt Jasmine's Cupcakes Order Form | Aunt Jasmine's Cupcakes Order Form |
|---|---|---|---|---|
| 47 | 56 | 39 | 87 | 62 |

**See the complete lesson plan in Appendix A on page 183.**

 This task can be downloaded for your use at resources.corwin.com/mathlessonplanning/k-2

**Why do you think this is a good first-grade task? Use the checklist to help you decide. Write any thoughts or concerns below.**

_____

_____

_____

_____

_____

_____

_____

_____

_____

When the second-grade teachers meet to plan lessons, Aliyah shares the following:

> After our discussion about developing robust tasks, I realized that my tasks were not very robust. I would like to see how we could change some of the tasks we are using to encourage students to incorporate multiple learning intentions. I would also like the tasks to encourage the students to communicate mathematically and to develop mathematical arguments to justify their reasoning. Do you think we could set up our place value task to do this?

Dwayne agrees and says, "I think this will also engage them in wanting to find a solution and prove they are correct."

Wilma exclaims, "Yes, let's do this!"

### Task:

#### Bucket of Blocks!

Elaine, Roberto, and Janine all grabbed a bucket of base-ten blocks. Elaine's bucket has 2 hundreds, 9 tens, and 2 ones. Roberto's bucket has 8 ones, 6 hundreds, and 5 tens. Janine's bucket has 50 ones and 20 tens. Elaine, Roberto, and Janine each think they have the greatest value. Help them figure out who has the greatest value. Represent and explain your thinking to prove who is right!

*See the complete lesson plan in Appendix A on page 188.*

 This task can be downloaded for your use at resources.corwin.com/mathlessonplanning/k-2

**Why do you think this is a good second-grade task? Use the checklist to help you decide. Write any thoughts or concerns below.**

**Under Construction**

Using your lesson plan that is under construction, add a task. Be sure it follows from your previous work and matches your instructional purpose.

**Task:**

 Download the full Lesson-Planning Template from resources.corwin.com/mathlessonplanning/k-2
Remember that you can use the online version of the lesson plan template to begin compiling each section into the full template as your lesson plan grows.

Chapter 6 ■ Choosing Tasks **77**

Standards

LI and SC

Purpose

Tasks

Materials

Student Thinking

Lesson Structures

Form. Assess.

Lesson Launch

Lesson Facilitation

Closure

# CHAPTER 7

# CHOOSING MATERIALS

## *Representations, Manipulatives, and Other Resources*

A new first-grade teacher, Okelo, had been not-so-patiently waiting to meet with his teammates, Electra and Amanda. He could hardly contain his excitement to begin the new school year. He mentally reviewed his list. He was pretty sure that this list was burned in his brain. Bulletin boards were up, desks were organized and labeled with nametags, and the book corner was ready for his first graders.

Okelo asked his colleagues, "What manipulatives will I have in my new classroom?"

Electra replied, "Unfortunately, we can't store the materials in our classrooms. In the past, we didn't have enough manipulatives for everyone to have them, and some people never got enough. Now we have a math supply room on the third-grade wing where we keep all of the manipulatives the school shares."

Okelo then asked, "Do you have a list of all the materials in the supply closet?"

Amanda replied, "I don't think I have ever seen one, although I remember that discussion coming up one time at a faculty meeting."

Electra added, "I just go down there when I am introducing a new topic and I scrounge around to find what will fit."

Okelo said, "But what if we need certain things, like plenty of counters for our first graders? I was hoping to gather tons of different kinds of counters for a big counting task I planned for the first week of school."

Electra stood up quickly and said, "Well, we better get up there and get what you need right now before everyone else starts collecting their manipulatives. And by the way, why don't you share this great task idea you have?"

**Resources vary. They can include anything from manipulatives, the amount of time devoted to mathematics, or your district-wide textbook. Resources can include teacher aides or special education collaborative teachers who join your class for certain lessons. Technology can vary from hardware, such as calculators, laptops, tablets, and document cameras, to software and applications. Likewise, manipulative materials can vary from school to school and from grade to grade. This chapter focuses on the resources that can help you create a rigorous and coherent set of math lessons. This chapter will answer these questions:**

- What is the role of representations in mathematics lessons?

- What is a **manipulative**?

- How are manipulatives used?

- What are other **resources**?

# WHAT IS THE ROLE OF REPRESENTATIONS IN MATHEMATICS LESSONS?

The Annenberg Learner Foundation (2003) offers this definition:

"Mathematical representation" refers to the wide variety of ways to capture an abstract mathematical concept or relationship. A mathematical representation may be visible, such as a number sentence, a display of manipulative materials, or a graph, but it may also be an internal way of seeing and thinking about a mathematical idea. Regardless of their form, representations can enhance students' communication, reasoning, and problem-solving abilities; help them make connections among ideas; and aid them in learning new concepts and procedures. (para. 2)

Since mathematical concepts are abstract, when teachers teach, they represent the concepts in a variety of ways. Representations can be thought of as a broad category of models. According to Van de Walle et al. (2016), there are seven ways to represent or model mathematical concepts:

1. Manipulatives
2. Pictures or drawings
3. Symbols
4. Language (written or spoken)
5. Real-world situations
6. Graphs
7. Tables

Selecting a representation is a vital part of your decision making while lesson planning. You must decide, "What representations will help achieve the learning intentions of today's lesson?" Here is an example of a teacher using a representation to help students make sense of rounding.

### Example: Alvaro

When planning a lesson that involves rounding two-digit numbers, Alvaro, a second-grade teacher, decided to use a number line from 20 to 30. When he asked his students to place the number 23 on the number line, he asked, "Is 23 closer to 20 or 30?"

Alvaro used a number line as a representation to model the relationship of the numbers from 20 to 30 in order. By using this representation, students can easily see that 23 is closer to 20 than 30, working toward a conceptual understanding of rounding.

The charts in Figures 7.1, 7.2, and 7.3 show examples of representations that can be used with selected standards.

### Figure 7.1

## Kindergarten

| Counting and Cardinality Standards | Representation |
| --- | --- |
| **Know number names and the count sequence.**<br><br>• Count to 100 by ones and by tens. |  |

*(Continued)*

**Figure 7.1** (*Continued*)

| Counting and Cardinality Standards | Representation |
|---|---|
| **Count to tell the number of objects.** | |

**Count to tell the number of objects.**

- Understand the relationship between numbers and quantities; connect counting to cardinality.

- When counting objects, say the number names in the standard order, pairing each object with one and only one number name and each number name with one and only one object.

- Understand that the last number name said tells the number of objects counted. The number of objects is the same regardless of their arrangement or the order in which they were counted.

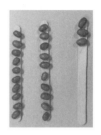

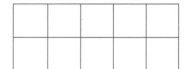

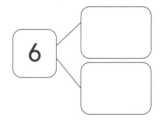

| 1 | 2 | 3 | 4 |
|---|---|---|---|
| 5 | 6 | 7 | 8 |
| 9 | 10 | 11 | 12 |
| 13 | 14 | 15 | 16 |
| 17 | 18 | 19 | 20 |

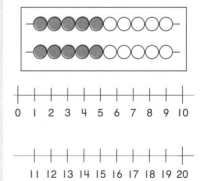

Figure 7.2

## Grade 1

| Place Value Standards (CCSS-M, 2010) | Representation |
|---|---|

**Place Value Standards (CCSS-M, 2010)**

- Understand that the two digits of a two-digit number represent amounts of tens and ones.

- Compare two two-digit numbers based on meanings of the tens and ones digits, recording the results of comparisons with the symbols >, =, and <.

**Representation**

Numbers, words, pictures, base-ten materials

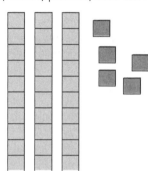

| 1 | 2 | 3 | 4 | 5 | 6 | 7 | 8 | 9 | 10 |
|---|---|---|---|---|---|---|---|---|---|
| 11 | 12 | 13 | 14 | 15 | 16 | 17 | 18 | 19 | 20 |
| 21 | 22 | 23 | 24 | 25 | 26 | 27 | 28 | 29 | 30 |
| 31 | 32 | 33 | 34 | 35 | 36 | 37 | 38 | 39 | 40 |
| 41 | 42 | 43 | 44 | 45 | 46 | 47 | 48 | 49 | 50 |
| 51 | 52 | 53 | 54 | 55 | 56 | 57 | 58 | 59 | 60 |
| 61 | 62 | 63 | 64 | 65 | 66 | 67 | 68 | 69 | 70 |
| 71 | 72 | 73 | 74 | 75 | 76 | 77 | 78 | 79 | 80 |
| 81 | 82 | 83 | 84 | 85 | 86 | 87 | 88 | 89 | 90 |
| 91 | 92 | 93 | 94 | 95 | 96 | 97 | 98 | 99 | 100 |

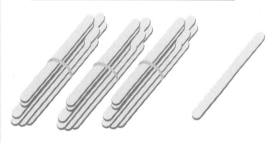

Standards

LI and SC

Purpose

Tasks

Materials

Student Thinking

Lesson Structures

Form. Assess.

Lesson Launch

Lesson Facilitation

Closure

## Figure 7.3

### Grade 2

**Numeric Relationships: Students will demonstrate, represent, and show relationships among whole numbers within the base-ten number system.**

- Count within 1,000, including skip-counting by 5s, 10s, and 100s starting at a variety of multiples of 5, 10, or 100.

- Read and write numbers within the range of 0 to 1,000 using standard, word, and expanded forms.

- Demonstrate that each digit of a three-digit number represents amounts of hundreds, tens, and ones (e.g., 387 is 3 hundreds, 8 tens, 7 ones).

- Demonstrate that 100 represents a group of 10 tens.

- Compare two three-digit numbers by using symbols <, =, and > and justify the comparison based on the meanings of the hundreds, tens, and ones.

| Hundreds 2 | Tens 3 | Ones 3 |
|---|---|---|

| 1 | 2 | 3 | 4 | 5 | 6 | 7 | 8 | 9 | 10 |
|---|---|---|---|---|---|---|---|---|---|
| 11 | 12 | 13 | 14 | 15 | 16 | 17 | 18 | 19 | 20 |
| 21 | 22 | 23 | 24 | 25 | 26 | 27 | 28 | 29 | 30 |
| 31 | 32 | 33 | 34 | 35 | 36 | 37 | 38 | 39 | 40 |
| 41 | 42 | 43 | 44 | 45 | 46 | 47 | 48 | 49 | 50 |
| 51 | 52 | 53 | 54 | 55 | 56 | 57 | 58 | 59 | 60 |
| 61 | 62 | 63 | 64 | 65 | 66 | 67 | 68 | 69 | 70 |
| 71 | 72 | 73 | 74 | 75 | 76 | 77 | 78 | 79 | 80 |
| 81 | 82 | 83 | 84 | 85 | 86 | 87 | 88 | 89 | 90 |
| 91 | 92 | 93 | 94 | 95 | 96 | 97 | 98 | 99 | 100 |

## WHAT IS A MANIPULATIVE?

A manipulative is one type of representation. Any concrete tool used to support **hands-on learning** can be considered a manipulative. Generally, manipulatives are concrete objects that students use to bring meaning to abstract mathematical ideas. Some common manipulatives used in mathematics at the primary level include (but are not limited to) snap cubes, pattern blocks, ten frames, teddy bear counters, square tiles, attribute blocks, GeoBlocks, and base-ten materials. Figures 7.1, 7.2, and 7.3 include some manipulatives used as representations. The chart in Figure 7.4 lists some materials available commercially.

Not all manipulatives need to be commercially produced. Beans, seashells, buttons, pennies, candy, marbles, toys, pebbles, straws, sand boxes, and so forth are all good objects to use for making sense of mathematical concepts.

Some manipulatives can be made. Examples include pattern blocks, attribute blocks, and fraction circles, which can all be constructed using a die-cut machine available at craft stores or from templates downloaded from the Internet.

Virtual manipulatives are available online for little or no cost. These are described as "interactive, Web-based, visual representations of dynamic objects that present opportunities for constructing mathematical knowledge" (Moyer, Bolyard, & Spikell, 2002). Virtual manipulatives are not static computer pictures because they are interactive. Research has shown that virtual manipulatives are effective representations. Reimer and Moyer (2005) described a study that showed statistically significant gains in students' conceptual knowledge using virtual manipulatives. Research by Steen, Brooks, and Lyon (2006) indicates that the use of virtual manipulatives as an instructional tool was extremely effective.

Standards

LI and SC

Purpose

Tasks

Materials

Student Thinking

Lesson Structures

Form. Assess.

Lesson Launch

Lesson Facilitation

Closure

**Figure 7.4**

| Description | Common Use | K | 1 | 2 | Picture |
|---|---|---|---|---|---|
| Attribute blocks: a set of five shapes in different sizes, thicknesses, and colors | Sorting, recognizing attributes | ✓ | ✓ | ✓ | 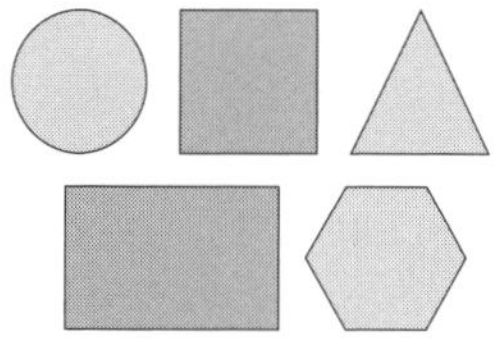 |
| Base-ten blocks: proportional representations of units, tens, and hundreds | Place value, addition, and subtraction | | | ✓ | 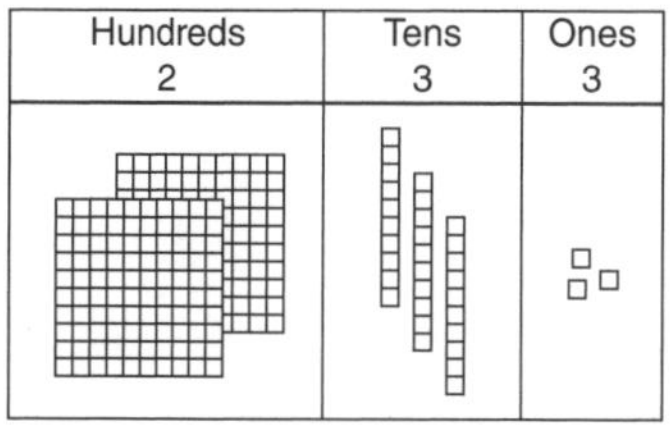 |
| Balance scale | Measurement | ✓ | ✓ | ✓ | 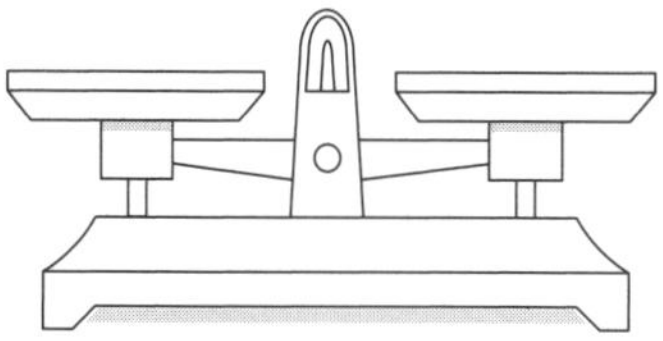 |
| Color cubes, tiles, squares | Counting, geometry, measurement | ✓ | ✓ | ✓ |  |
| Fraction circles | Fractions | ✓ | ✓ | ✓ | 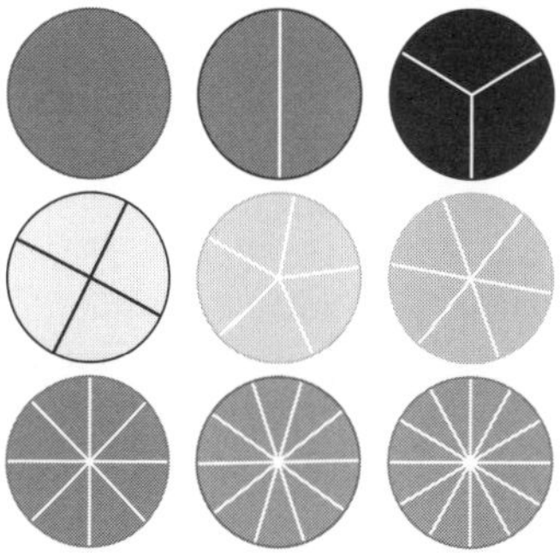 |
| Pattern blocks: six proportional shapes in six colors | Fractions, patterning, geometry | ✓ | ✓ | ✓ | 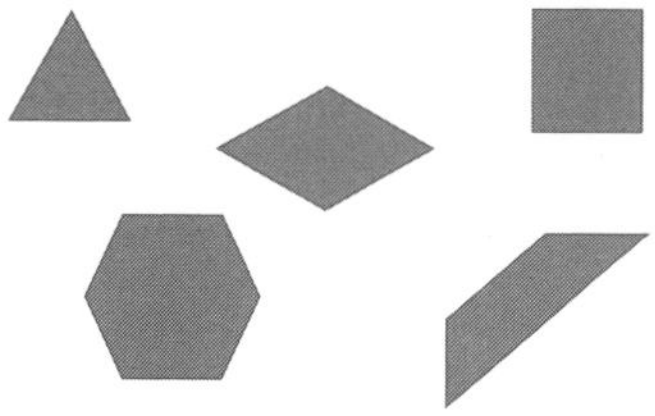 |

*(Continued)*

Figure 7.4 (*Continued*)

| Description | Common Use | K | 1 | 2 | Picture |
|---|---|---|---|---|---|
| Rekenreks: a two-tier abacus with 10 beads of two colors on each tier | Composing and decomposing numbers, addition and subtraction | ✓ | ✓ | ✓ | |
| Snap cubes: interlocking plastic cubes | Number sense, operations, counting, tens and ones, measurement, patterning | ✓ | ✓ | ✓ | |
| Counters: can be one or two colors | Counting, number sense, and for use with ten frames | ✓ | ✓ | ✓ | |

Two free sources for virtual materials are the Library of Virtual Manipulatives found at http://nlvm.usu.edu/ and The Math Learning Center at https://www.mathlearningcenter.org/resources/apps.

## HOW ARE MANIPULATIVES USED?

"I hear and I forget. I see and I remember. I do and I understand." This ancient quote from Confucius sums up the current beliefs about using manipulatives in mathematics. It reminds us that we need to provide learning tools to help students make sense of mathematical concepts. In 2009, the U.S. Department of Education's What Works Clearinghouse, a trusted source for scientific evidence of what works in education, made *using manipulatives* one of their top research-based recommendations. It is important to note that the mathematics is not in the manipulatives, but, rather, students use their interaction with a manipulative to construct mathematical conceptual understanding. In other words, students form ideas about mathematics while working with the manipulatives. They use the manipulatives to test out hypotheses, model/create meaning for algorithms, find patterns and relationships, and so forth, all of which help them construct the abstract concepts.

When introducing a new manipulative to your class, give the students time to explore before giving them any specific instructions. Not only does this give your students a chance to explore the characteristics of the manipulative, but it also helps cut down on behavior issues where students want to play with the manipulative later instead of following instructions.

The most popular use of manipulatives is to introduce a concept. Here is an example.

Example: Eli

Eli, a first-grade teacher, wants to introduce the commutative property of addition on Monday. She asks students to make snakes using three dark snap cubes and four light snap cubes as in the following diagram:

Eli asks, "How many cubes are in your snake?"

Then she asks her students to flip the snake over end to end to get the following representation:

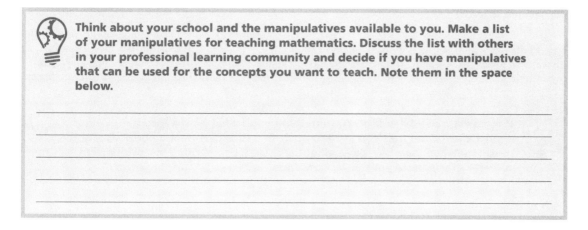

She asks, "Is four light cubes and three dark cubes the same amount as three dark cubes and four light cubes? How do you know? Explain your thinking to me."

After Eli uses manipulatives to introduce the concept of commutativity, she wants the students to be able to transfer their knowledge from objects to representations or mental images of the concept. In this example, Eli uses snap cubes and other manipulatives initially for two or three days to ensure that her students constructed the concept of commutativity. Then she is ready to have her students create pictorial representations. She says to her students, "Class, I have forgotten to bring in our snap cubes today. Can you draw for me snap cubes that show that five plus three is the same as three plus five?"

After several practices at the pictorial representation level, Eli wants to assess if her students are ready to work with the concept of commutativity abstractly. She gives them the following scenario:

> On Monday, Ruth put 5 pennies in her piggy bank. On Tuesday, Ruth added 6 more pennies to her piggy bank. On Monday Lois put 6 pennies in her piggy bank. She put 5 pennies in her piggy bank on Tuesday. Without doing any math on paper, can you tell me who had more pennies in her piggy bank, Ruth or Lois? Explain your thinking.

In Eli's scenario, she works with students concretely with manipulatives. Then she helps them move to a pictorial representation. Finally, she assesses to see if they are understanding and applying the concept abstractly.

> **Think about your school and the manipulatives available to you. Make a list of your manipulatives for teaching mathematics. Discuss the list with others in your professional learning community and decide if you have manipulatives that can be used for the concepts you want to teach. Note them in the space below.**
>
> _____
>
> _____
>
> _____
>
> _____
>
> _____

As Eli's example shows, teachers can use representations for assessment as well as instruction because the manipulatives give insight into what students do or do not understand. You can then use this knowledge to help you make decisions about future lesson planning. To begin, you can tie these questions, suggested by NCTM Past-President Skip Fennell, into your formative assessment.

- How are students using representation to model and interpret the mathematics presented?
- What do the representations that a student is using tell about that student's understanding of the mathematics?
- What do students provide when asked to use diagrams, sketches, or equations to explain their solution to a problem or task? (Fennell, 2006)

See Chapter 10 for more information on formative assessment and lesson planning.

When students can use different representations to model a concept, they demonstrate their ability to understand the concept. Conversely, when students are introduced to only one representation, their misconceptions may be enhanced. For example, students who are exposed only to fraction circles may believe that it is not possible to divide a rectangle into fractional parts. It is good practice to use multiple representations for a concept.

Standards

LI and SC

Purpose

Tasks

Materials

Student Thinking

Lesson Structures

Form. Assess.

Lesson Launch

Lesson Facilitation

Closure

In addition to representations, you have many other resources at your disposal. One of the most common is the **textbook,** but a textbook is only as good as the teacher who uses it. A skilled builder with a hammer and nails can create an architectural masterpiece. In the hands of an unskilled builder, the same blocks of wood made into furniture will fall apart in your living room. As you consider the most effective way to use your textbook for instruction, keep these suggestions in mind:

- Carefully select portions of the text for your students to use. Consider the readability level of what you select and the complexity of the explanations and the level of questions offered. Look for tasks that have multiple entry points, are low-floor and high-ceiling, and for which students may have multiple strategic approaches. Choose higher-level questions rather than low-level questions (e.g., recall, carry out an algorithm).

- Discover your students' prior knowledge before preselecting any material based on lessons written for the general K to 2 population.

- Supplement your lessons with suggestions from the teacher ancillary materials that accompany your text.

Textbook lessons are written for the general student population, which means that the lesson design may not address the individual needs of all of your students. For this reason, creating your own lessons—incorporating the best of what your textbook has to offer—is advantageous.

Another resource you may have is a **district-wide curriculum.** Usually district lesson plans are aligned closely to the state required mathematics standards. Most plans are based on big ideas, conceptual understandings, real-world applications, and hands-on experiences. The district plans will likely engage your students and keep them excited about learning mathematics; these plans may even have ideas for differentiating instruction. Always prepare the district lesson plans thoroughly, using our guidelines, but in class remember to teach your students, not the plan.

The Internet is an endless source of teaching materials. A word of caution: The learning intentions and success criteria you create for your lessons should be of paramount importance. Before jumping to any website with what appear to be cute, engaging lessons or ideas, be sure to match them with your learning intentions and success criteria and think deeply about your standards, big ideas, essential questions, and the purpose of your lesson.

> **Using a copy of your textbook, something you found on the Internet, or your district curriculum that you used recently in a lesson, reflect on how closely the lesson matched your big ideas, essential questions, learning intentions, and success criteria. Note your reflections here.**

## Building Unit Coherence

You can create coherence and appropriate rigor across a unit by carefully attending to how and when you use particular resources, particularly the manipulatives. It can be tempting to use the same manipulative throughout a unit, but students need to see how particular manipulatives connect to one another.

Example: Misha

When Misha teaches first-grade place value, she knows that first graders need ample time to create and build sets of ten by making sticks of ten using single cubes first. When she notices that students are ready, she moves them to the commercially prepared place value materials, which represent sticks of ten but cannot be broken apart. She needs to ensure that students are able to make this conceptual link.

Notes

Standards

LI and SC

Purpose

Tasks

Materials

Student Thinking

Lesson Structures

Form. Assess.

Lesson Launch

Lesson Facilitation

Closure

## Material Selection

Kindergarten teacher Rena has been using snap cubes with her students. For this lesson, she wants to introduce a new manipulative so that students will get comfortable knowing that anything can be counted. She adds two-color counters to the lesson. In contrast, her colleagues, Eliza and Marilyn, decide to provide their students with a choice of manipulatives for this lesson because they want to see what kinds of manipulatives the students will select.

**Materials (representations, manipulatives, other):**

Two-color counters

*See the complete lesson plan in Appendix A on page 178.*

How does the representation for this lesson enhance or further the learning intentions and success criteria of this lesson? Write your thoughts below.

Standards

LI and SC

Purpose

Tasks

Materials

Student Thinking

Lesson Structures

Form. Assess.

Lesson Launch

Lesson Facilitation

Closure

## First-Grade Snapshot

## Material Selection

Jen is a first-year teacher. She remembers from her methods courses in school that tens and ones is an important concept. Students need it to build deep understanding for developing procedural fluency. She discusses her ideas about using manipulatives with her teammates, Karlo and Sarita. In this introductory lesson, she wants to use beans as simple counters for students to put into groups of ten. She also provides her students with some blank ten frames so the children can organize their counting. Karlo and Sarita both agree that beans and ten frames are excellent choices.

### Materials (representations, manipulatives, other):

Counters, base-ten blocks, blank ten frames, order form, chart paper

*See the complete lesson plan in Appendix A on page 183.*

**How do the representations for this lesson enhance or further the learning intentions and success criteria of this lesson? Write your thoughts below.**

Second-grade teachers Wilma, Dwayne, and Aliyah have made an effort to communicate frequently with the first- and third-grade teachers in their school. Wilma has an excellent professional relationship with Kendra, the first-grade teacher in her building. They chat often about the students in Grade 1 and their prior knowledge entering second grade. Wilma finds it really helpful to learn about the kinds of learning activities that Kendra is teaching. Wilma knows that her present students spent a lot of time building tens and ones using linking cubes in first grade. Based on this information, she decides to use commercially prepared base-ten materials.

> ### Materials (representations, manipulatives, other):
>
> Base-ten blocks

*See the complete lesson plan in Appendix A on page 188.*

**How do the representations for this lesson enhance or further the learning intentions and success criteria of this lesson? Write your thoughts below.**

**Under Construction**

Now it is your turn! Decide what representations will help meet your learning intentions and success criteria for the lesson you are building.

## Materials (representations, manipulatives, other):

online resources

Download the full Lesson-Planning Template from resources.corwin.com/mathlessonplanning/k-2
Remember that you can use the online version of the lesson plan template to begin compiling each section into the full template as your lesson plan grows.

# CHAPTER 8

# CEMENTING THE CRACKS
## *Anticipating Student Thinking*

A team of primary teachers were making plans for the upcoming school year while thinking about their previous year. First-grade teacher Dion made the following comment: "You know, I thought I was doing a great job last year focusing on geometry with shapes. We used pictures and drew shapes in shaving cream and traced triangles on a sand table, and yet toward the end of the year, a student named Shanna insisted that a yield sign was not a triangle because it was upside down! When I probed further, she told me, 'A triangle sits on its bottom and points to the sky.' Now, I know I never taught her that!"

One of his colleagues, Isabella, shared a similar experience: "I know what you mean. I really focused on equations last year. I know my students understood equations and could find the solution to eight plus nine or five plus six with no problem. Yet when I turned the equation around to blank equals five plus six, they didn't seem to make the connection. I was so curious about this confusion. I asked Loreen why she thought this was so hard. You remember Loreen. She was my top student last year! Well, she told me that there was something wrong with the equation because the answer always comes after the equal sign. I know I never said that!"

"Right!" exclaimed Dion. "I don't understand where these ideas come from sometimes. We teach with hands-on materials and really get our students involved, and then they come up with these ideas we never taught."

Isabella added, "You know, I was with some friends this summer. We weren't discussing teaching, but the term unintended consequences came up in discussion. It reminds me of what we're talking about. We teach one idea but for some reason a few students—sometimes more than that—end up with a completely different conclusion."

Dion concluded, "It might help this year if we are more proactive on these topics that we know get turned around in their minds. Let's make a list now while we are thinking about it. Perhaps we could even plan with the student misconceptions in mind."

---

**Dion and Isabella are frustrated about how their students' thinking, in some cases, is not aligned with what they believe the students should have learned. In this chapter, we will consider the factors that lead to these situations and explore how advance planning and anticipation can be crucial. This chapter will focus on the following questions:**

- What are misconceptions, and where do they come from?

- How can you plan to minimize misconceptions?

Standards

LI and SC

Purpose

Tasks

Materials

Student Thinking

Lesson Structures

Form. Assess.

Lesson Launch

Lesson Facilitation

Closure

# WHAT ARE MISCONCEPTIONS, AND WHERE DO THEY COME FROM?

One problem that leads to very serious instructional issues for teachers and students is misconceptions. **Common errors** and misconceptions occur when children make incorrect or inappropriate generalizations of an idea (Resnick, 1982; Resnick & Omanson, 1987). Misconceptions may result from several sources: preconceptions, informal thinking, or poor memory.

Students do not come to school with a blank slate of knowledge. They come with background knowledge gathered from prior learning experiences both within and outside of school, such as home or the playground. Some of this knowledge relates to the topics taught in school (Bransford, Brown, & Cocking, 1999; Gelman & Lucariello, 2002; Piaget & Inhelder, 1969; Resnick, 1983). Learning builds on and is related to this prior knowledge. Prior knowledge is based on intuition, everyday experiences, and what students have previously been taught. Before beginning instruction, you need to know your students' prior knowledge. Your instruction depends on whether this knowledge is accurate or not (Lucariello, 2012).

Example: Annie

Annie, a second-grade teacher, noticed the following work by Kelly, one of her students.

$$23$$
$$\underline{-7}$$
$$24$$

Annie was puzzled by the answer, particularly since the class had spent a lot of time using base-ten blocks for regrouping. She asked Kelly to explain how she arrived at her answer.

Kelly said, "Last year, Mr. Williams taught us to subtract the smaller number from the larger, so I did seven minus three equals four. Then I just brought the two down because there was nothing left to subtract."

Annie was amazed that the prior knowledge Kelly brought to her class was so powerful that it interfered with Kelly's ability to make sense of the new concepts in her second-grade class.

Other misconceptions arrive from everyday experiences. Children form many ideas about numbers, shapes, fractions, time, and money from their environment, including talk on the playground, what they see on television, computer games they play, children's literature that is read to them, and so forth. It's no wonder some children develop very interesting and perhaps incorrect ideas about mathematical concepts (Bamberger, Oberdorf, Schultz-Ferrell, & Leinwand, 2011). For example, parents may read the children's book *The Legend of Spookley the Square Pumpkin* by Joe Troiano (2001) to their children. (Reading to children is an excellent prereading activity to help them develop language.) In the touching story, Spookley starts out as a misfit but ends up a hero. The problem is this: Spookley is described as a square pumpkin, but all illustrations of Spookley in the book depict him as a cube. This misconception can be very hard to correct as students become emotionally attached to Spookley as a character. Mohyuddin and Khalil (2016) explain that students become emotionally and intellectually attached to misconceptions because they have actively constructed them. They often find it difficult to accept new concepts that are different from their misconception.

Not all misconceptions come from prior knowledge. Some are the **unintended consequences** of the best-intentioned teaching. Here is an example.

Example: Sean

The primary teachers at Martin Luther King Elementary School frequently work together to bring cohesion to their mathematics instruction. They check in with each other often. One of their group decisions has been to portray equations the same way in kindergarten and first grade so students will not get confused seeing different representations. They have set the format $3 + 4 = 7$ as the standard.

In Grade 2, Sean, a teacher new to the school, displays the equation $8 = \_\_ + 5$ to his second-grade students. He is surprised to find that many put 13 on the line. When he questions his students' reasoning, they tell him that the equal sign indicates that the answer comes next. He is shocked to hear this and has a discussion with the primary teachers. None of them has ever taught that definition for the equal sign. However, students have formulated that definition on their own by picking up on the pattern of the format $3 + 4 = 7$, where the answer always followed the equal sign. The definition of "equals" that the students have formulated was unintentional on the teachers' part, but the misconception has occurred anyway.

To summarize, misconceptions are a problem for two reasons. First, students become emotionally and intellectually attached to the misconceptions because they have actively constructed them, as in the example with *Spookley the Square Pumpkin*. Second, they interfere with learning when students use them to interpret new experiences, as in the example with Kelly and Annie and with Sean's second-grade students.

For more exploration of unintended consequences, check out "13 Rules That Expire" (Karp, Bush, & Dougherty, 2014). This NCTM article highlights 13 generalizations that are often taught in elementary school because they work for the lesson at hand, but they do not hold true over the long term. For example, early educators often tell students that a larger number cannot be subtracted from a smaller number because they do not want to confuse students by introducing negative numbers. However, students do not have to be taught explicitly about negative numbers to know they exist. The focus of your lessons should always be on developing conceptual understanding instead of adhering to a rule.

> **How do you identify your students' common misconceptions? Note some of the main ones here.**
>
> _____
>
> _____
>
> _____
>
> _____

## HOW CAN YOU PLAN TO MINIMIZE MISCONCEPTIONS?

According to Steven Leinwand (2014), effective teachers have always understood that mistakes and confusion are powerful learning opportunities. Moreover, they understand that one of their critical roles is to anticipate these misconceptions in their lesson planning and have at their disposal an array of strategies to address common misunderstandings before they expand, solidify, and undermine confidence.

Before we can plan to minimize misconceptions, because they can never be eliminated totally, it is helpful to know some of the more common K–2 mathematics misconceptions that students form. Note that the table in Figure 8.1 is not an exhaustive list.

### Figure 8.1

| Misconception | Student Example |
| --- | --- |
| Zero is not a number. | How many pennies are in the empty jar? Students respond "none" but will not write 0. |
| Subtraction is commutative. | $8 - 5 = 5 - 8$ |
| Key words tell us which operation to perform, such as *more* and *altogether* always mean add. | John has 3 toy cars and Mary has 4 toy cars. Who has more toy cars? Student will answer 7. |
| We can only add two numbers at a time. | $3 + 4 + 7 =$ ___ Students do not know what to do since they believe we cannot add three numbers. |

**Figure 8.1 (Continued)**

| Misconception | Student Example |
|---|---|
| Equal sign means "the next number is the answer." | Students respond to $12 = \underline{\phantom{xx}} + 6$ as 18. |
| Always subtract the smaller number from the larger number. | $24 - 7 = 23$ because student subtracted $7 - 3 = 4$. |
| Inverting a shape changes the shape. | A gravity-based triangle is no longer a triangle when it is turned upside-down. triangle △ not a triangle ▽ |
| When using a ruler, the markings are the inches, not the spaces between the markings. | For example, when asked to show an inch on the ruler, the student points to the mark for 1 inch. |
| The value of a coin is directly related to its size. | A penny is worth more than a dime. |
| Coin value is based on the number of coins instead of the value of each individual coin. | When asked the value of three coins (penny, nickel, and dime), students respond 3. |
| Using English-language names for shapes as opposed to mathematical names. | Naming this shape a diamond. ◇ |
| Using the denominator of a fraction as a whole number to determine relative size of a fraction. | Fourths are larger than halves because 4 is bigger than 2. |
| Using the term "the biggest half." | My half is bigger than yours. |

Because misconceptions tend to be strongly held student beliefs, it does not work well to simply repeat a lesson or tell a student that his or her idea is a misconception. Instead, you need to plan so you can diagnose, anticipate, and uncover student misconceptions that are related to the lesson you create.

Misconceptions that result from prior knowledge can be diagnosed. Formative assessments and questioning techniques are two ways to do this; a third way is to anticipate misconceptions. Let's take a quick look at each of these approaches.

## Formative Assessment

**Formative assessment** can include techniques such as observations, interviews, show me, hinge questions, and exit tasks as explained in the book *The Formative 5* (Fennell, Kobett, & Wray, 2017). Each of these techniques can be used to uncover prior knowledge. Chapter 10 will focus on using formative assessment strategies.

Standards

LI and SC

Purpose

Tasks

Materials

Student Thinking

Lesson Structures

Form. Assess.

Lesson Launch

Lesson Facilitation

Closure

## Questioning

Questioning is another way to uncover prior knowledge. Some questioning techniques that work for this purpose include the following:

1. Prepare and pose questions that probe prior knowledge related to the lesson you are planning.

2. Avoid asking questions that require one-word answers (Kazemi & Hintz, 2014).

3. Ask follow-up questions to both correct and incorrect answers (Moyer-Packenham & Milewicz, 2002; Walsh & Sattes, 2005).

## Anticipating

Anticipating misconceptions is another way to minimize them. Here are three ways you can add steps to your lesson plan to anticipate, diagnose, and correct the misconceptions.

1. Use Figure 8.1 to anticipate misconceptions.

2. Consider your experience with previous students.

3. Discuss the situation with your colleagues.

> Example: Nancy
>
> Nancy, a first-grade teacher, includes this word problem in her lesson plan on addition to determine if her students have any preconceived ideas about solving word problems using key words.
>
> > Sam has 4 seashells and Sara has 5 shells. How many more shells does Sara have?

In particular, Nancy is looking to see if any students answer 9. If they do, she will follow up with additional questions, such as, "How did you get nine for your answer? Does it make sense that Sara could have nine more? Can you convince me that one is the correct answer?"

Notice that Nancy does not ask any one-word-answer questions. They are all questions that probe thinking for a specific piece of prior knowledge.

Nancy discovers that three of her students had the misconception that the key word *more* means *add*. To address this, she adds the following activity to her lesson the next day.

Nancy announces to the class that today they are going to be math actors and actresses. She gives the students seashells and asks the students to work in pairs to act out the story as Sam and Sara. She encourages the students, especially those with the misconception, to line up the seashells next to each other to see that Sara has one more seashell and not nine more shells.

 Sara's shells

Sam's shells

Nancy is deliberately providing the students with other experiences that allow them to reconstruct the concept they misunderstood. This is a necessary step for students who are truly vested in their misconceptions because they constructed them and used them successfully.

## Building Unit Coherence

To increase coherence, you can also identify the misconceptions that students may develop across a unit.

> Mariya, a kindergarten teacher, always jots down misconceptions that she anticipates the students may develop or have already developed. This allows her to plan lessons that will help her prevent the misconception from occurring.

Mariya developed this practice after a particularly difficult year when her students insisted that skip counting could only begin with the first number they were skip counting! At the time, a particularly precocious kindergartener wanted to skip count by tens starting at 5. Because Mariya did not want to confuse the other children, she told him that he couldn't do that, and thus the misconception began. She regretted that moment for a long time because she knew that she had never intended to promote that misconception. Now, she charts the big idea misconceptions so she will be ready (Figure 8.2).

### Figure 8.2

**Unit: Counting and Cardinality**

**Misconceptions:**

Idea that counting must always begin with one

Issues with the teen numbers (remembering sequence)

Mismatch between the oral words and counting objects

Mismatch between counting and answering the question "How many?"

Notes

Standards

LI and SC

Purpose

Tasks

Materials

Student Thinking

Lesson Structures

Form. Assess.

Lesson Launch

Lesson Facilitation

Closure

Kindergarten teachers Marilyn, Eliza, and Rena are discussing their students' counting abilities. Rena says, "Sometimes I notice students leaving out zero when I ask certain questions, but I have not seen a pattern in those responses."

Eliza says, "I have had a few students like that too. I wonder if maybe they are not doing enough work with the concept of zero as a number. After all, when students come to kindergarten and are asked to count, they usually begin at one."

To check out whether this is a student misconception, they decide to pay extra attention to zero in their instructional tasks. They also add a special task to their lesson plan to target this potential misconception.

> ### Misconceptions or Common Errors:
>
> Students may count every dot without subitizing.
>
> Students cannot decompose teen numbers.
>
> Students may struggle with one-to-one correspondence.
>
> Students read teen numbers like 11 as onety-one or one-one.

*See the complete lesson plan in Appendix A on page 178.*

**Why do you think that simply informing students of a misconception will not change their thinking? What role does anticipating a misconception play in helping you focus your lesson plan? Record your thoughts below.**

_____

_____

_____

_____

_____

_____

_____

_____

_____

_____

_____

_____

_____

_____

_____

_____

_____

_____

Standards

LI and SC

Purpose

Tasks

Materials

Student Thinking

Lesson Structures

Form. Assess.

Lesson Launch

Lesson Facilitation

Closure

### First-Grade Snapshot

## Student Thinking

Sarita, Jen, and Karlo are planning their lessons on tens and ones. Karlo says, "My students are always able to fill in those place value charts where students just write in the digit under the place names. However, I do not feel comfortable that the children really understand the meaning behind it."

Sarita agrees. She adds, "I wonder what the students really know about tens and ones when they get to first grade."

Jen added, "I am always wondering how well they really understand decomposing numbers. Could we keep this on our minds as we teach and look for evidence of their thinking?"

---

**Misconceptions or Common Errors:**

Difficulty decomposing numbers into tens and ones

Difficulty counting

---

*See the complete lesson plan in Appendix A on page 183.*

**Why do you think that simply informing students of a misconception will not change their thinking? What role does anticipating a misconception play in helping you focus your lesson plan? Record your thoughts below.**

At a team meeting where they are planning lessons on place value, second-grade teachers Aliyah, Wilma, and Dwayne discuss how, in the past, by using place value charts often, their students never really understood that the 3 in 367 means 300. The teachers add this misconception to their lesson plan, hoping it will help them focus on using different representations when they write their lessons.

### Misconceptions or Common Errors:

Some students will think of a three-digit number as three separate digits and not hundreds, tens, and ones.

*See the complete lesson plan in Appendix A on page 188.*

Why do you think that simply informing students of a misconception will not change their thinking? What role does anticipating a misconception play in helping you focus your lesson plan? Record your thoughts below.

Now it is your turn! Decide on whether you are anticipating a misconception or need to probe prior knowledge. Add it to your lesson plan.

## Misconceptions or Common Errors:

Download the full Lesson-Planning Template from resources.corwin.com/mathlessonplanning/k-2
Remember that you can use the online version of the lesson plan template to begin compiling each section into the full template as your lesson plan grows.

Standards

LI and SC

Purpose

Tasks

Materials

Student Thinking

Lesson Structures

Form. Assess.

Lesson Launch

Lesson Facilitation

Closure

# CHAPTER 9

# FRAMING THE LESSON
## Formats

Imani, along with her colleagues, Diamond and Bonnie, had been teaching kindergarten the same way every day for the past five years. At this point, Imani really wanted to shake up the way they had been organizing the math class. She felt like it had not been meeting all of her students' needs, particularly the stragglers, who were not working unless she was constantly reminding them, and she wanted to try some new things to engage them and all of her students. They needed more opportunities to talk with one another and learn how to work together on problems. In order to facilitate this kind of shared experience, Imani knew that she would need to be available to monitor the students while they were working; she did not want to be tied up in an instructional group. She still believed in small-group instruction; she just felt that her students needed to be working together more often.

As Imani sat down with her team, she shared the following: "I think we really need to take a look at our lesson format. We have been using the same center/math rotations for years. I am not sure we are building enough opportunities for math discourse between the students. I know they are talking to each other at the centers, but I am not hearing much math talk. I think we need to build some more strategic tasks that we could facilitate through a combination of whole-group and small-group instruction. Students can work in pairs or small groups while we facilitate the task. What do you think?"

Diamond agreed. She said, "I would love to try some different formats. Perhaps we can begin with pairs and see how that goes. I think the students will be very excited about solving some problems together. We can also work on the social learning intentions at the same time!"

Bonnie was also on board. She said, "Let's do it! I suggest that we begin with the inventory task we did in the workshop last week. Let's plan this conceptual lesson first, try it out, and come back and share our thoughts."

> **Lessons need structure. Lesson formats give you that structure. Lesson formats refer to how you organize your class for the lesson. Some lessons work better when students are in collaborative groups, and some are more effective when students move around to different centers. For instance, rotating stations may be a good decision for a procedural fluency lesson but not for the introductory lesson on a new concept. As you select a lesson format for a particular lesson, you should base your decision on the purpose of the lesson. Lesson format can and should vary depending on the purpose of the lesson as Imani, Diamond, and Bonnie agree. This chapter will address the following question:**
>
> - What are some different lesson formats?

# WHAT ARE SOME DIFFERENT LESSON FORMATS?

Seemingly, everyone has their own preferred **lesson format**, but the fact is that there is not one mathematics lesson format that should be implemented every day. Adhering to one model can be limiting, and it may not best support your students' learning because the format is taking precedence over the students' needs. Effective teachers use more than one type of lesson format. As you think about selecting lesson formats, ask yourself if the mathematics lesson structure meets the following criteria.

- Does it support student discourse?

- Does it support differentiation?

- Does it place the big ideas front and center in the lesson?

- Does it enhance opportunities for formative assessment?

As you decide on a lesson format, you will need to analyze the standards you will teach. In particular, you should consider which of the standards point to developing conceptual understanding and which ones point to procedural fluency.

The following formats are just four ways you might structure your lessons. Flexibility is the key to selecting lesson formats. You should structure your lessons with a deep consideration of your students' needs and mathematics standards. Note that these lesson formats provide many opportunities to formatively assess students, provide timely feedback, and foster student-to-student interactions.

## Four-Part Lesson Format

Structure your class using this format for problem-solving lessons. The four parts are known as *before, during, after,* and *reflection* (see Figure 9.1). This is an adaptation of the format from the book *Elementary and Middle School Mathematics: Teaching Developmentally* by Van de Walle et al. (2016).

### Figure 9.1

| | **Before** | |
| Activate prior knowledge | Be sure the problem is understood | Whole group |

⬇

| | **During** | |
| Students work | Teacher provides support | Small group |

⬇

| | **After** | |
| Class discussion | Students present their conclusions/conjectures | Whole group |

⬇

| | **Reflection** | |
| Students make sense of the lesson | Closure | Individual |

Standards

LI and SC

Purpose

Tasks

Materials

Student Thinking

Lesson Structures

Form. Assess.

Lesson Launch

Lesson Facilitation

Closure

### Before

In the *before* stage, your students are in a **whole group.** The goal of this part of the lesson is to prepare students for the mathematics to come by having them revisit concepts, procedures, and strategies previously learned. You can do this by focusing on vocabulary, starting with a similar problem, or having students reword, act out, or model the problem. You also introduce the problem during the before stage.

### During

In the second part of the lesson, the *during* stage, students work in small groups. They work on solving the problem, and they prepare to present their ideas to the class. They can use manipulatives or any representations they choose. This is when they actively engage with the task. You can use this time to support the groups through questioning. Use several different questioning strategies to support your students' higher-order thinking, such as the following:

- Ask group members to share their strategies with other group members.
- Pose questions to provoke further thinking when groups are at an impasse.
- Ask probing questions.
- Provide extensions when appropriate.

In this part of the lesson, take note of student thinking and the strategies used so that you can begin to organize the *after* part of the lesson. Be as hands-off as possible so that your students can engage in productive struggle.

### After

In the *after* part of the lesson, students come back together in a whole group to share their work. The purpose of this part of the lesson is for students to analyze their classmates' thinking. In the *during* stage, you noted the students' strategies so that you can now organize student presentations, posters, or other products in an order that leads to discourse around their work. For example, you may decide to have the students with partial or incorrect solutions make their presentations first so you can ask the class for input. This will allow you to start a class discussion on the effectiveness of the strategy used. Alternatively, you may have students do a gallery walk or try another method to share student thinking and encourage discourse. During the *after*, your students make sense of the mathematics. They form conjectures and link the new ideas to their previous understandings.

### Reflection

Reflection refers to the process of thinking about learning. In the *reflection* piece of the lesson, students get the time they need to cement their learning individually. It is during reflection that new student learning takes place. During reflection, students examine ideas and seek out evidence to support or refute ideas they have previously held. To ensure this reflection, you should provide students with a prompt they can use to reflect on the class discussion and the mathematics involved. Here are some sample prompts for reflection that you might try.

- How was your strategy different from those of your classmates?
- What was your favorite strategy, and why?
- Explain a strategy used by a classmate that was not yours.
- How did this lesson connect to what we did yesterday?

Reflection is a proactive way to support students' mathematical development. You should never skip the reflection portion of the lesson. In fact, you may wish to use reflection time as your closure (see Chapter 11).

### Game Format

There are some lessons where you want students to practice what they have learned so they can make connections. The game format works well for this purpose and gives you a chance to assess your students formatively.

During planning, assign all students into groups of two or three, and decide on a game or activity for each group or pair. Select games or activities they are familiar with so they can practice the concept or skill they need.

For example, if you know that three of your students all have some difficulty naming the number word before or after a given number, then group them together and let them play "Before and After" (Figure 9.2).

**Figure 9.2**

### Before and After

Using blank dice, mark three faces of one die with the letter "A" and three faces with the letter "B." For the other blank die, mark the faces with numbers that the students need to practice naming the number before or after such as the decade numbers or numbers within 1 to 10. Give a group of two or three students one of each marked die. Students roll both dice in turn. An "A" means to say the number that comes AFTER the number rolled on the number die. A "B" means to say the number BEFORE the number rolled on the number die.

Rich games and activities such as "Before and After" lend themselves well to this lesson format.

To begin a lesson structured in the game format, gather the whole group together as shown in Figure 9.3. Assign partners or triads to games or activities. Then let students get to work. Use this time to move from game to game, observing, formatively assessing, and joining in when necessary. Note that students remain with the same activity throughout the lesson. This is not a student rotation format; instead, the teacher moves from group to group.

**Figure 9.3**

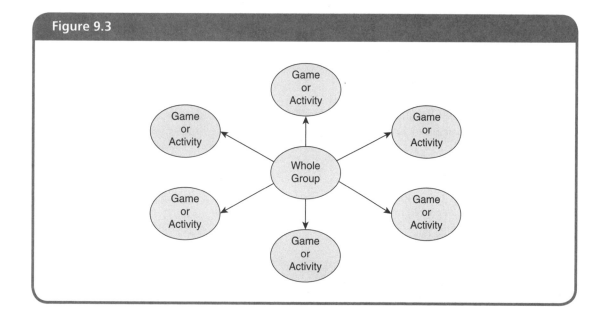

## Small-Group Instruction

In this lesson format, you have the opportunity to work with small groups of students for instruction while the other groups work independently. Research shows that students who work in groups on rich tasks, problems, assignments, and other mathematical investigations display increased achievement (Protheroe, 2007).

You begin instruction with a whole-group minilesson that takes 10 to 15 minutes. For instance, you might review a previous concept, introduce a new concept or vocabulary, play a short game on the day's topic, model a game that students will play independently, and so forth.

After the minilesson, you ask two or three small groups to engage in independent tasks that allow students to explore, practice, apply, and/or review the topic for the lesson. Students can play games, use the computer, solve problems, explore concepts with manipulatives, practice counting or writing numbers, and so forth.

Standards

LI and SC

Purpose

Tasks

Materials

Student Thinking

Lesson Structures

Form. Assess.

Lesson Launch

Lesson Facilitation

Closure

While most students are working in small groups independently, another group works with you. Be sure to form the groups in a way that makes sense for their learning. For example, you may choose to work with a small group of students with a particular misconception about zero that you noticed the previous day.

You can vary how you use this format. Figure 9.4 shows how you can move from whole group into small groups and remain in those groups for the entire class time. This works well for students who need time to fill in knowledge gaps or who need extra time on a concept with you. Remember that not all students learn at the same pace. Some need more instructional time to cement concepts or practice procedures. If you work with only one group during the class period, then you reconvene the whole class at the end of the lesson to share ideas from the day. You may use this time to preview the next lesson and/or review the day. See Chapter 13 for more on closure activities.

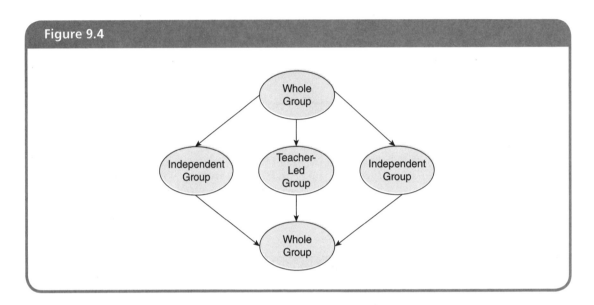

Figure 9.4

You can use this format two or three days in a row if you use the small-group instructional time to work on deepening knowledge on a topic. For example, if you work with a small group on a misconception about zero and it takes the entire class time allotted, then the next day you may work the entire class time with another group that needs work on decomposing numbers. In this scenario, you can see one group each day for instruction with you while the others work independently. This also works if you have three or four groups and they need different levels of depth.

Alternatively, you can use the format as shown in Figure 9.5. Here you get the opportunity to work with a rotation of small groups during the class time. For example, you may decide that the introduction to place value needs to be differentiated. You group students accordingly and rotate groups during the class time so that you work with each group and can differentiate the lesson to meet the needs of the group members. Students working independently also get a chance to rotate among two or three different activities or stations.

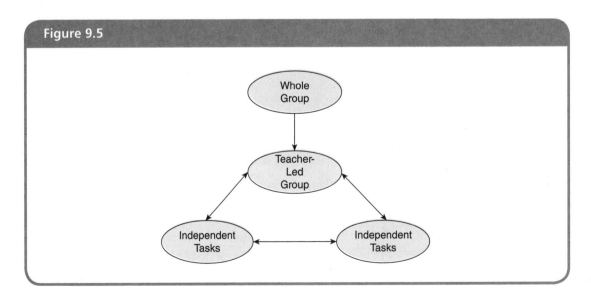

Figure 9.5

This format lends itself to procedural fluency lessons because you can use the small-group instruction time to target students who need additional scaffolding to link the concept to the procedure. On the other hand, you can use this model to reinforce a concept or to practice procedural fluency with a group of students who, based on your formative assessment from the previous day, need additional attention immediately. Students learn concepts at varying rates. Not all students make sense of mathematics at the same pace. This model provides you with the opportunity to bridge this gap.

A benefit of this model is that students are engaged at all times, either directly with you or in an independent setting. It allows your students to fluidly move within groups based on their needs. In other words, you can change the makeup of the groups often to meet specific needs.

## Pairs

With this format, students work in pairs to answer questions throughout the lesson. For example, you may begin the lesson by presenting two shapes and asking the students to decide with their partners what is the same about those shapes. Then they discuss their answers as a whole group. Next, you further the discussion by asking pairs to discuss how the shapes are different. After a brief discussion, they share as a whole group. The lesson continues in this fashion. It may involve a series of short tasks or one long task that students engage in with their partner.

You can pair students of similar abilities, different abilities, differing language strengths, and so forth depending on your goals for that particular lesson. Frequently changing the way you pair students is a good practice.

This format encourages student discourse. The smaller the number of students in a group, the more the children get individual opportunities to express themselves. This structure works well for helping students build conceptual understanding.

These are just a few lesson formats. You may have a few of your own to add to the list, or you may adapt any of these presented as long as the format supports the purpose of your lesson.

**Why do you think more effective teachers use multiple formats? Is there anything inherent in changing formats that might be described as good instruction? Write your responses below.**

_____

_____

_____

_____

### Building Unit Coherence

When you use multiple lesson formats, you often create stronger coherence because you are matching the format to the content and to your learning intentions. In other words, you are facilitating your lesson using a format that best meets the needs of your learners. Forcing lessons into the same format day after day chips away at coherence because you are trying to make the lesson fit the structure instead of deciding which structure best suits the lesson content.

Example: Chris

Chris, a second-grade teacher, used to teach small-group lessons every day. He rotated the students through the lessons, but he found that he did not always have enough time to develop the concept. Many days he ended up giving directions instead of asking good questions. Now, he plans the unit using multiple structures. He finds that he can develop better connections between concepts, and he can create that unit coherence he was craving.

Standards

LI and SC

Purpose

Tasks

Materials

Student Thinking

Lesson Structures

Form. Assess.

Lesson Launch

Lesson Facilitation

Closure

After selecting the task, Rena, Marilyn, and Eliza review some of the lesson elements discussed in previous chapters, including prior knowledge, big ideas, learning intentions, task selection, and misconceptions. Rena shares the following: "I would like to pair the students at the beginning of the lesson before we move them to small groups. I really think it will be good for them to work on the task with partners to give them an opportunity to discuss their ideas. I can also determine places where I can differentiate if needed. What do you both think?"

Marilyn says, "I have really been wanting to do this, too. I think my ELL students will love the opportunity to share their ideas in the safety of a pair."

Eliza agrees.

### Format:

☐ Four-Part Lesson     ☐ Game Format     ☐ Small-Group Instruction

☑ Pairs             ☐ Other_____

*See the complete lesson plan in Appendix A on page 178.*

**What kind of format might best meet the needs of your learners' collaboration skills? Record your thoughts below.**

_____

_____

_____

_____

_____

_____

_____

_____

_____

_____

_____

_____

_____

_____

_____

_____

_____

_____

_____

_____

Sarita, Jen, and Karlo discuss different types of structures that they might begin implementing in their first-grade classrooms. Karlo shares the following: "I have to admit, I think we are stuck in a bit of a rut. We tend to teach using math rotations every day, no matter what content we are using. We need to think about how we can use these classroom formats to better meet our students' learning needs and align those needs to the content we are teaching. Whole group can work if students are working in small groups most of the time. Are you ready to try the four-part lesson plan format?"

Sarita and Jen respond in unison, "Let's do it!"

### Format:

☑ Four-Part Lesson ☐ Game Format ☐ Small-Group Instruction

☐ Pairs ☐ Other_____

*See the complete lesson plan in Appendix A on page 183.*

**What kind of format might best meet the needs of your learners' collaboration skills? Record your answers below.**

_____

_____

_____

_____

_____

_____

_____

_____

_____

_____

_____

_____

_____

_____

_____

_____

_____

_____

_____

_____

Standards | LI and SC | Purpose | Tasks | Materials | Student Thinking | Lesson Structures | Form. Assess. | Lesson Launch | Lesson Facilitation | Closure

*Lesson Format*

Wilma tells her second-grade colleagues, "I would like to make heterogeneous groups for this lesson. I want them to spend time developing their understanding and have them share their ideas with others."

Dwayne adds, "I like this idea because they can hear each other's perspectives."

Aliyah agrees. She says, "If we use the four-part lesson structure, we can monitor the groups and encourage them to collaborate to share their ideas."

**Format:**

☑ Four-Part Lesson     ☐ Game Format     ☐ Small-Group Instruction

☐ Pairs     ☐ Other_____

*See the complete lesson plan in Appendix A on page 188.*

**What kind of format might best meet the needs of your learners' collaboration skills? Record your thoughts below.**

Standards

LI and SC

Purpose

Tasks

Materials

Student Thinking

Lesson Structures

Form. Assess.

Lesson Launch

Lesson Facilitation

Closure

## Under Construction

Now it is your turn! Select the lesson format you would like to use for your lesson that is under construction. Be able to justify for yourself how this format supports the purpose of the lesson.

### Format:

☐ Four-Part Lesson      ☐ Game Format      ☐ Small-Group Instruction

☐ Pairs      ☐ Other_____

**online resources** Download the full Lesson-Planning Template from resources.corwin.com/mathlessonplanning/k-2

Remember that you can use the online version of the lesson plan template to begin compiling each section into the full template as your lesson plan grows.

Notes

# CHAPTER 10

# EVALUATING IMPACT
## *Formative Assessment*

Shae, a first-grade teacher, glanced at her observation checklist and noted that she hadn't been able to record observations for Emilio and Andrea in almost two weeks. She liked to gather observation evidence on every student at least once a week. She had always observed what students were doing, of course, but this new more formalized observation practice had truly empowered her teaching. She was making better decisions in the moment of teaching and could adjust her instruction using the information she was gathering. Today she was going to use the Show Me technique (Fennell et al., 2017) and capture students' work with pictures during small-group instruction. She had family conferences coming up and thought it would be helpful to be able to show pictures of the students' work.

She planned to pose this question: "How many ways can you make eight using blue and red connecting cubes? Please show me." She anticipated that some students would say one and others would say eight. She was also curious about how the students would find the combinations. In prior lessons, she had been working with the students to use a pattern to find the combinations systematically. For example, for the total 6, students began with 6 and 0, then 5 and 1, 4 and 2, 3 and 3, 2 and 4, 5 and 1, and 0 and 6. She was curious to see if the students would transfer this method to a new total.

Shae began by asking the students to make predictions. She recorded the predictions next to their names on the board. She then posed the question and gave the students the connecting cubes and a recording sheet.

As the students worked, Shae noted that Rosa and Amir worked systematically through the combinations. She was fascinated to see that Rosa first made a stick with eight blue cubes and then made a stick with eight red cubes. She asked Rosa to tell her about her cubes and explain why she made eight cubes of each color.

Rosa answered, "It is eight blue plus zero red equals eight blue. Then it is zero blue plus eight red equals eight red!"

Shae was pleasantly surprised to see Rosa immediately use 0 in her combinations.

Amir began making his combinations with four blue plus four red. Then he adjusted the combination of colors from there by adding one more blue and taking one red away.

A third student, Adrian, counted each cube. Each time he placed a new cube in the row, he recounted the total cubes to make sure there were eight. Shae asked him, "Is there any way to find out how many cubes you have without counting each cube?"

Adrian replied, "Nope! You have to keep counting!"

Shae took photos using her phone and uploaded them to the recording sheet. Then she adjusted her instruction to help the students focus on showing a pattern to find all of the combinations. She asked, "How can you use a pattern to find all the combinations for eight total cubes?"

> Shae used formative assessment to design a prompt to understand her students' thinking, gather assessment data, adjust instruction using that data, and communicate the information to the students' families. This chapter will explore the following questions:
>
> - What is formative assessment?
> - What are specific formative assessment techniques?

# WHAT IS FORMATIVE ASSESSMENT?

Formative assessment, also called **formative evaluation** (Hattie, 2009), focuses on collecting information about student learning in the moment—as it is happening—and responding to that information by adapting instruction to improve learning. Consistent and thoughtful formative evaluation can be leveraged to produce the largest student-learning gains (Hattie, 2009). Formative assessment can be thought of as *assessment for learning* because teachers adjust their teaching practices in response to what they learn about student understanding. On the flip side, *assessment of learning* may also be called *summative learning*. Schools use **summative assessment** to determine students' achievement levels at particular points in time, particularly at the end of units, quarters, and even entire grade levels. Wiliam and Thompson (2008) recommend the following five key formative assessment strategies.

Consider the following examples:

1. *Clarifying and sharing learning intentions and criteria for success.* The first step in formative assessment involves letting your students know what they will learn and what it means when they have learned it. This is a critical but often misunderstood part of formative assessment. You will recall from Chapter 4 the importance of establishing and communicating learning intentions and success criteria for every student. When you let students know what they are supposed to be learning and help them determine or self-evaluate their own success, you empower them!

2. *Engineering effective classroom discussions, questions, and learning tasks that elicit evidence of learning.* By posing questions, responding to students' thinking, and designing and conducting tasks that prompt deep mathematical thinking, you set the stage for responsive formative assessment. Chapters 6 (tasks), 8 (student thinking), and 12 (facilitating lessons) emphasize the need for and importance of eliciting student thinking. As the engineer, you carefully plan for these opportunities to formatively assess and adapt your instruction.

3. *Providing feedback that moves learning forward.* Feedback that is built upon student thinking and reasoning is powerful because you are targeting exactly the next right instructional move for your particular students. You are charged with evaluating your students to give some type of grade or score, but grades are not actionable feedback. You take the daily collection of student evidence to the next level by offering explicit feedback to students that builds on prior learning, stretches their thinking, and unpacks misconceptions. This feedback is a key component to formative assessment because you are meeting students where they are and advancing their learning during the lesson without delay. Feedback is not a punitive opportunity to catch students when they are wrong but an opportunity to uncover interesting thinking.

Consider the following examples:

> Great job explaining what an odd number is, Chelsea!

> Liam, I like how you explained that an odd number does not have a partner. Can you show me what you mean using manipulatives?

Note how the second example provides explicit feedback to the child and asks for further clarification from the student to represent his thinking using manipulatives. Primary teachers are so very positive with their students! Extend your current warm, positive, and inviting approach by specifically linking your feedback to what students do and say.

4. *Activating students as instructional resources for one another.* Students can and do provide each other with instructional support. They often recognize each other's misconceptions and can remediate confusion naturally and effortlessly. Other times, they work together through shared learning and serve as instructional supports to each other by asking questions. They also clarify their own understanding by explaining their thinking to others. When you build this kind of co-construction of learning in your classroom, you empower your entire learning community by equally distributing the responsibility of learning to everyone.

5. *Activating students as the owners of their own learning.* When you stimulate students to own their learning, you communicate confidence to them about their ability to advocate for themselves. Students become "in tune" with their own understanding and can convey their levels of understanding to their classmates, teachers, and families.

Standards

LI and SC

Purpose

Tasks

Materials

Student Thinking

Lesson Structures

Form. Assess.

Lesson Launch

Lesson Facilitation

Closure

Example: Molly

Second-grade teacher Molly distributes the image of a stoplight (Figure 10.1) to her students during small-group instruction. At strategic points, she asks students to place a cube on the stoplight to show their readiness to move on in the lesson. When Molly first introduced this approach, her second graders expressed reticence to evaluate their own understanding, but she persevered and encouraged them to self-evaluate. Now, they are quite comfortable sharing. One of the students, Chet, explains, "I was nervous to say I didn't understand. Now I know that Ms. Lynard wants to know if we are confused. She just smiles and doesn't get mad at us."

**Figure 10.1**

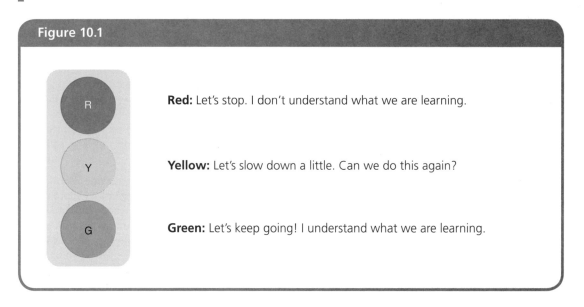

**Red:** Let's stop. I don't understand what we are learning.

**Yellow:** Let's slow down a little. Can we do this again?

**Green:** Let's keep going! I understand what we are learning.

As you review these strategies, you may note the shared responsibility that teachers and students hold in the mathematics learning community. You and the students work together to build one another's understanding and probe each other to clarify reasoning. Be sure to communicate that misconceptions are a normal part of every lesson that should be expected and celebrated (Hattie et al., 2016) and express appreciation for their efforts. Also ensure that students understand that they are expected to explain and show their mathematical thinking, ask questions, and evaluate their own understanding.

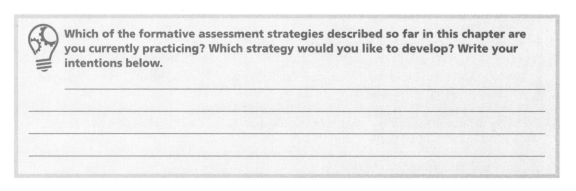

**Which of the formative assessment strategies described so far in this chapter are you currently practicing? Which strategy would you like to develop? Write your intentions below.**

_____

_____

_____

_____

## WHAT ARE SPECIFIC FORMATIVE ASSESSMENT TECHNIQUES?

The Formative 5 assessment techniques (Fennell et al., 2017) include the following:

- Observation
- Interview
- Show Me
- Hinge questions
- Exit tasks

Each of these techniques includes five important phases:

1. Anticipating student responses
2. Implementing the technique
3. Collecting evidence
4. Adjusting instruction
5. Providing feedback to students

Let's take a close look at each technique, including the five different phases, so you can determine how to implement them in your classroom.

## Observation

You observe your students every day! **Observation** is perhaps the most comfortable of all the classroom-based formative assessment strategies because you are constantly informally observing your students as they engage in mathematics activities. Observational evidence is particularly powerful when you document what you observe to inform your instruction (Fennell et al., 2017).

*Anticipating Student Responses:* How might students respond to the mathematics concepts you are teaching? What will students do during the lessons? What kinds of behaviors or actions will you observe? Think about potential misconceptions (Chapter 8) students might make (Figure 10.2).

**Figure 10.2**

| Mathematics Standard | Anticipate | |
| --- | --- | --- |
| | **Observations** | **Misconceptions** |
| Add and subtract within 20, demonstrating fluency for addition and subtraction within 10. Use strategies such as counting on, making ten, decomposing a number leading to a ten, using the relationship between addition and subtraction, and creating equivalent but easier or known sums. | Students will vary in their use of different strategies. Students will use primarily one or two strategies. Students will invent their own strategies. | Students will use the count-all strategy and will not be able to recognize when strategies could be used. Students will incorrectly apply a strategy. |

*Implementing the Observations:* How and when will you conduct the observation during your lesson? Consider the strategic points during the lesson to conduct observations and collect data.

*Collecting Evidence:* What kind of tool will you use to record your observations? As you conduct the observation, you will want to use a simple recording tool. Figure 10.3 shows a completed example of a form that first-grade teacher Aida used to collect evidence during a lesson.

Standards

LI and SC

Purpose

Tasks

Materials

Student Thinking

Lesson Structures

Form. Assess.

Lesson Launch

Lesson Facilitation

Closure

Figure 10.3

Standard: Add and subtract within 20

Prompt: Addition equations: $9 + 8 =$ __  $7 + 8 =$ __  $6 + 7 =$ __
$6 + 6 =$ __

| Names | Observations |
|---|---|
| Eli | Used make ten (sums that make ten) and doubles strategies. |
| Micah | Counted on even when the equation was presented with the larger number first but did not count on when the larger number was second in the equation. |

*Adjusting Instruction:* How will you immediately adjust instruction using the feedback from the observation? For example, using the evidence collected in Figure 10.3, Aida prompted Eli to see if he could use another one of the strategies they had learned about. She asked, "Which strategy is more efficient for you? Why?"

For Micah, Aida leaned over, covered some of the unit cubes with her hand, and said, "How can you find out the total for seven plus eight without counting each cube?"

*Providing Feedback to Students:* How will you do this during the lesson to move learning forward? It's important to give feedback swiftly, after students have supplied evidence of their learning. Immediate feedback helps students positively connect the feedback with their explanation or representation. You also need to ensure that the feedback is explicit and connects specifically to the student's learning needs. In Aida's example, she said to Eli, "I can see that you are using the make ten and doubles addition strategies with your addition facts. I am wondering if you would like to use what you know about the doubles facts to solve the doubles plus one facts (six plus seven) strategy."

Aida positively reinforced Eli's knowledge of two of the addition fact strategies and then prompted him to add a related addition fact strategy.

Aida's feedback to Micah was also careful and thoughtful. She said, "Micah, you are a very good counter, and I see that you are always able to get the correct total. Have you noticed that sometimes it takes a long time to count on? Let's take a look at this fact, six plus six, and see if we can figure out a way to find the total without counting on."

Once again, Aida gave explicit feedback to Micah and then deftly positioned a new task to move his thinking along. If teachers wait too long to give feedback to students, the magical moment can be lost, and students will not be able to connect the feedback to their actions.

## Interview

The formative assessment **interview** is a brief interview that you tuck into a lesson when you want to collect more information about a student's thinking. The interview is brief, is on the spot, and can be conducted as a response to something you observed students doing. Interviews can help you dig deeper into the source of student misconceptions.

*Anticipating Student Responses:* Consider the kinds of responses students might give you during the interview. You can decide ahead of time that you will interview particular students or a group of students. You might also decide to interview students who respond in particular ways to the lesson. Interview questions include these:

Why did you decide to solve it that way?

Can you explain your thinking?

*Implementing the Interview:* When and how will you conduct it? You can also plan to insert interviews in a lesson during small-group instruction.

*Collecting Evidence:* You gather student data to inform your instructional decisions. For example, Olga, a second-grade teacher, designed an interview recording sheet for each of her small groups (Figure 10.4). Although she only meets with her small groups twice a week, she finds that this is the best time to conduct the interview because she can concentrate on her students' thinking.

**Figure 10.4**

Group:

| Date | Name | Interview Question | Interview Notes |
|------|------|--------------------|-----------------|
|      |      |                    |                 |
|      |      |                    |                 |

*Adjusting Instruction:* As you interview students, you can gain insight into those sticky misconceptions that prevent students from learning. For example, during an interview about the place value unit, Olga interviewed a student named Harry by asking him to represent 304 using place value blocks and explain his thinking. Harry showed her:

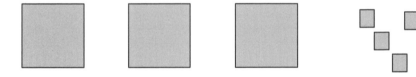

Olga replied, "Now tell me about the value of each of the digits in three hundred four, and show me where the value is represented in the place value blocks."

Harry explained, "Well, there are three hundreds [pointing to the three hundred blocks], and there are four ones [pointing to the four ones]."

Olga asked, "What about the zero? What does that mean?"

Harry responded, "Well there is a zero, which means nothing, so it does not count."

Olga then showed Harry the following and asked him to write the number.

Harry wrote 15. Olga asked him to explain how his number matched the blocks. Harry explained, "Well there are five ones [pointing to the five ones] and there is one hundred. So, I wrote one hundred five."

Olga asked Harry to read the number he wrote again.

Harry said, "Hmmmmm, it is fifteen—no, it's not!"

Standards

LI and SC

Purpose

Tasks

Materials

Student Thinking

Lesson Structures

Form. Assess.

Lesson Launch

Lesson Facilitation

Closure

Olga's interview revealed Harry's tentative understanding of zero and place value in the hundreds, particularly when zero is in the tens place. The interview helped Olga gain a better understanding of Harry's inconsistency in representing and writing place value.

*Providing Feedback:* Once again, timely *feedback* is critical. However, note that in Olga's interview, she did not start providing feedback to Harry before she gathered evidence of his thinking. She needed to fully understand the extent of his misconception in order to provide appropriate feedback.

Olga next said to Harry, "You explained to me that three hundred four is three hundreds and four ones. Then you showed me one hundred block and five ones and told me that it represents fifteen. Does that make sense to you? What should we do about the zeros in each of the numbers?"

In this example, Olga reflected back what Harry said and did in the interview, and then she asked a question to prompt more thinking. While it would have been easier for Olga simply to tell Harry what to do, she knew that providing feedback by reflecting back to Harry about his own actions would promote new learning.

## Show Me

The **Show Me** technique is "a performance response by a student or group of students that extends and often deepens what was observed and what might have been asked within an interview" (Fennell et al., 2017, p. 63). This technique is nicely suited for primary teachers because you can easily integrate the Show Me technique into lessons by asking students to show understanding using manipulatives and/or drawings, digit cards, whiteboards, and/or response cards.

*Anticipating Student Responses:* As you plan to use the Show Me technique, think about the potential responses students might provide. For example, Tatiana, a kindergarten teacher, gave each student a 1 to 10 number path. She planned to ask the students to pinch the number path when she posed *one more* questions. For example, she showed the students a card with three dots and asked the students, "Pinch the number that is *one more* than three." She anticipated that some students would struggle and prepared some number paths so that the numbers were on one side and the corresponding dot values were on the other side. She decided to begin by allowing the students to choose which side they would use.

*Implementing Show Me:* Consider at what points you will want to use it. Tatiana planned to implement the Show Me technique during the brief whole-group lesson after she read *Just One More* by Jennifer Hansen Rolli (2014). During the class, she prompted the kindergartners, "Show me a number one more than six." Kindergartners pinched the number path and then held it up for her to see. Tatiana scanned the room and could easily see which of her students were struggling.

*Collecting Evidence:* You can collect evidence using the Show Me technique by taking photographs, jotting down notes, and using technology applications like Go Formative (Goformative.com), which collects representations of individual students' work. Tatiana often snaps a photo of the students as they are showing their work.

*Adjusting Instruction:* As you conduct the Show Me technique, consider how you will adjust instruction using the evidence you are collecting. Show Me prompts, in particular, often reveal trends in student thinking because you can see everyone's response at one time. For example, as Tatiana was prompting the students with the "one more" questions, she noted that a few students were not able to fluently find one more than the number she said. She decided to show the students a ten frame and ask them to show her one more than what she was showing on the ten frame. She thought that this adjustment would help the students see the value of the number and then count on to find one more.

*Providing Feedback:* The Show Me formative assessment offers the perfect opportunity for students to provide feedback to each other by explaining their own thinking and probing each other's thinking. For instance, as Tatiana scanned the room, she noticed that Jorge quickly pinched one more, almost before she even posed the prompt. She decided to put the students in pairs while she posed the prompts so they could explain their thinking to each other. She purposely paired Jorge with Ann Marie because she noticed that Ann Marie found one more by placing her finger on each number and then counting up. She heard Jorge say, "Ann Marie, when Ms. Ramos says one more than five, find five first and then ask yourself to move your finger one more!"

## Hinge Questions

As a teacher, you craft and ask hundreds of questions throughout the course of one day! The **hinge question** is a special kind of question that essentially provides a check for understanding at a pivotal moment in your lesson (Wiliam, 2011). In other words, the next part of your lesson hinges on how students respond. According to Wiliam (2011), students should respond in one minute or less. Fennell et al. (2017) suggest that this could be expanded to two or three minutes, particularly as you consider the developmental needs of your primary students.

*Anticipating Student Responses:* The key to writing a good hinge question is to anticipate the possible interpretations or incorrect responses that students might give. Hinge questions take several forms, including multiple choice and short, open-ended prompts. For example, Bailey, a second-grade teacher, developed a multiple-choice hinge question for the following standard:

Add up to four two-digit numbers using strategies based on place value and properties of operations.

Here is Bailey's hinge question.

Marco solved 36 + 59 = ___ in four ways. Circle all correct solutions.

A. 30 + 50 + 10 + 5 = 95

B. 30 + 50 + 14 = 95

C. 36 + 50 = 86

   86 + 8 = 95

D. 40 + 60 = 100

   100 − 5 = 95

Bailey anticipated that all or most of her students would select A. She wanted to see if the students would recognize the composing and decomposing strategies they have been working on.

*Implementing Hinge Questions:* To implement hinge questions, you can pose them at the beginning, middle, or end of the lesson. The key idea is to pose the question at a strategic point to assess if students are ready to move on to the next concept. For example, Bailey decided to ask her question after a task on using place value to add two-digit numbers, which was at the midpoint of her lesson.

*Collecting Evidence:* You can collect evidence of students' responses to the hinge questions by using small slips of paper, journals, or technology. For example, Bailey displayed the prompt for her students on a whiteboard and distributed small slips of paper with the same prompt.

*Adjusting Instruction:* Many teachers choose to regroup students to adjust instruction after collecting evidence from the hinge question. For example, Bailey planned to move her students into math stations so she could provide additional instruction for her struggling students in a small group while the other students rotated through the stations, which included word problems with two-digit numbers. Bailey used the hinge question to flexibly group her students, using real evidence from the lesson. She loved that she was immediately responding to the students' learning needs.

*Providing Feedback:* You can provide feedback on the hinge question in many ways. Some teachers reveal the correct answer and have students gather in pairs or small groups to discuss the solutions. Other teachers, like Bailey, use the hinge question to provide explicit instructional feedback to the students during the lesson, either in small groups or individually. The key is to take an immediate call to action based on the evidence.

## Exit Tasks

The **exit task** is a "capstone problem or task that captures the major focus of the lesson for that day or perhaps the last several days and provides a sampling of student performance" (Fennell et al., 2017, p. 109). You may be familiar with the term **exit ticket** or **exit slip.** However, an exit task extends beyond a simple question that may assess only a small portion of the student's understanding. Instead, the exit task is a high-cognitive task (see Chapter 6) that includes opportunities for students to connect procedures to concepts, explore mathematical relationships, use representations, and apply self-monitoring and self-regulation skills as they work to solve the problem (Smith & Stein, 2011).

Kyle, a first-grade teacher, considered the prompts in Figure 10.5 for his exit task.

Standards

LI and SC

Purpose

Tasks

Materials

Student Thinking

Lesson Structures

Form. Assess.

Lesson Launch

Lesson Facilitation

Closure

## Figure 10.5

| Task A | Task B |
|---|---|
| Find the number that makes 10. <br><br> $6 + \rule{1cm}{0.15mm} = 10$ <br><br> $3 + \rule{1cm}{0.15mm} = 10$ <br><br> $8 + \rule{1cm}{0.15mm} = 10$ | Use a ten frame to find combinations to ten. Find as many combinations as you can. |

Kyle chose Task B because he wanted the students to figure out their own combinations. Task A wasn't going to give him good information about the students' understanding of combinations.

*Anticipating Student Responses:* Once again, it is critical to *anticipate* the results of the formative assessment, particularly as you consider how you will assess your students' understanding of the concept you just taught. You can also differentiate the exit task or design it so that students can enter into the task from different points. For example, students can find between one and nine combinations to solve Task B in Figure 10.5. Kyle can also determine how students find combinations by examining their work to see if they found patterns or randomly listed combinations.

*Implementing Exit Tasks:* As the description of the task indicated, you can implement an exit task at the end of a concept or lesson. Some teachers design exit tasks to reflect standards that they have been teaching for a long time. Other teachers design and conduct exit tasks toward the end of the lesson. The key is to make sure you give students plenty of time to solve the task!

*Collecting Evidence:* Review the students' responses to the exit task to collect evidence for overall trends in their understanding. After that, you can examine each group for individual strengths and needs. For example, Emily likes to use an exit task summary sheet (Figure 10.6) to analyze student work from the whole class. She uses the same format for each exit task and supplies the specific criteria for each task. She then records the names of the students below the appropriate criteria.

## Figure 10.6

**Exit Task:** Use a ten frame to find combinations to ten. Find as many combinations as you can find.

| Does Not Meet Expectations (Describe) | Meets Expectations (Describe) | Exceeds Expectations (Describe) |
|---|---|---|
| Supplies only one or two combinations. | Provides three or more combinations. Combinations are recorded without pattern. | Provides all combinations and uses a pattern to record the combinations. |
| Renya <br><br> Marcy | Carey <br><br> Colby | Toya <br><br> Mariella |

*Adjusting Instruction:* Your exit task evidence is quite important in deciding how you will adjust instruction. For instance, you may decide that your students are ready to move on or, perhaps, that they need additional, targeted instruction. The exit task is particularly suited to differentiation as you see the particular needs of your students. You may be tempted to divide them into same ability groups, but you might also wish to consider mixed-ability groups, which allow students to share strategies and construct new ideas together. The key is to use student evidence to make your decisions about how you will adjust instruction.

*Providing Feedback to the Students:* Since the exit task is often conducted at the end of the lesson or series of lessons, you will want to provide feedback that is directly connected to the success criteria. You can do this when you move to your next instructional step, whether you choose to work with students individually, in small groups, or in large groups. Exit task data are also great data to share with families. For example, Emily collects five exit tasks per quarter to place in the students' portfolios for family conferences. In her school, students lead the conferences by sharing their work, thus providing even more opportunities to receive feedback.

As you can see, formative assessment is intricately tied to your planning and teaching. If you are just beginning to use formative assessment techniques, begin with those that are most comfortable to you, and build your repertoire as you develop ease with the techniques.

 **Which of the formative assessment techniques will you try first? Why? How will you begin integrating this technique into your teaching practice? Record your ideas below.**

_____

_____

_____

_____

### Building Unit Coherence

As you design and collect daily formative assessment evidence, you develop comprehensive knowledge of your students' mathematical understanding. You can support unit coherence by varying the techniques and kinds of formative assessment data you collect.

Example: Natasha

Natasha, a first-grade teacher, realizes that she is primarily using the observation technique for her students. This technique produces a lot of anecdotal evidence, but although it is rich in detail, she wants to use more student work evidence. Consequently, she decides to incorporate more Show Me assessment prompts over the course of the unit. She feels that the combination of anecdotal notes and student work nicely captures her students' mathematical understanding and, over the course of the unit, creates a coherent picture of all of the students' learning.

Standards

LI and SC

Purpose

Tasks

Materials

Student Thinking

Lesson Structures

Form. Assess.

Lesson Launch

Lesson Facilitation

Closure

The kindergarten teachers are deciding which formative assessment technique to try first. Eliza says, "I am the newest member, and I don't feel comfortable with my observations yet. Do you think we could develop a specific observation checklist for this lesson? I would like to try it out as a team and then share what we observed. This will help me feel like I am on the right track."

### Formative Assessment:

Use observation checklist to observe the following:

- One-to-one correspondence
- Grouping of tens and some ones
- Counting technique
- Conservation

*See the complete lesson plan in Appendix A on page 178.*

Why would it be helpful to design an observation checklist that aligns specifically to the lesson you are teaching? Note your thoughts below.

_____

_____

_____

_____

_____

_____

_____

_____

_____

_____

_____

_____

_____

_____

_____

_____

_____

_____

_____

## Formative Assessment

Sarita bounds into the planning meeting. With great excitement in her voice, she shares, "We got the individual whiteboards! Now, we can design regular Show Me prompts in our lessons!"

Karlo chuckles and says, "We have already been doing them, Sarita!"

She replies, "I know, but now we can do them more efficiently!"

**Formative Assessment:**

Show Me prompt: Show me 34 using base-ten blocks. How many tens and ones?

Interview prompt: How did you figure out how many tens and ones are in 34?

*See the complete lesson plan in Appendix A on page 183.*

**How might you capture students' work while using the Show Me formative assessment technique?**

_____

_____

_____

_____

_____

_____

_____

_____

_____

_____

_____

_____

_____

_____

_____

_____

_____

_____

_____

_____

_____

Standards | LI and SC | Purpose | Tasks | Materials | Student Thinking | Lesson Structures | Form. Assess. | Lesson Launch | Lesson Facilitation | Closure

*Formative Assessment*

Dwayne, Aliyah, and Wilma are working to develop brief formative assessment interviews to use with their second graders. They previously decided that they will interview individual students and/or student pairs about their solutions. Now they agree to collect information from the interviews to inform their long-range planning for the place value unit.

> **Formative Assessment:**
>
> Brief formative Interview
>
> How did you decide to represent the number?
>
> Which value is greatest? How do you know?

*See the complete lesson plan in Appendix A on page 188.*

How could you integrate brief formative assessment interviews into your practice? Note your ideas below.

_____

_____

_____

_____

_____

_____

_____

_____

_____

_____

_____

_____

_____

_____

_____

_____

_____

_____

_____

_____

_____

_____

Now it is your turn! Decide on the formative assessment(s) that will best suit the lesson you are building.

**Formative Assessment:**

Download the full Lesson-Planning Template from resources.corwin.com/mathlessonplanning/k-2
Remember that you can use the online version of the lesson plan template to begin compiling each section into the full template as your lesson plan grows.

Standards
LI and SC
Purpose
Tasks
Materials
Student Thinking
Lesson Structures
Form. Assess.
Lesson Launch
Lesson Facilitation
Closure

# PART III

# PULLING ALL THE PIECES TOGETHER

# CHAPTER 11

# PLANNING TO LAUNCH THE LESSON

Amirah, a second-grade teacher, began her lesson by displaying the picture in Figure 11.1.

**Figure 11.1**

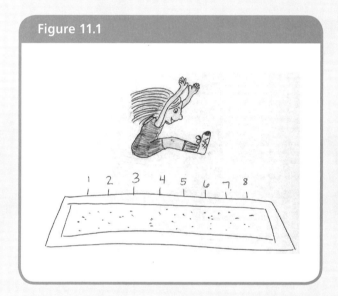

She told her students that she would give them one minute to See, Think, and Wonder (Ritchhart, Church, & Morrison, 2011) about the picture. After a minute of silence, she told the students to find their Turn and Talk Buddies to discuss what they see, think, and wonder about the picture. The classroom buzzed with excitement. Amirah noticed some of the students waving their arms and legs as if they were acting out the movement, while others appeared to be counting objects in the picture.

Amirah asked, "What do you notice about the picture? Please let me know about something your Turn and Talk Buddy noticed."

Hands waved wildly in the air as students strained to share their partners' observations. Amirah wrote quickly to include what they saw. Then she asked her students to share their think and wonders (Figure 11.2).

**Figure 11.2**

| See | Think and Wonder |
| --- | --- |
| It looks like a sandbox. | Will she fall? |
| The girl is jumping. | What team is she on? |
| The girl is in the air. | How high is she in the air? |
| The girl might fall. | How far can she jump? |
| There are numbers. | What are the numbers for? |
| | Is this how far she jumped? |

Amirah announced that today they would find out some of the answers, because they would be measuring their own jumps using different kinds of manipulatives. She asked, "How far do you think you can you jump? What if we measured your jump with counting cubes? Paper clips? How many of each? What is the best measuring tool we should use to find out?"

**This chapter explores ways to begin your lesson. We will explore the following questions:**

- What is a lesson launch?
- How can you launch a problem-solving lesson?
- What kinds of lesson launches focus on mathematics concepts?
- What are number routine lesson launches?
- What do you anticipate students will do?

## WHAT IS A LESSON LAUNCH?

Imagine you are opening to the first page of a book or turning to a new television show. How quickly do you decide whether you will continue to read or watch or abandon? In a similar way, students may also make conscious or unconscious decisions about whether they will engage in a lesson. This possibility highlights the importance of the **lesson launch**.

Your lesson launch can be implemented in many ways and should be designed with just as much purpose and planning as the main body of your lesson. For example, lesson launches may include a number routine to help students think and talk about numbers, equations, and computation. Or, your lesson launch might introduce a specific problem-solving task. Your lesson launch can be tied directly to the big idea and learning intention for the day, particularly if you plan to use the lesson launch to set up the lesson you are about to teach. Or you might use the lesson launch to circle back to a big idea or concept that the students previously learned because you want to make sure the children continue to build understanding of that concept. This is called **interleaving**, and it increases the students' retention and performance on assessments (Rohrer, 2012).

The way that you construct how your lesson will be launched will depend greatly on your students' learning needs, the content standards, Standards for Mathematical Practice or process standards, learning intentions, and lesson purpose. Lessons can be launched by creating interest around a problem-solving task (like in the vignette at the start of this chapter), connecting to prior knowledge or previous lessons, or implementing a number routine. Lesson launches can be facilitated in 5 to 15 minutes and are typically conducted in a whole-group setting.

Many teachers use the same routine, like calendar math, to launch a lesson every day. While there are benefits to building a routine into your mathematics lesson, such as calendar math, teachers report that many students passively watch one or two students perform the calendar math exercises. Rather than beginning your mathematics lesson in the same way every day, vary your lesson launch as it connects to the students' learning and math content needs. As you read this chapter, consider ways you might launch your mathematics lessons to stimulate *all* students' interests and boost conceptual understanding.

## HOW CAN YOU LAUNCH A PROBLEM-SOLVING LESSON?

Launching a lesson with a focus on problem solving gives you an opportunity to help students unpack a problem before trying to solve it. The following problem-solving lesson launches also nicely connect to the Standards for Mathematical Practice or process standards. You can focus on helping students make sense of problems, develop ways to communicate their ideas, ask questions of their peers, and critique each other's reasoning and thinking.

### See, Think, and Wonder Lesson Launch

The See, Think, and Wonder (STW) (Ritchhart, Church, & Morrison, 2011) routine summons students to carefully observe, make some predictions, and expand the predictions into questions. Along with Notice and Wonder (Math Forum, 2015), which is described later in this chapter, STW capitalizes on students' keen observational skills and natural curiosity about what they are learning. When you use this launch, you invite students to bring their own thoughts and questions forward before you instruct them to engage in particular ways with the content. Both strategies can help students draw on prior knowledge, and they motivate students to reason before receiving formal instruction, which is particularly useful for ELL learners or other learners who struggle. The two strategies have slight but important variations.

Example: Melanie

Melanie, a kindergarten teacher, has always noticed that her kindergartners are very inquisitive, and she likes to engage their curiosity as much as possible. Instead of giving the students perfect models of a triangle and then directly telling them why a triangle is a triangle, she decides to capitalize on their natural curiosity to engage and motivate them.

To launch the lesson, Melanie shows students the illustration in Figure 11.3 and asks them to SEE quietly.

**Figure 11.3**

This quiet reflection time allows students an opportunity to make observations without being hindered by another student's thoughts. Melanie makes sure that students have enough time to notice important details in the picture. She then asks the students to share with a partner what they saw. She reminds them that she wants them to share by making "I SEE" statements. She then asks the student pairs to share something their partners noticed that they didn't. She records their answers in a chart that everyone can view (Figure 11.4).

**Figure 11.4**

**I SEE**

Six things

One has crooked lines

Two sides and a squiggle

One looks like an ice cream cone

Three sides that are straight

Triangles

Three shapes on the top and three shapes on the bottom

Two and two and two

Only one triangle

One side is ripped

Melanie then asks the students to THINK. To remind her students that this is when they make predictions about what they are seeing, she says, "Using what you observe, make a prediction about what you are seeing. What do you think is going on here?" She again gives them quiet time to think. This time she calls on students to share their ideas. Then she records their answers (Figure 11.5).

Figure 11.5

**I THINK**

A teacher asked a kid to draw funny shapes.

Someone was drawing and another person moved the paper.

Someone was trying to draw an ice cream cone.

Someone was trying to draw a sign on the road.

Someone ripped one.

A dog took a bite.

Melanie then asks students what they WONDER after Seeing and Thinking about the shapes. She records the Wonders (Figure 11.6). Students may also record their own wonders on individual whiteboards and then post them for everyone to see.

Figure 11.6

**I WONDER**

If we are going to make them.

Which ones are triangles?

If we will find out who drew them.

If the shapes have a name.

If we can touch them.

Melanie then uses the Wonders to launch into her lesson about what makes a triangle a triangle.

## Notice and Wonder Lesson Launch

While similar to the See, Think, and Wonder approach, the Notice and Wonder protocol, developed by the Math Forum (2015), simplifies the process into two distinct steps. It was originally designed to focus students

Standards

LI and SC

Purpose

Tasks

Materials

Student Thinking

Lesson Structures

Form. Assess.

Lesson Launch

Lesson Facilitation

Closure

on unpacking word problems to enhance students' understanding of "the story, the quantities, and the relationships in the problem" (p. 2). The Math Forum suggests the following steps.

Notice

- Display or read a portion or complete problem to students.
- Ask the students, "What do you notice?" Be sure to encourage wait time.
- Record all of the students' ideas without commenting.

Wonder

- Ask the students, "What are you wondering?"
- Record all of the students' ideas without commenting.
- Ask the students if they have additional questions or clarifications.

At the conclusion of the Notice and Wonder, you can encourage students to tell the story in partners or small groups before solving the problem.

Example: Lynae

Second-grade teacher Lynae often uses Notice and Wonder to introduce routine and nonroutine word problems. Her students are so accustomed to this approach that they can even conduct their own Notice and Wonder sessions in small groups.

One day she shares the following problem with her second graders:

Patty traveled 216 miles to pick up her niece. The entire trip took six hours. She traveled 42 miles the first hour and 23 miles the last hour. ████████████████████████ ██████████████ ? (Note that the question is covered.)

The second graders notice the following:

- She had to travel 216 miles.
- She traveled more miles the first hour than the last hour.
- She traveled 65 miles the first and last hour.

They wondered the following:

- Why did it take so long?
- Where was her niece?
- What would they do?
- How many more miles did she travel in the first hour than the second?
- How many miles did she travel in the middle?

Lynae then reveals the question: "How many miles did she travel during the other four hours?" to the delight of the second graders! They clap gleefully, excited that they have once again wondered the question in the word problem.

## Numberless Word Problem Lesson Launch

Students may be so distracted by the numbers in the word problem that they are tempted to perform any operation regardless of what makes sense. The **numberless word problem** launch encourages the students to make sense of the word problem without the numbers.

Example: Terry

Terry, a first-grade teacher, displays and reads the following problem to his students.

Ariele and Marcus cut out stars to decorate the classroom. Ariele cut out gold stars. Marcus cut out silver stars. How many more stars did Ariele cut than Marcus?

Terry has purposely selected a word problem with the word *more* in it because he has noticed that many students think that they need to add when they see the word *more*. Terry asks student pairs to talk with each other and share their ideas about what is happening in the word problem. As he looks around the classroom, he notices that the students are excitedly talking about how many stars they can cut out. He has purposely paired the students because there are two students in the word problem. Prior to the lesson, he anticipated that the students might supply numbers and begin trying to solve the problem.

After about five minutes of paired discussion, Terry asks, "What is this word problem asking us to solve?" Here are the students' replies.

Maria: I think we are adding together the stars, but Kevin does not think we should do that.

Arnold: We thought that too, but then we realized that Ariele cut out more than Marcus so we have to find how out how many more stars Ariele cut out than Marcus.

Rosita: Ya, like if Ariele cut five stars and Marcus cut four, then Ariele cut one more than Marcus because five minus four equals one.

Terry smiles. This is exactly the kind of discussion he had hoped to elicit. Without the numbers in the problem, the students are able to reason about the problem and even supply their own numbers to prove their ideas.

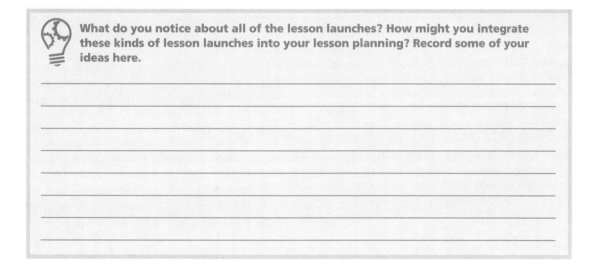

**What do you notice about all of the lesson launches? How might you integrate these kinds of lesson launches into your lesson planning? Record some of your ideas here.**

_____

_____

_____

_____

_____

_____

## WHAT KINDS OF LESSON LAUNCHES FOCUS ON MATHEMATICS CONCEPTS?

You can use the following lesson launch routines to focus students on recalling, using, and applying prior knowledge; using, developing, and applying appropriate vocabulary; and noticing and examining the structure of mathematics.

### One of These Things Is Not Like the Others

You may remember the old *Sesame Street* song:

> One of these things is not like the others,
> One of these things just doesn't belong (Raposo & Stone, 1972)

In this lesson launch, students examine three related numbers or pictures and one unrelated number or picture and try to determine why one of the choices does not belong. Students must select one of the options and then construct a viable argument about why they believe a particular picture or number does not belong. The key to this launch is to provide examples that reveal different entry points for students.

Standards

LI and SC

Purpose

Tasks

Materials

Student Thinking

Lesson Structures

Form. Assess.

Lesson Launch

Lesson Facilitation

Closure

Example: Debbie

Debbie's students have been working diligently on representing numbers using place value materials and have recently been recording the values using word form. She wants to see if the students will notice and talk about how 70 tens can also be represented as 700. She also wants to see if students will notice when a choice is not written in order of value.

Debbie designs the prompt in Figure 11.7 to elicit conversation about place value, odd and even numbers, and expanded form. Whenever Debbie uses this type of prompt, she typically displays it and then gives the students time to think about and prepare a mathematical argument for which one is not like the others. Sometimes she even challenges the students to create a mathematical argument for all of the choices. In this case, she ensures that any of the choices can be selected as the one not like the others, if students can explain their reasoning.

**Figure 11.7**

| 3 hundreds<br>5 tens<br>9 ones | 70 tens<br>5 ones |
|---|---|
| 2 ones<br>4 hundreds<br>9 tens | 637 |

Debbie asks, "Which one of these things is not like the others?"

Debbie's students quickly notice that 637 is the only choice written in **standard form**. Only a few noticed that 2 ones, 4 hundreds, and 9 tens should be written as 492. Even fewer students connected 70 tens to 700.

This lesson launch offers Debbie good insight into her students' thinking about place value. She is able to use the student work from this lesson launch to transition to her lesson that focuses on multiple ways to represent a number.

You can also tailor this lesson launch to focus on particular kinds of reasoning that your students exhibit. For more examples like this, you can check out the Which One Doesn't Belong website (http://wodb.ca) created by Mary Barousa (2017) with contributions by teachers from all over the country. Also, check out Christopher Danielson's (2016) book, *Which One Doesn't Belong*, which focuses on shapes.

## WHAT ARE NUMBER ROUTINE LESSON LAUNCHES?

**Number routines** focus on strategies that help students understand number concepts and build computational fluency. Most important, you are providing opportunities for students to derive their own strategies, hear the strategies their peers use, and develop fluency using those strategies. Number routines also offer opportunities for students to engage in **spaced practice**, which occurs when you expose students to an idea over several days and then *space* opportunities to practice the learned skill (Hattie et al., 2016). Select your number routines purposely, either as a launch to link to the content you are about to teach or as an opportunity to provided spaced practice. The following number routine lesson launches encourage the students to develop understanding and reasoning about numbers, flexibility with numbers, and number fluency.

## Counting Jar

You can use counting jars to provide multiple opportunities for your students to count with purpose. Kindergartners can develop one-to-one correspondence, rote counting, and rational counting. First and second graders can count and group objects into sets of ten to develop place value understanding. You can develop K–2 students' reasoning about number magnitude by having them estimate before counting.

> **Example: Leo**
>
> Leo, a kindergarten teacher, uses counting jars both as a lesson launch and as a center in his classroom. He uses the counting jars as a launch when he wants to create a discussion with students about efficient ways to count, keep track of objects counted, develop skip counting concepts, and make connections to subitizing and numerals. For a lesson on skip counting by twos, Leo launches the lesson by distributing counting jars and two egg cartons to groups of students. He asks them to estimate how many groups of two they think are in the counting jar and write it on a sticky note. Then he asks the students to pull the objects out of the counting jar in groups of two and place them in the egg carton. Finally, he has the students place numeral cards next to each row and orally skip count as a group. Later, Leo places different counting jars in a center for students to continue to practice counting by twos to develop fluency.

## Number Paths and Number Lines

The number path and number line are ideally suited to support students as they develop meaning about numbers and understanding about number relationships. A number path is a representation that models counting. Rectangles are connected and labeled with each number (Figure 11.8).

**Figure 11.8**

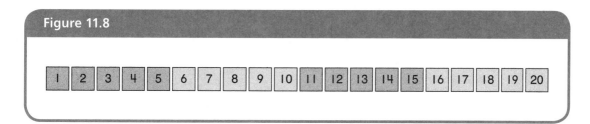

You can use the number path (Grades K and 1) and number line (Grades 1 and 2) as a number launch routine to help students construct conceptual understanding and develop fluency.

Some students struggle with the number line representation because they have difficulty seeing the units; they need to see objects, so they focus on the numbers instead of on the lengths. As a result, they may "count the starting point 0 and then be off by one, or they may focus on the spaces and become confused by the location of the numbers at the end of the spaces" (Committee on Early Childhood Mathematics, 2009, p. 167). When this is the case, you may wish to have them use a number path instead.

> **Example: Adi**
>
> First-grade teacher Adi uses a number path to encourage students to construct a way to add 8 + 7 = ____ using the *make ten* and *doubles plus one* strategies. She poses the prompt and distributes laminated number paths to the students. Students then record their thinking. Finally, she posts the students' ideas, and students discuss what they notice about the strategies (Figure 11.9).
>
> Happily, she notes that many students are thinking about the power of ten as an efficient strategy.

Standards

LI and SC

Purpose

Tasks

Materials

Student Thinking

Lesson Structures

Form. Assess.

Lesson Launch

Lesson Facilitation

Closure

Figure 11.9

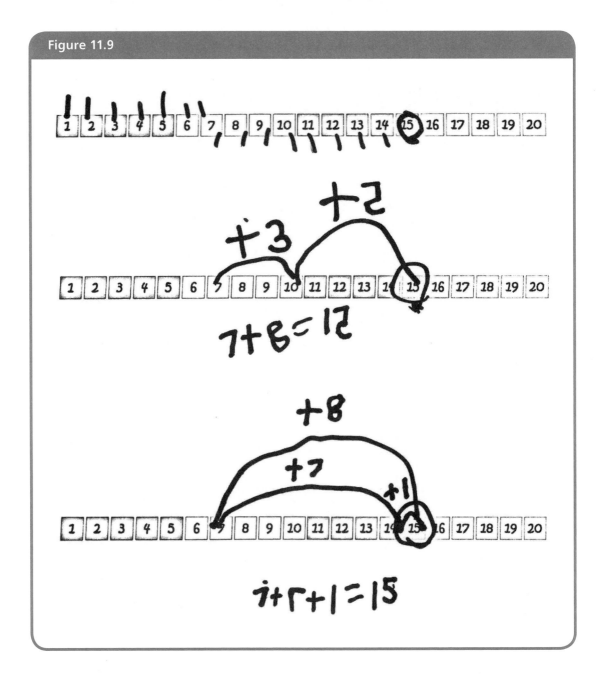

## Number Talk

A **number talk**, also called a **math talk**, is a brief classroom routine that focuses on number relationships, mathematical structures, and strategies to build computational fluency. During a number talk, you present students with one or more computation problems to solve mentally. Then you encourage them to explain and justify their strategy while you record their ideas for the rest of the class to see. These explanations help the students work toward accurate, efficient, and flexible strategies (Parrish, 2011). You may conduct a number talk by following these important steps.

1. Present the number problem to your students. You might display subitizing cards, rekenreks, manipulatives, written math equations, and word problems.

2. Give students time to think about the solution. Encourage your students to think quietly. Some teachers encourage students to signal when they are ready to share a strategy.

3. Elicit students' strategies. Record the students' strategies as they explain their thinking. You may also want to record the students' names next to each strategy.

4. Encourage students to ask clarifying questions. You can also ask students to determine efficient and flexible strategies.

5. Repeat with a new problem if there is time.

Example: Kelsie

Kelsie (Ms. Rites), a second-grade teacher, conducts number talks at least twice a week with her students. One day, she displays the following prompt and waits for the students to think of at least one strategy:

$$25 + 26 =$$

Students begin holding one finger up to show that they have at least one strategy. Some students show two or three fingers, indicating that they have two or three strategies. Kelsie calls on Sammy to share a strategy.

Sammy: Well, I just break 26 into 25 and 1. So I add 25 plus 25 plus 1 equals 51.

Ms. Rites: You used the doubling strategy with 25, Sammy! How many of you also used the doubling strategy? Sara, do you have a strategy to share?

Sara: I broke 25 into 20 plus 5 and 26 into 20 plus 6. Then I added 20 plus 20 equals 40. Then I added 5 plus 6 equals 11. After that, I added 40 plus 11 equals 51.

Ms. Rites: Sara, you broke apart your numbers by place value. How many of you also used place value to add? We have time for one more person to share. Mansoor, it looks like you have a strategy.

Mansoor: I added 4 plus 26 to make 30. Then I added 25 plus 30 equals 55. Then, I subtracted 55 minus 4 equals 51.

Ms. Rites: How come you subtracted 4?

Mansoor: I had to subtract the 4 because I added it in the beginning. I had to make sure that I subtracted it in the end.

Kelsie is pleased with the number talk. She notices that many students are using the place value strategy. She is also excited about Mansoor's solution. She had hoped that a student might introduce the idea of flexibly changing the number to make it easier to add or subtract. Even though the numbers in this problem did not necessarily need to be changed, this has been a great opportunity for students to think about this strategy and hear Mansoor's thinking.

> **What do you notice about the number routine lesson launches? How might these kinds of number routine lesson launches be integrated into your lesson planning? Note your responses below.**

_____

_____

_____

_____

_____

_____

_____

_____

_____

Standards

LI and SC

Purpose

Tasks

Materials

Student Thinking

Lesson Structures

Form. Assess.

Lesson Launch

Lesson Facilitation

Closure

As you plan your lesson launch, it is critical to anticipate how your students will respond to the launch you have designed. Consider the information in Chapter 1, Surveying Your Site: Knowing Your Students. As you plan instructional activities for your class, anticipate how particular students will react to particular activities. This can help you respond in a way that moves your students' learning forward. If you anticipate and include some typical student responses in your lesson plan, you can also plan for your next instructional move.

> **How do you anticipate your students' responses to your instructional activities? Note your response below.**
>
> _____
>
> _____
>
> _____
>
> _____
>
> _____
>
> _____
>
> _____
>
> _____
>
> _____
>
> _____
>
> _____

### Building Unit Coherence

While your lesson launches should be connected to the content you are teaching, you can support unit coherence by varying your lesson launches to reflect different Standards for Mathematical Practice and mathematical habits of mind. You can also use the lesson launch to anchor the current lesson within the unit. You can connect the lesson you are currently teaching to prior learning and forecast what you will be teaching next. Students can then eagerly engage in the launch knowing fully the place this lesson has within the unit.

The launch is also a great point to showcase rigorous tasks. The way you choose to launch the lesson should invite students with varying abilities to enter into the task with confidence.

Example: Brittany

First-grade teacher Brittany regularly chooses the See, Think, and Wonder and Notice and Wonder lesson launches because they invite her English Language Learners to talk and share ideas with partners. She ensures that they have multiple opportunities to talk with their partners. She believes that this supports them in making connections from one lesson to another.

## Kindergarten Snapshot

### Launch the Lesson

Kindergarten teachers Eliza, Marilyn, and Rena implement regular number talks with their students. The teachers have been focusing students on **subitizing**, which is the instant recognition of a number, and they now decide that they want to have their students subitize values of ten dots in a ten frame by showing the students sets of ten frames. They believe this will be a good way for students to connect the big idea of the lesson to the lesson launch.

### Launch:

*Number Talk:*

First, "flash" the ten-frame cards to the students in a series. Ask the students to show how many dots they see using their fingers or numeral cards. Then post all the ten-frame cards on the board. Pose these questions:

- What do you see?
- What do you notice about the ten-frame cards?

*Anticipate:*

Some students will still need extra time to mentally count the dots on the cards.

Some students will instantly see how many dots are on the cards.

Some students may need to see how the dots can fill in the spaces.

Questions to help the students make the connection:

- Do you notice anything about the arrangement of the dots that will help you find out how many dots are on the ten-frame card?
- Is there a way you can figure out how many dots are there without counting all the dots?

**See the complete lesson plan in Appendix A on page 178.**

How can you select and use number talks to launch your lessons and help students connect their strategies to important math concepts? Record your thoughts below.

_____

_____

_____

_____

_____

_____

_____

Sarita, Jen, and Karlo decide to design a launch that will set up the problem-solving task for the first-grade students. They want to develop a purpose for grouping objects into sets of ten. They really want to use Notice and Wonder after seeing it at a conference presentation and are excited to try it out!

## Launch:

(This is the *before* part of the four-part lesson format.)

Pose the first part of the problem and tell the story to the students.

Aunt Jasmine has a new cupcake business. Uncle Ronnie is helping Aunt Jasmine keep track of how many she sells. He wants to know how many cupcakes she sold last week, but she doesn't know! She is so busy making cupcakes that she cannot keep track of her orders!

Record students' notices and wonders on a chart for all the students to see. Then, introduce the second part of the problem and ask students if they have more notices and wonders they would like to add to the chart.

Aunt Jasmine needs your help sorting the cupcake orders. Uncle Ronnie needs to know how many groups of ten are in each order and how many leftovers are in each order. Can you help find the number of groups of tens and ones? You must be able to show and explain all of your thinking. The orders they received today are 47, 56, 39, 87, and 62.

| Aunt Jasmine's Cupcakes Order Form | Aunt Jasmine's Cupcakes Order Form | Aunt Jasmine's Cupcakes Order Form | Aunt Jasmine's Cupcakes Order Form | Aunt Jasmine's Cupcakes Order Form |
|---|---|---|---|---|
| 47 | 56 | 39 | 87 | 62 |

*Anticipate student responses for Part I Notice:*

Lots of cupcakes

They don't know how many they sold

Very busy business

*Anticipate student responses for Part I Wonder:*

How many cupcakes?

What are the kinds of cupcakes?

How many cupcakes are in an order?

*Anticipate student responses for Part 2 Notice:*

*Cupcakes will need to be in groups of ten*

*Leftover cupcakes*

*Find the groups of tens and ones*

*Students explain their thinking*

*Anticipate student responses for Part 2 Wonder:*

*How big will the order be?*

*What does left over mean?*

*How will we organize the cupcakes?*

**See the complete lesson plan in Appendix A on page 183.**

**How might you use the SEE, THINK, and WONDER technique to launch a lesson? Write your thoughts below.**

_____

_____

_____

_____

_____

_____

_____

_____

_____

_____

_____

_____

_____

_____

_____

_____

_____

_____

_____

Standards

LI and SC

Purpose

Tasks

Materials

Student Thinking

Lesson Structures

Form. Assess.

Lesson Launch

Lesson Facilitation

Closure

Aliyah, Dwayne, and Wilma are working on developing reasoning about place value with their students. They are wondering how students might reason through a problem when the actual values are not given upfront. They decide that they will launch the lesson with a numberless word problem to invite the students to think about place value when the numbers are missing. After allowing the students time to discuss the word problem, they will reveal the actual values and then ask the students to solve it. They also decide to use the SEE, THINK, and WONDER technique to encourage the students to think about their own ideas before sharing.

## Launch:

This is the *before* part of the four-part lesson.

Present the following numberless word problem to the students:

Elaine, Roberto, and Janine all grabbed a bucket of base-ten blocks. Elaine's bucket has hundreds, tens, and ones. Roberto's bucket has ones, hundreds, and tens. Janine's bucket has ones and tens. Elaine, Roberto, and Janine each think they have the greatest value. Help them figure out who has the greatest value. Represent and explain your thinking to prove who is right!

Ask the students to talk with a partner about what is happening in the word problem. Next ask the students to share their ideas.

Anticipate student responses:

- Notice that Janine's bucket has only ones and tens

- Notice that Roberto's bucket information is presented in a different order

- Want to know the exact numbers

- Assume that Elaine's bucket has more

- Need manipulatives to determine the actual value

*See the complete lesson plan in Appendix A on page 188.*

How can you use the numberless word problem technique as a lesson launch?

_____

_____

_____

_____

_____

_____

Now it is your turn! Develop a lesson launch and anticipate how your students will respond.

**Launch:**

Download the full Lesson-Planning Template from resources.corwin.com/mathlessonplanning/k-2
Remember that you can use the online version of the lesson plan template to begin compiling each section into the full template as your lesson plan grows.

Standards

LI and SC

Purpose

Tasks

Materials

Student Thinking

Lesson Structures

Form. Assess.

Lesson Launch

Lesson Facilitation

Closure

# PLANNING TO FACILITATE THE LESSON

Janey, a kindergarten teacher, had always imagined herself as an educator. As a child, she collected worksheets from her teachers and stored them in her basement, which she set up as a school. She cajoled neighborhood friends into playing school with her for hours on end.

By the time that Janey actually started teaching, she knew that the approach to education had shifted from her own days as a student. She recognized the need to encourage her students to construct meaning through carefully planned activities and to allow her students to talk to each other, explain their thinking, and even productively struggle, but she still felt conflicted with how to best support her students' communication skills. She hated to watch them struggle, even a little bit. She frequently found herself falling right into the trap of saving a student way too early instead of asking a question or providing a suggestion. Just the other day, one of her students, Jeremy, had asked for help, and she had picked up a pencil and started showing him what to do. She hadn't even realized it until she glanced at him and caught him grinning from ear to ear!

Janey shared her concerns with her coteacher, David, and they decided that they would help each other by specifically planning how they would facilitate lessons so there would be more chances for students to explain and justify their thinking, more questioning from both students and teachers, and more opportunities for students to productively struggle.

As they began their planning, their math coach suggested that Janey and David think about a lesson that had gone well because students were actively engaged in mathematical discourse as inspiration for their planning. Both Janey and David agreed that a good example was the lesson in which the students measured the principal, Mrs. Palmer.

The lesson had developed after the students read *The Principal's New Clothes* (Calmenson, 1991), which had inspired the children to try to make new clothes for their own very fashionable principal. For this lesson, the students traced their principal on paper, measured, and designed clothes for her paper cutout to wear. The project concluded with a fashion show of all the paper principal cutouts and clothing designs, complete with measurements. Both Janey and David had been amazed at how well the kindergartners had worked on the project, particularly as they had negotiated decisions about who would measure Mrs. Palmer. Janey and David had spent all of their time supporting the students and questioning them as they worked.

As the teachers discussed this lesson with their math coach, David asked, "So how can we capture that kind of energy and student-centered learning every day?"

**Witnessing those moments when students are engaged productively in mathematical thinking, reasoning, and communication is so exciting to see. Sometimes they just happen, but most likely they happen when all of your hard work in planning comes together. Planning to facilitate a lesson incorporates the selection of effective instructional activities and strategically planning how you will support and facilitate student learning during the instructional activities. Good tasks, problems, games, and activities are only just that—good—until you mindfully use care and purpose to design a teaching and learning environment that supports your students' learning through discourse and appropriate productive struggle. This chapter will discuss the following questions.**

- What is mathematical communication?
- How do you facilitate meaningful mathematical discourse?
- How do you plan for and pose purposeful questions?
- How do you facilitate productive struggle?

# WHAT IS MATHEMATICAL COMMUNICATION?

Communication is an essential part of mathematics and mathematical education. *Principles to Actions: Ensuring Success for All* (NCTM, 2014b) notes that "effective teaching of mathematics facilitates discourse among students to build shared understanding of mathematical ideas by analyzing and comparing student approaches and arguments" (p. 29). Students need multiple opportunities to exchange ideas, explain and defend their reasoning, use mathematical vocabulary, and consider one another's ideas (NCTM, 1991, 2000, 2014b). There are several facets to good mathematical communication, including the following:

- *Precise use of vocabulary*. Teachers must use precise mathematical vocabulary consistently and facilitate students' use of mathematical language to promote mathematical understanding. This means that all students learn and use the correct mathematics vocabulary, even when first learning new mathematical concepts.

- Some teachers may want to focus on key words or simplify the language by using simple terms, but that can ultimately confuse students. For example, teaching students that they should always add when they see the words "*in all*" in a word problem will lead students to believe that this will always work, when in reality it will work only in particular situations and cannot be transferred to all word problems.

- *Verbal discussion or* **mathematical discourse**. Mathematical discourse occurs when students talk about the mathematics they are learning with each other and the teacher. During this discussion, they demonstrate their understanding and reveal their reasoning. Teachers should plan for and facilitate multiple opportunities for discourse throughout the lesson to provide students many different ways to engage in conversation about the mathematics they are learning. Often, the most powerful mathematical conversations occur between students as they reason with each other to make sense of their learning.

- *Writing*. Writing in the mathematics classroom allows students to record their thinking so they can remember how they thought through a problem or how they solved it. Writing helps students focus on and build precise mathematical language, whereas words "disappear" once spoken. For students who feel shy when talking aloud, writing gives them the opportunity to explain their thinking.

- If some of your students have difficulty with writing, give them sentence starters such as, "I think the answer is ____ because____" or allow them to use pictures and diagrams in their written explanations. These approaches will help them fully participate. In addition, you can show students examples of writing to help them improve their discourse skills. To do this, you can use student work on chart paper or under a document camera to show examples of what you mean by phrases like "Use pictures to explain your solution."

> **What are some strategies you use to facilitate discourse? List a few below.**
>
> _____
>
> _____
>
> _____
>
> _____
>
> _____

# HOW DO YOU FACILITATE MEANINGFUL MATHEMATICAL DISCOURSE?

Providing for and teaching mathematical communication requires explicit attention to planning lessons (Walshaw & Anthony, 2008). Building a classroom community that supports discourse requires some shifts in the traditional student and teacher roles. In particular, the students assume greater responsibility for their learning, and the teacher no longer serves as the primary source of mathematical authority. Instead, the teacher consistently encourages student engagement and strategically uses questioning to position students as mathematical leaders in the classroom. *Principles to Action* (NCTM, 2014b) notes the critical roles by considering what teachers and students are *doing* in classrooms where rich mathematical discourse is occurring. For example, teachers are designing learning activities that prompt students to use multiple representations, describe their solutions, and explain their reasoning. Teachers also strategically facilitate conversations among students about the mathematics they are learning. When teachers are promoting mathematical discourse, a peek inside these classrooms shows students presenting their ideas to other students while other students are listening and asking questions.

You can promote effective discourse by monitoring and responding to the students as they work. You can ask particular questions that will support students to explain their thinking and reasoning. Here are some sample questions you may wish to ask.

- Was this the first strategy you tried? Why did you give up on the first strategy?

- How did you decide what to do?

- Did you try something that did not work? How did you figure out it was not going to work?

- How does what you are doing make sense to you?

The questions help students reflect on their work but also give you more information to determine which of the student strategies you want to select for the class discussion. In this way, you can plan a purposeful discussion on the strategy(s) to focus on in the lesson. Once you make the decision about which student work you will present to the class (one, some, all), you also decide the order in which they will be presented. This purposeful planning of the discussion allows concepts to unfold in a coherent manner that you predetermine to match the learning intention (Smith & Stein, 2011). Once the students are presenting their work, you facilitate the discussion through questions that connect the strategies and concepts studied. Here are some additional sample questions.

- Is there anything in Graham's strategy that is like something we have done before?

- What mathematical words did he use that we have learned?

- Is there something in this solution that reminds you of anything we did yesterday in class?

- How is Graham's solution like or different from Gail's solution?

You should also encourage the students to ask questions of one another, thus promoting student-to-student interaction and engagement in constructing viable arguments and critiquing the reasoning of others (National Governors Association and Council of Chief State School Officers, 2010). You can encourage classroom discourse by establishing an environment and expectation for students to engage in some type of discourse every day (Rasmussen, Yackel, & King, 2003; Wood, Williams, & McNeal, 2006; Yackel & Cobb, 1996).

Many teachers of young students find it helpful to **unpack** what it means to be in a mathematics **learning community.** You can do this by holding classroom discussions about what math talk looks like in your classroom. You may also find it helpful to explicitly teach students how to share their ideas, actively listen, and give appropriate responses to peers (Wagganer, 2015).

Here are some additional suggestions.

- Encourage student-to-student discourse by asking students to address each other's questions: "Antonio, can you answer Jamal's question?" Or "Jamal, did you understand Antonio's solution? You can ask him a question to help him explain what he meant."

- Use a Think Aloud technique to model your own thinking and reasoning through a problem that focuses on mathematical thinking that you want your students to develop (Trocki, Taylor, Starling, Sztajn, & Heck, 2015).

- Model how to ask questions and instruct students to ask questions of each other. You can show students that it is okay to be confused and to ask for an explanation. Model a question you would like to students to ask: "Class, I am confused about this problem. Can someone help me?" Or "Jamal, why don't you ask Antonio a question about his solution."

- Ask follow-up questions when students respond with a right or wrong answer that will lead them back to the conceptual understanding. For example, you might ask, "Can you start at the beginning and explain your thinking?"

- Use sentence stems (Wagganer, 2015) to jumpstart student thinking and student-to-student discourse. This is helpful for all students, but especially for English language learners. Here are some sentence stems you might try with your students.

    I agree with _____because …

    This is what I think …

    I have a different perspective because …

    I made a connection with what _____ said because …

    When I thought about that question, I remembered …

    I chose this method because …

- Use language frames to scaffold math talk (Hattie et al., 2016) and enhance student conversations while collaborating. Some language frames for mathematics include the following:

> Another way to solve this would be …
>
> In order to solve this problem, I need to know …
>
> We think this answer is reasonable because …
>
> If I change _____, my answer would be different because …
>
> I can check my answer by …

Like most communication, mathematics discourse is messy. Young students, in particular, may struggle to find the right words to explain their thinking and reasoning. Your patience and willingness to let students participate in lots of discourse is key to building a rich discourse community.

> **Which discourse strategies resonate most with you? Why? Note your ideas below.**
> _____
> _____
> _____

## HOW DO YOU PLAN FOR AND POSE PURPOSEFUL QUESTIONS?

Questioning is at the center of effective mathematical discourse. The National Council of Teachers of Mathematics' (2014b) *Principles to Actions: Ensuring Mathematical Success for All* states, "Effective teaching of mathematics uses purposeful questions to assess and advance students' reasoning and sense making about important mathematical ideas and relationships" (p. 35). When you plan questions to ask during a lesson, you also increase access and engagement for all students because you are mindful about whom you will be calling on.

The roles of both the teacher and the students are important as teachers pose purposeful questions that advance students' mathematical understanding (NCTM, 2014b). As a teacher, you must be intentional in your planning, consider what you are doing as you ask questions, and consider what your students are doing in response to your questions. Plan and ask higher-level questions that prompt your students to provide explanations, justifications, and reasoning about the mathematics they are learning. Also be sure to provide plenty of wait time for students to ponder, reflect, and make sense of the question. When you take these actions, your students provide deeper responses and justify their thinking with evidence. They also ask you questions to clarify and build new understanding (NCTM, 2014b).

The questions a teacher asks are the key to orchestrating positive and productive classroom discourse. As you formulate questions to challenge students to think deeply, draw conclusions, and extend the student inquiry in the lesson (Van de Walle et al., 2016), consider the purpose and type of question. The *Principles to Actions: Ensuring Mathematical Success for All* (NCTM, 2014b) organized question types into four distinct categories: gathering information, probing thinking, making the mathematics visible, and encouraging reflection and justification. NCTM's 2017 publication, *Taking Action: Implementing Effective Teaching Practices*, introduced a fifth category: engaging with the reasoning of others. The question types can also be connected to the Standards for Mathematical Practice (National Governors Association and Council of Chief State School Officers, 2010). Let's briefly look at each type of question in more detail.

### Gathering Information

Teachers ask these types of questions to elicit procedural information by asking "What is" and "how to" questions. Some examples appear in Figure 12.1. When students answer probing questions, they provide factual information or steps. You can also use this type of question to elicit students' precise use of mathematics vocabulary. Typically, these kinds of questions elicit right or wrong answers.

Standards

LI and SC

Purpose

Tasks

Materials

Student Thinking

Lesson Structures

Form. Assess.

Lesson Launch

Lesson Facilitation

Closure

**Figure 12.1**

| Teachers | Students |
|---|---|
| What is the sum of 5 + 9 = ____? | 14 |
| What is the value of the number in the tens place? 54 | The value of the number in the tens place is 50. |
| How did you count? <br><br> ● ● ● ● ● ● | I pointed at each one and counted. |

## Probing Thinking

Teachers ask these kinds of questions to encourage students to explain their thinking and demonstrate their reasoning. Figure 12.2 gives some examples.

**Figure 12.2**

| Teachers | Students |
|---|---|
| Why did you decide to add all the tens together first in this equation? <br><br> 23 + 41 + 27 = | I wanted to see how big my number would be so I added the tens first. |
| Can you tell me about how you solved this problem? <br><br> Some children were in the backyard playing. 4 children are on the slide and 2 children are on the swings. How many children are in the backyard? | When I saw that the problem started with *some children were in the backyard,* I knew that I didn't know how many I started with, so I made this number sentence [points to ____ = ___ + ___]. Then I saw that four kids were on the slide and two were on the swings, so I knew that I should put the 4 and 2 on the parts. Then I knew that 6 was the whole. |
| How did drawing a picture help you solve this problem? <br><br> 6 envelopes are in the mailbox. 4 are white and the rest are blue. How many are blue? | I need to draw pictures to keep track of what I am subtracting. So I drew six squares and then crossed out four. Two are leftover. |

## Making the Mathematics Visible

Teachers ask these kinds of questions to help the students build connections between mathematical ideas, see patterns, and understand the underlying structure of mathematical ideas. Figure 12.3 gives some examples.

Standards

**Figure 12.3**

| Teachers | Students |
|---|---|
| What patterns do you notice in the following?<br><br>5 + 5, 4 + 4, 8 + 8, 7 + 7 | All of those have the same number to add, so it is a double! |
| How are these two problems alike? Different?<br><br>10 − 6 = 4 and 10 = 6 + 4 | They are using the same numbers, but one is addition and one is subtraction. They are a fact family. They are related. |

## Encouraging Reflection and Justification

Teachers ask these kinds of questions when they want to encourage students to develop mathematical arguments and justify their solutions with thorough explanations. Figure 12.4 includes some examples.

**Figure 12.4**

| Teachers | Students |
|---|---|
| How do you know that 23 is closer to 0 on the number line?<br><br>0—23——————100 | I put 23 on the number line in that spot because 23 has two tens and 100 has ten tens. I also thought about where five tens or fifty would go. |
| How many ways can you make 10? How do you know when you find all the ways? | I know I found all the ways to make 10 when I make the combinations in a pattern.<br><br>I start with 10 + 0, 9 + 1, 8 + 2, and keep going. The pattern helps me find all the ways. See? One of the numbers goes up and the other goes down, and they all equal 10! |
| Why did you use that representation to explain your solution? | I drew base-ten blocks because I wanted to show that I counted by tens to add 12 + 52. |

Standards | LI and SC | Purpose | Tasks | Materials | Student Thinking | Lesson Structures | Form. Assess. | Lesson Launch | Lesson Facilitation | Closure

Teachers ask these kinds of questions when they want to encourage students to explain their own thinking, construct a viable argument, and listen to the reasoning of their peers. They also ask these types of questions to encourage students to ask questions to each other. Figure 12.5 shows some examples.

**Figure 12.5**

| Teachers | Students |
|---|---|
| I am noticing that you and Maria solved the problem in different ways. Explain Maria's solution, and tell why you think Maria solved it that way.<br><br>51 – 34 = | Maria solved the problem by adding 6 to each number to make the equation 57 – 40 = ____. I think she did this because she can then subtract it easily. |
| Do you agree or disagree with Maria's idea? Why or why not? | I agree with Maria because it is still the same amount between the two numbers. I can show you on a number line. See how there is the same amount in between the numbers?<br><br>40 41 42 43 44 45 46 47 48 49 50 51 52 53 54 55 56 57<br><br>34 35 36 327 38 39 40 41 42 43 44 45 46 47 38 49 50 51 |

Without strategic planning, teachers tend to ask the most questions at the lowest cognitive level (fact, recall, or knowledge) and wait less than one second before calling on a student after asking a question (Walsh & Sattes, 2005). Instead, you should strive to ask higher-level questions that require students to explain and elaborate on their ideas, make the mathematics visible, and encourage justification. For example, think about the questions that Anna Melbourne, a first-grade teacher, asks in the following scenario.

Mrs. Melbourne: What is the shape of the door?

Margot: It is a rectangle.

Mrs. Melbourne: Margot, how do you know it is a rectangle?

Margot: It has four sides.

Emilee: I think it is a square!

Mrs. Melbourne: Hmmmm…. What an interesting idea! Now we have two ideas about the shape of the door. Can anyone else tell us how we know the door is a rectangle or a square? Let's turn and talk to our partners about the shape of the door. In a few minutes I am going to ask you to be ready to add to the ideas you heard and tell whether you agree or disagree and why.

The first question, "What shape is the door?" is at the gathering information level. But the teacher continues to raise the level of the students' thinking by encouraging a conversation about how they know the door is a rectangle; this occurs when she asks Margot follow-up questions and then engages the whole class in the discussion.

Have you ever asked a question, called on a student who gave the correct answer, and watched all hands disappear quickly? Good questions prompt students to provide more than answers. Note how Anna was able to move the discussion forward instead of closing it down. When you pose purposeful questions, you promote student understanding because you are asking students to make connections by building upon what they know.

Teachers tend to use two kinds of main questioning techniques: funneling (Herbel-Eisenmann & Breyfogle, 2005) and focusing (Herbel-Eisenmann, 2010; NCTM, 2014b).

- *Funneling questions* lead students in a particular direction to provide evidence of student learning; for this reason, they can squash students' thinking because the teacher is asking questions with a particular answer in mind. These kinds of questions often offer only a superficial assessment of what students know.

- *Focusing questions*, on the other hand, encourage students to think on their own and provide explanations and justifications. While the teacher has an endpoint in mind, the students' reasoning is most important.

Consider the questions in Figure 12.6 and note how a funneling question can be opened up to become a focusing question. Anticipate the different kinds of responses each type of question will elicit.

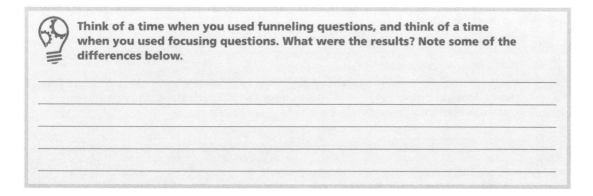

**Figure 12.6**

| Funneling | Focusing |
|---|---|
| What is the value of the 2 in 726? | Describe all of the values in 726. |
| Is 23 even or odd? | Convince me why a number is even or odd. |

As you plan to facilitate your lesson, it is important to consider how you will plan for and implement purposeful and rich questions that support rich student thinking.

> **Think of a time when you used funneling questions, and think of a time when you used focusing questions. What were the results? Note some of the differences below.**
>
> _____
>
> _____
>
> _____
>
> _____
>
> _____

## HOW DO YOU FACILITATE PRODUCTIVE STRUGGLE?

By consistently providing students with high-quality, engaging mathematics instruction, you will also invite them to productively struggle because they will be actively involved in making sense of the mathematics they are learning (NCTM, 2014b). Your students will be better able to apply their learning to new situations if you routinely ensure that they participate in mathematics learning that stretches their thinking and promotes opportunities to make and analyze their mistakes (Boaler, 2015) and that prompts them to engage in higher-level thinking (Kapur, 2010).

Standards

LI and SC

Purpose

Tasks

Materials

Student Thinking

Lesson Structures

Form. Assess.

Lesson Launch

Lesson Facilitation

Closure

As you construct lessons to engage students in productive struggle, you must keep the needs of your own learners in mind. While it is tempting to rescue students by giving them answers or by overscaffolding lessons, this does not, in the long run, support their learning. On the other hand, you also do not want to send your students into an unproductive spiral of struggle. Simply telling students to try harder does not promote productive struggle when students feel that they are, in fact, trying very hard.

Creating this "sweet spot" of productive struggle for your students can be challenging, which is why it is critical to consider how you will create an environment that promotes productive struggle during the planning process. You can do this by following these steps:

1. Be explicit about what struggle looks like and feels like so students understand that it will help them.

2. Discuss perseverance with students, and actively recognize when students demonstrate it.

3. Provide plenty of time for students to struggle with tasks and move through the struggle so they know what it feels like on the other side of the struggle.

4. Plan for how you will respond when students are struggling by asking scaffolding questions.

5. Celebrate and use confusion and mistakes (yours and theirs) as an opportunity for furthering and deepening understanding.

6. Create opportunities for students to ask questions, help each other, and share how they moved through a struggle.

7. Reflect on how you respond to student confusion and struggle and plan strategic moves.

---

Example: Fatima

Fatima, a first-grade teacher, doesn't like to watch her students struggle, even a tiny bit, but she knows that she needs to make this a class focus for the year. She recently watched Jo Boaler's (2017) video, *Brains Grow and Change,* and she wants to be able to translate that information to her first graders. She knows that many of them worry about getting all the answers correct.

She decides to begin the school year by making each student a small, laminated nametag in the shape of the brain. She tells them that "mistakes grow your brain" and that she wants to be able to know when their brains are growing. She encourages the students to make a tally mark on the laminated nametags every time they make a mistake.

At the end of the week, they count up the totals from the whole class and celebrate their growing brains. Then she has students share their "Favorite Mistake" of the week. She also keeps track of the weekly tallies during the year.

Fatima is surprised by the positive impact of this effort on her classroom environment as students become relaxed and thoughtful about their mistakes. One of the students, Joey, tells her, "At first I thought my mistakes were bad and I should hide them away. But then I found out that my mistakes tell me I am learning. They aren't bad at all."

---

**How might you integrate conversations about productive struggle in your own classroom? Write a few notes here.**

_____

_____

_____

_____

_____

_____

_____

_____

## HOW DO YOU MAKE SURE YOU ENGAGE STUDENTS IN THE PROCESS STANDARDS AS YOU FACILITATE THE LESSON?

The examples throughout this chapter show many ways that you can engage students in communicating mathematically, developing problem-solving behaviors, demonstrating reasoning, making connections between and among mathematical ideas, and using representations to explain and justify thinking. You can ensure that you are encouraging students to demonstrate the process standards by planning for one or two process standards for each lesson. As you plan to facilitate your lesson, consider the questions you will ask and the task you design or select that will elicit particular student mathematical behaviors. For example, Jenna wants her second graders to notice and use mathematical structures and designs a word problem sorting task. She gives students eight word problems and tells them they must not solve the problems. She explains that she wants them to read the word problems and then group word problems that are alike together and explain how they are alike. Jenna's students quickly notice that particular word problems represent addition while others might be solved using addition or subtraction.

> How can you make sure to incorporate questioning that will support students in engaging in the process standards?
>
> _____
>
> _____
>
> _____
>
> _____

### Building Unit Coherence

Similar to the launch, the lesson facilitation shapes coherence because you are constantly connecting prior learning to new learning. You ask questions and invite robust discourse that stimulates mathematical learning. You can do this by asking students to record their ideas and explain their thinking to peers. You can post their ideas and refer to them throughout the unit. Each new lesson offers opportunities for you to call upon students' ideas and work samples to support new mathematical concepts. With this combination of teaching moves, you create coherence because students begin to connect and link their ideas from one day to the next. Every day, you may also wish to ask the students, "Why are we learning this?" This question can help them understand that the mathematics they are learning is connected to their lives and to the new mathematics they will learn.

Notes

_____

_____

_____

_____

_____

Standards

LI and SC

Purpose

Tasks

Materials

Student Thinking

Lesson Structures

Form. Assess.

Lesson Launch

Lesson Facilitation

Closure

Kindergarten teachers Eliza, Marilyn, and Rena gather together to plan their lesson facilitation. They really want to focus on providing many experiences for students to talk with each other in partners and share their work publicly during a gallery walk. They want to ensure that the children have many opportunities to explain their thinking using mathematical vocabulary and listen to each other's ideas. They decide to conduct a whole-group lesson so they can monitor the students and highlight their kindergartners' reasoning. Then they will pair the students for center work to encourage collaboration and discussion.

## Facilitate:

Include plans for mathematical discourse and questions.

Present students with *How Many Insects?* problem and visual.

1. Conduct a Notice and Wonder (see lesson launch chapter) with the students, and record their notices and wonders.

2. Connect the notices and wonders and ask, "How can we find out how many insects are on the leaves?"

3. Ask the students to write an estimate on a sticky note and post the estimates in order from least to greatest.

4. Elicit from the students that they can count the insects on the leaves.

5. Ask the students,
   - What tools might be helpful to keep track of your counting?
   - How can we find out if there is a group of ten insects on the leaves?

6. Explain that this lesson will include the following success criteria:
   - Count a group of objects and record or write the number I counted.
   - Stick with a problem even when I am not sure at first how to solve it.
   - Listen to my classmates' explanations about counting and ask questions that show I understand counting.

7. Arrange the students in pairs to use counters, ten-frames cards, and the recording sheet to decompose the number of insects on the leaves (give pairs different amounts). Monitor the students as they work, and ask questions like, "How did you figure out how many tens? How many leftovers? How did you organize your counting? Did you and your partner count the same way? How did you keep track of the insects you counted on the leaf?"

8. Encourage the students to explain their thinking by asking questions.

9. Have the students record the number of ten ones and some more ones on the recording sheet and explain how they figured it out.

10. Have student pairs post their work and conduct a gallery walk. Give students a sticky dot and ask them to post a sticky dot on students' work that is interesting.

11. Select three student pairs to share how they counted, decomposed, and used the blank ten-frame card to find out how many insects were on the leaf. Have student pairs share based on clarity of examples. As the pairs share, encourage them to comment on each other's ideas. Ask, "How was your strategy alike or different than _____?"

**12.** Ask, "What do you notice about all the leaves?" Elicit from the students that every leaf has ten ones and some more ones.

**13.** Use students' work to highlight the pattern. For example, begin with ten. Each time, highlight student work to reveal the pattern. Ask students to Turn and Talk about the patterns they are noticing.

10 = 1 group of ten insects and 0 more
11 = 1 group of ten insects and 1 more
12 = 1 group of ten insects and 2 more
13 = 1 group of ten insects and 3 more
14 = 1 group of ten insects and 4 more
15 = 1 group of ten insects and 5 more
16 = 1 group of ten insects and 6 more
17 = 1 group of ten insects and 7 more
18 = 1 group of ten insects and 8 more
19 = 1 group of ten insects and 9 more

**14.** Ask the students, "What do you notice about the teen numbers? How many groups of ten are in all the teen numbers? What do you notice about the *some more* part?"

**15.** Close by asking the students to Turn and Talk about the patterns in the teen numbers. "What do you notice about all the numbers that had a ten and some more ones?"

**16.** Connect back to the sticky-note estimates. Ask the students to Turn and Talk. "What do you notice about your estimates and the actual number of insects?"

*Anticipating student responses:*

Some students will need organizational help. Encourage them to use a ten-frame organizer and other tools to help them keep track.

Some students will want to work independently rather than collaboratively. Give pairs one sheet of large chart paper to encourage them to work together. Call attention to pairs and groups that work together and remind them what working together means. Connect their struggle to the success criteria.

Pairs and groups will work at different rates. Organize the pairs and small groups to reflect differing learning needs to support each other's learning.

*Monitoring the students' productive struggle:*

Scaffold as needed by identifying mini-goals for some students. For example, ask students to find one leaf first and then check in with the teacher. Reward the students' "stick with it" behavior by calling attention to their perseverance.

*See the complete lesson plan in Appendix A on page 178.*

 **What do you notice about the opportunities for student discourse? Record your response below.**

_____

_____

_____

_____

Standards
LI and SC
Purpose
Tasks
Materials
Student Thinking
Lesson Structures
Form. Assess.
Lesson Launch
Lesson Facilitation
Closure

First-grade teachers Sarita, Jen, and Karlo have just planned the lesson facilitation for their problem-solving task. They want to make sure that the students have plenty of manipulatives and recording space for their work. They also plan to group the students in pairs to encourage collaboration. They will make sure to pair students with varying learning needs.

## Facilitate:

*During*

1. Connect the students' notices and wonders to the task by explaining to the students that they are going to have a chance to help Uncle Ronnie find out the number of groups of tens and ones.

2. Explain that this lesson will include the following success criteria:

   - Group objects by their place value and record.

   - Show a two-digit number using base-ten blocks or by drawing.

   - See a number and represent that number using place value.

   - Stick with a problem even when I am not sure at first how to solve it.

   - Listen to my classmates' explanations about counting groups, and ask questions that show I understand how they counted.

3. Arrange the students in pairs or groups of three. Say to the students, "You will receive a cupcake order form with the number of cupcakes, chart paper to record all of your thinking, counters, and blank ten frames. Your task is to find out how many groups of tens and ones are in the cupcake order."

4. As the pairs and groups work together, monitor their work by asking questions such as these:

   - How can you represent the tens and ones on the chart paper?

   - How will you show your thinking?

   - How will you keep track of your work?

   - How will you get started?

   - What ideas did your partner have?

   - How can you use the ten frame as a tool to show your thinking?

   - How are you working with your partner?

   - What are you noticing?

5. Conduct a group gallery walk: Have the students hang their posters around the room. Have the students do a gallery walk to view everyone else's work. Give the students a sticky note or a sticker and ask them to post a sticker or a comment on another group's work they have a question about or on one that is different from their own.

*After*

6. Conduct a group Notice: As students finish looking at others' work, bring them back together as a group. Ask them to Turn and Talk with their partners to discuss what they noticed or had a question about.

7. Highlight strategies the students used by selecting three posters for students to share. Look for evidence of use of ten frames to find groups of ten, accuracy, and explanation.

8. Record the students' work from each poster on a chart like the following, moving in order from least to greatest:

| Cupcake Order | Groups of Ten | Ones |
|---|---|---|
| 27 | 2 | 7 |
| 35 | 3 | 5 |

9. Have the students Turn and Talk to a partner and ask, "What do you notice?" Elicit from the students that there is a pattern. The number of the groups of ten is the same as the digit in the tens place.

*Anticipating student responses:*

Some students will need organizational help. Encourage them to count out the total using counters and then organize the total on the ten frames. Have plenty of extra ten frames if students want to draw a dot on the ten frame and then glue the ten frame to the poster.

Some first graders will want to work independently rather than collaboratively. Give them one sheet of large chart paper to encourage them to work together. Call attention to pairs and groups that work together and remind the first graders what working together means.

Pairs and groups will work at different rates. Differentiate the numbers of the order forms for groups that might need more time. Have extra order forms for groups that would like to work on another order form.

*Monitoring students' productive struggle:*

Monitor the students carefully, encourage students to solve their own problems, and collaborate with each other. Scaffold the questions if students need more time to work on the problem.

*See the complete lesson plan in Appendix A on page 183.*

**What do you notice about how the lesson moves the students back and forth between whole-group and paired discussion? Record your response below.**

_____

_____

_____

_____

_____

Second-grade teachers Wilma, Dwayne, and Aliyah anticipate that the students might want to work independently rather than collaboratively. They plan to monitor the students closely to encourage discussion and collaboration. They decide that the students will construct their mathematical argument as a pair to present their idea to another pair in a small group. They are hoping that this will encourage rich discussion among the students.

---

## Facilitate:

*During*

1. After ideas have been shared from the launch, transition to the task to reveal the actual problem.

2. Elaine, Roberto, and Janine all grabbed a bucket of base-ten blocks. Elaine's bucket has 2 hundreds, 9 tens, and 2 ones. Roberto's bucket has 8 ones, 6 hundreds, and 5 tens. Janine's bucket has 50 ones and 20 tens. Elaine, Roberto, and Janine each think they have the greatest value. Help them figure out who has the greatest value. Represent and explain your thinking to prove who is right!

3. Ask the students to discuss with a partner what they are noticing. Elicit ideas from the students, but make sure that they do not give any answers away!

4. Arrange the students in pairs or groups of three. Say to the students, "You will solve this problem with your partner or group of three. Each group will receive a piece of chart paper to show all of your work. You may also use, but are not required to use, base-ten blocks, hundreds charts, and blank ten frames. Your task is to determine and prove who has the greatest value. You must show all of your thinking on the chart paper. Here is your success criteria for this lesson:

   • Explain and construct the place value and value of numbers when presented in varying orders, such as 3 tens, 4 hundreds, and 5 ones.

   • Show the place value of three-digit numbers using base-ten blocks or pictures when presented with the number.

   • Stick with a problem even when I am not sure at first how to solve it.

   • Listen to my classmates' explanations about place value and ask questions that show I understand place value.

5. As the pairs and groups work together, monitor their work by asking questions such as these:

   • How can you represent the hundreds, tens, and ones on the chart paper?

   • How will you show your thinking?

   • How will you keep track of your work?

   • How will you get started?

   • What ideas did your partner have?

   • How can you use the manipulatives and tools to show your thinking?

   • How are you working with your partner?

   • What are you noticing?

*After*

6.  Conduct a group gallery walk: Have the students hang their posters around the room. Have the students do a gallery walk to view everyone else's work. Give the students a sticky note or a sticker and ask them to post a sticker or a comment on another group's work they have a question about or on one that is different from their own.

7.  Conduct a group Notice: As students finish looking at others' work, bring them back together as a group. Ask them to Turn and Talk with their partners to discuss what they noticed or had a question about.

8.  Highlight strategies the students used by selecting three posters for students to share. Look for evidence of use of place value to prove the values. Note if students were able to notice the values even when the order was different. Select groups based on understanding of place value, accuracy, and explanation.

*Reflect*

Ask the students to work individually to determine which of these numbers has the greatest value:

9 ones, 5 hundreds, 7 tens OR 6 hundreds, 4 ones, 9 tens

*Anticipating student responses:*

Some students will need organizational help. Encourage them to use a place value organizer and other tools to help them keep track.

Some students will want to work independently rather than collaboratively. Give them one sheet of large chart paper to encourage them to work together. Call attention to pairs and groups that work together and remind them what working together means. Connect their struggle to the success criteria. Pairs and groups will work at different rates. Organize the pairs and small groups to reflect differing learning needs to support each other's learning.

*Monitoring students' productive struggle:*

Scaffold as needed by identifying mini-goals for some students.

**See the complete lesson plan in Appendix A on page 188.**

**How can you facilitate effective student collaboration? Record your response below.**

_____

_____

_____

_____

_____

_____

Now it is your turn! What will you do to facilitate your lesson?

**Facilitate:**

online resources

Download the full Lesson-Planning Template from resources.corwin.com/mathlessonplanning/k-2

Remember that you can use the online version of the lesson plan template to begin compiling each section into the full template as your lesson plan grows.

**160**   The Mathematics Lesson-Planning Handbook, Grades K–2

# CHAPTER 13

# PLANNING TO CLOSE THE LESSON

The second-grade team members at Hollins Elementary School were discussing some of their closure experiences.

"Closure?" questioned Abe, a third-year teacher. "I hardly ever get a chance for closure. My lessons always go to the last minute and sometimes even run over into recess."

"I have that problem sometimes," chimed in Jane, the veteran teacher in the group. "I am getting better, but last week my class had to remind me to stop because it was time for lunch! My goal for this year is to improve my closure. I'm working on it."

Cilia, a second-year teacher, spoke up. "I went to a workshop this summer and they talked about how important closure is to determine how students are grasping a lesson. I have been trying some of the suggestions. I like using exit slips, and my kids seem to like them. I let them write me notes at the end of the lesson to tell me if there was anything they didn't understand. I have been using those notes to help me launch my next lesson."

"Exit slips? And you have time to fit them in?" asked Abe.

Cilia replied, "Most days, but not every day."

Jane said, "It's funny that you mentioned a workshop. I went to a workshop about closure two years ago. We discussed how closure is about reflection. And we used exit slips too, but we learned that there are other things you can do, like pair sharing. Another option is to do a more in-depth exit task, like we learned in the formative assessment workshop."

"Stop keeping all these ideas a secret!" Abe said. Then he smiled and added, "You two need to do a closure workshop for me!"

> If you have ever looked at the clock and realized that you not only lack time for closure but also have run overtime, you are not alone. Abe, Jane, and Celia have been working on closure for a few years and continue to struggle to fit it all in. Planning for closure is the first step in using it your classroom. This chapter will discuss closure and several different closure formats while answering the following questions:
>
> - Why do you need closure in a lesson?
>
> - What are some different closure activities?
>
> - What is an extended closure?

## WHY DO YOU NEED CLOSURE IN A LESSON?

Closure is widely accepted as an important feature of lesson planning (Ganske, 2017), yet it is often neglected as a teaching practice because it gets sacrificed for critical instructional time. By making time for this essential lesson feature, you can help students solidify learning.

While the word *closure* indicates an ending, it is more like a pause in the learning so students can reflect on or demonstrate what they learned, and teachers can collect feedback to determine next steps for learning.

**Closure** has two purposes—one for the teacher and one for the students. For the teacher, closure helps determine what students have learned, and it gives direction as to where to go next: reteach, correct misconceptions, or move on. Through closure activities, you collect formative assessment information to inform instructional decision making and provide valuable feedback to students (Wiliam & Thompson, 2008). For the students, closure is a cognitive activity that helps them focus on what they learned and whether the learning made sense and had meaning (Sousa, 2014) by connecting to the learning intentions and success criteria (Hattie et al., 2016).

During closure, you help students circle back to clarify the learning intentions and success criteria to focus students on the intended learning for the lesson. Closure provides the opportunity to reorganize the information from a lesson in a meaningful way by asking them to summarize, review, and demonstrate understanding of the big ideas from the lesson. Students may reflect on what occurred in the lesson, make sense of it, and link ideas to prior knowledge. An effective closure increases retention and helps students internalize what they have learned (Pollock, 2007). Closure activities that require students to think, respond, write, and discuss concepts improve learning (Cavanaugh, Heward, & Donelson, 1996).

To ensure that closure is effective and benefits both you and your students, you need to devote enough time to it because it is a reflective process that every learner must experience to make sense of the lesson. It can seldom be done in one hurried minute before recess or lunch. You must also be mindful of the format you use, because many closure formats require students to work in pairs or small groups. In these situations, you need to be sure every student has a chance to make meaning from the lesson.

You must also attend to the students' responses. It is not enough to just collect their work as with an exit slip. When you collect any reflection/closure response in writing, use a two-pile protocol. You sort the students' responses into two piles. The first pile is for student responses that show an understanding of the lesson. Pile two is for student responses that indicate additional instruction is needed. You can then decide where you go next with your lesson, how you organize grouping, and other lesson options based on these piles. For example, if a pile indicates that more than half of the students need more help, then you may choose to reteach the entire lesson using a different representation. If a pile reveals that only a few students need more help, you can plan to use a lesson format to reach these individuals and correct their misconceptions or misunderstandings. Note that closure activities should not be graded.

## WHAT ARE SOME DIFFERENT CLOSURE ACTIVITIES?

There are too many different lesson closure activities to name all of them here. However, the chart in Figure 13.1 provides a sampling that you can use in K–2.

### Figure 13.1

| Name and Description | Sample Prompts |
| --- | --- |
| **Exit slips:** Students respond in writing to a prompt and hand in these responses. | Look at the clock and write down the time.<br><br>How many counters do I have on the screen? |

**Figure 13.1** *(Continued)*

| Name and Description | Sample Prompts |
|---|---|
| **Journal entries:** Students respond to a prompt using numbers, symbols, pictures, or words in their journals. This activity takes more time as the prompt requires a deeper explanation than one required on an exit slip. | What comes next in the pattern?  ● ▲ ● ▲ ● ▲ |
| **Selfie:** Students engage in self-reflection that allows them to assess their own learning. This can be as simple as a checklist for students to complete. | ☺ I totally understand.  😐 I kinda get it.  ☹ I am confused. |
| **3-2-1:** Students have the opportunity to express thoughts about specific learning from the lesson. | Write three things you learned today about the equal sign.  Write two different examples of when you use the equal sign.  Write one thing you want me to know about your learning and the equal sign. |
| **Text message:** This approach allows students to share what they learned with a specific audience. Use a template of a cellphone screen for students to write their message. | Provide the template with a prompt such as: create a text to your parents about what you learned in math today about tens and ones. |
| **Play teacher:** Students play the role of teacher by writing a math quiz. | Create a five-question quiz on the material from today's lesson. |
| **Draw a picture:** This is primarily for kindergarten students who do not have any writing skills but can express themselves with pictures. | Draw a picture of what you did in math class today. |
| **The 3 Whats:** On a prepared sheet, ask students to reflect on specific questions. Teachers can tailor the "whats." | *What?* (What did I learn today about graphing?)  *So what?* (Why is graphing important?)  *Now what?* (Where have you seen graphs outside of school?) |

*(Continued)*

Standards | LI and SC | Purpose | Tasks | Materials | Student Thinking | Lesson Structures | Form. Assess. | Lesson Launch | Lesson Facilitation | Closure

Figure 13.1 (*Continued*)

| Name and Description | Sample Prompts |
|---|---|
| **Pair/share:** Students each tell their partner the answer to a specific question about the lesson. Then each of the pairs shares with the class. The teacher can take notes for the two-pile protocol. | Tell your partner the most important thing you learned today about triangles. |
| **Whip-around:** While tossing a ball around the room, students who get the ball respond with one thing about today's class. It can be a fact (e.g., the clock is a circle) or a self-reflection (e.g., I am good at patterning). This is a fast-paced activity. The teacher should allow students a minute or two to think of what they want to say prior to starting the activity. The teacher can take notes for the two-pile protocol. | Name a fact.<br><br>Share a self-reflection. |
| **S-T-O-P:** Students summarize the lesson orally or in writing by finishing sentence starters. | We **S**tarted the lesson _____.<br><br>Our **T**opic was _____.<br><br>**O**pportunities to do the math included _____.<br><br>The **P**urpose of the lesson was _____. |
| **Footprint:** Students each receive a cutout footprint and then use words, pictures, or symbols to show what they will *walk away* from the lesson with. | What will you walk away from the lesson with? |

## EXTENDED CLOSURE

Some lessons may call for a more in-depth closure than the ones previously listed. This is called an extended closure. When you teach a rich problem-based task that invites students to engage deeply with conceptual understanding, you will want to provide plenty of time for students to make sense of each other's work, connect representations, construct viable arguments, and link new learning to the learning intentions. During the lesson facilitation, you monitor the students as they work to represent their solutions and ask probing questions along the way. Just as you provide ample time for your students to work on the rich task, you will also want to make sure you leave plenty of time for your closure. During this time, you will want to strategically connect the students' solutions to the learning intention. Many teachers conduct a gallery walk to invite student feedback before formally closing the lesson.

Megan poses a rich fraction task by asking students to examine state flags, estimate the fractional amount of red in the flags, and then order the flags by the fractional amount by gluing the flags to a large poster. While the students are working, Megan also thinks about how she will select and sequence the students' work (Smith &

Stein, 2011) to best facilitate her students' conceptual understanding during the closure. As the student groups complete their work, Megan hangs their posters around the room and hands each student five green and five yellow sticky dots. She asks them to place a green sticky dot on solutions that are the same or similar to their solutions. She also asks them to place a yellow sticky dot on student work that they have a question about.

When the gallery walk is complete, Megan directs her students' attention to the posters and asks, "I am noticing a lot of green stickers on several posters. What strategies did many of you use to figure out a fraction for the amount of red in the flag?"

> Thomas: Lots of us put fraction pieces on the flag to match it up.

Megan had previously selected one of the groups that used fraction pieces to share their solution strategy and asks them to present their solution to the group.

> Bertie: We got a bunch of the fraction tiles and just started covering up the flag with the tiles. Then we compared it to the part that wasn't covered up. We could tell if the flag had more or less, but we weren't sure how to name it after that because there were lots of different pieces in the red part.
>
> Megan: Hmmmm. I see what you mean. You had a ½ piece and a ¼ piece in the red part of the flag.
>
> Bertie: Ya. So then we thought we should add that up together and ran into a big problem.
>
> Megan: What was that big problem?
>
> Bertie: Well, that was when we noticed that the fraction tile for the whole was not the same size as the flag so we couldn't really compare them.

Megan smiled. This is exactly what she wanted the students to understand. The extended closure allowed time for her to use the students' work to this particular concept. She then said, "Nice work, you realized that in order to compare fractional parts, the wholes must be the same size. I noticed that many of you put yellow stickers on this poster because this group used a strategy different than you. Let's have this group share their solution."

> Malachi: Well, we tried fraction circle pieces first and that was terrible because nothing was matching up! So, we decided to fold the flags into equal parts so we could compare the flags! We started folding them into halves and then fourths. We liked the fourths better because we needed the smaller parts to be able to compare them.
>
> Megan: I like how the folding helped you compare the flags to each other.
>
> Malachi: Yes, because then we were comparing the same parts.
>
> Megan: These are very nice explanations because the groups are explaining their ideas and the representations on the posters help us understand our thinking. From this lesson, we can see how important it is to compare fractions when the wholes are the same size! Let's take a look at our learning intention and reflect on our learning for today.

Megan facilitates the extended closure to highlight and use the students' representations and build conceptual understanding. She explicitly states the mathematical concept that she wants to learn after they have had lots of time exploring and explaining their ideas.

---

> You may have seen other ideas for closure. With your team, compile a list of more closure activities that are appropriate for your grade level. Be sure each meets the purpose for the teacher and the student. Record the ones you would like to try first.
>
> _____
> _____
> _____
> _____

**Building Unit Coherence**

Closure provides a perfect opportunity for you to build coherence among your lessons. You can connect student reflection on the day's lesson to previous lessons to help your students make sense of the big idea/essential question that is the thread throughout the unit. For example, asking students to team up with a partner to answer the question, "How are the patterns we looked at today different from or the same as the patterns we looked at yesterday?" is an effective and simple way to tie lessons together and build the big ideas across the unit.

During closure, students share new mathematical ideas and reflect on their learning. During this time, you co-construct opportunities for coherence. You bring together the big ideas from the lesson and forecast new learning for the next day. As you devote essential time to the closure, you create space for students to make important connections between and within lessons.

Notes

## Close the Lesson

Eliza, Marilyn, and Rena decide to conduct a performance exit task. They want to be able to monitor the students as they work and see if the children can transfer their learning from the lesson to a new task. They also plan to differentiate this exit task as needed if they notice that some students are struggling during the lesson.

### Closure:

Exit task: Give each student a baggie that contains 17 cubes. Students write down the number of ten cubes and leftover cubes:

_____ group of tens

_____ leftover

**See the complete lesson plan in Appendix A on page 178.**

**How does the closure activity in this lesson satisfy the purpose for closure for the teacher and student? Note your ideas below.**

Standards | LI and SC | Purpose | Tasks | Materials | Student Thinking | Lesson Structures | Form. Assess. | Lesson Launch | Lesson Facilitation | Closure

Sarita, Jen, and Karlo decide to have their students use journals to conduct closure activities. They believe that this record will provide them with valuable information about their students. They decide that even though they will give all of the children the same prompt, they will adjust the prompt as needed depending on the students' learning needs.

**Closure:**

Journal prompt: Represent the number 29 two different ways using pictures, words, and/or numbers.

(Teddy bear counters provided for students not at the abstract level.)

**See the complete lesson plan in Appendix A on page 183.**

**How does the closure activity in this lesson satisfy the purpose for closure for the teacher and student?**

_____

_____

_____

_____

_____

_____

_____

_____

_____

_____

_____

_____

_____

_____

_____

_____

_____

_____

_____

_____

_____

_____

Aliyah, Dwayne, and Wilma note that this lesson will engage the students in many opportunities for discourse. They decide to design a short closure using one of the students' favorite closure activities, writing a "text" to their parents. The teachers also want to see how the students perform independently.

### Closure:

Text: On a phone text template, students write a text to their parents telling them what 629 means.

*See the complete lesson plan in Appendix A on page 188.*

**How does the closure activity in this lesson satisfy the purpose for closure for the teacher and student? Note your ideas below.**

Standards

LI and SC

Purpose

Tasks

Materials

Student Thinking

Lesson Structures

Form. Assess.

Lesson Launch

Lesson Facilitation

Closure

Now it is your turn! Add an appropriate closure activity to your lesson plan that is under construction.

**Closure:**

Download the full Lesson-Planning Template from resources.corwin.com/mathlessonplanning/k-2
Remember that you can use the online version of the lesson plan template to begin compiling each section into the full template as your lesson plan grows.

# CHAPTER 14

# SURVEYING YOUR RESULTS
## *Lesson Reflection*

First-grade teacher Hannah sat down at her desk after the last bell rang. She was tired as always, but it was a good tired. As usual, she allowed herself an extra 10 to 15 minutes to reflect on the day before moving on to the next thing. She didn't always get this time when there were after-school meetings, but she had learned that this brief period to reflect was very important to her professional practice. Before she had built reflective practice into her teaching, she had found herself getting burned out and focusing on only the hard things that had happened during the day. A mentor had shared her own reflection practice with Hannah before she retired, and Hannah was pretty sure it had changed her professional life.

Hannah mentally went through the day and took a couple of notes. Her mentor had suggested that she always start with successes. Hannah thought about her math lesson that day. Her students had been so excited to work in pairs and showcase their work during the gallery walk. The students' understanding of place value was coming along nicely.

Knowing that this standard crossed over two instructional quarters helped her feel less panicked about staying on a particular schedule. She just about had the students working in pairs smoothly, an approach she had been working on since the beginning of the year.

As she continued to reflect on the day, she decided that she would move two of the students, Bryan and Kelly, to work with different partners. Bryan struggled with some math anxiety and Kelly still had trouble getting along with others unless the group did what she wanted.

Hannah was also pleased to note that the students were settling nicely into the number talk routine. A couple things nagged her, though. First, she recognized that she still couldn't conduct the number talk in a timely fashion. As she reflected on the situation, she decided to make sure she adheres to the time constraints and also lets the students know that they will be stopping at a certain time.

Second, she reminded herself that she needs to think about her questions more—an issue she had been working on steadily ever since she noticed that she often slips back into funneling questions with students who struggle. She recognized that her good intentions to help her students can actually interfere with their learning. She decided to ask her teammate, Beverly, who seemed to have an endless supply of good questions.

Hannah's teammates had learned not to disturb her reflection now. Now Beverly called into her classroom, "Your 10 minutes are up, Hannah!"

"Perfect," Hannah thought. "Maybe I will have a few minutes to talk to Beverly about my questioning before our meeting starts."

---

**No doubt your day is filled with endless decisions and lots of rushing from one thing to the next. Teaching young learners does not allow much space for thinking about the day. However, teaching is an emotional and often physical challenge that requires deep processing. This chapter will consider the following questions:**

- Why is it important to reflect upon lessons?
- What kind of reflection cycle supports teacher growth?

Teachers can use **reflection** as way to focus on what works, recognize challenges, and move forward in productive ways. Your reflection should be centered on a healthy curiosity about student learning that helps you better understand and learn about your teaching practice (Danielson, 2008; Smyth, 1992). You can reflect as you are teaching, which is called **reflecting in action** (Schön, 1983), to monitor and adjust to the ebb and flow of your learners' needs. You can also reflect after you have taught, which is called **reflecting on action** (Schön, 1983), by thinking about your students and instruction after a lesson ends.

You are probably already asked to reflect as a formal part of your professional practice. Many teacher evaluation systems require some sort of reflection about teaching. These reflection prompts formalize what good teachers already do every day and focus on established criteria.

Perhaps the most powerful reflection occurs when teachers pose their own questions about their teaching because those questions help them make meaningful connections between their teaching decisions and student learning. In an analysis of John Dewey's (1933, 1944) writing on the importance of reflection, Carol Rodgers (2002) extracted four essential criteria that define effective reflection.

1. *Reflection is a meaning-making process.* Your reflection should support your ability to make connections. As it moves beyond ruminating, hashing over, or contemplating the day's events, your reflection should support a deeper understanding of your teaching choices and your students' response to those choices.

2. *Reflection is a rigorous, disciplined way of thinking, with its roots in scientific inquiry.* Your reflection should always begin with a question that probes and pushes your thinking. Inquiry nudges teachers to tell their teaching stories in new ways. Consider these questions:

   - What do I believe about how students learn? How is this reflected in my instructional planning?

   - What kinds of questions did I ask during this lesson? How was student learning affected?

   - How does planning my questioning affect my lesson facilitation?

   - What does student-centered teaching mean to me?

   - How do I know my students are learning?

   - What data did I collect today that were most powerful?

3. *Reflection needs to happen in a community, in interaction with others.* Personal reflection is important and necessary. However, reflection that happens in a community of teachers is also powerful as other teachers provide unique perspectives, ask questions, and offer insight that can reveal new ways of thinking about teaching.

4. *Reflection requires attitudes that value your personal and professional growth as well as the personal and professional growth of other teachers and leaders.* Reflection is cathartic and powerful. Without it, learning and change are not likely to happen. Making time to reflect is essential to maintaining your professional health, and this approach will support you in making good decisions about teaching and learning (Constantino & De Lorenzo, 2001; Day, 1999; Harris, Bruster, Peterson, & Shutt, 2010).

**Describe your reflective practice. When, how, and with whom do you reflect? Write your response here.**

_____

_____

_____

_____

_____

When you take time to mindfully unpack your professional teaching practice, you can gain insight into improving your future practice. If you focus on successes before challenges, you can gain new understandings about the factors that promote success and shape new teaching decisions. Consider the reflection cycle in Figure 14.1.

**Figure 14.1**

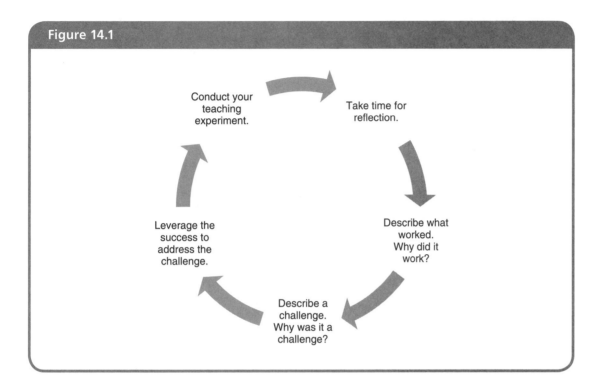

Let's look at each component of the reflecting cycle in more detail.

## Take Time for Reflection

Unless you set a designated time for reflection, it can be difficult to move beyond musings about the day. Teachers are very hard on themselves and tend to focus on those most difficult moments or the problems of the day. Making time for reflection, using a specific cycle, can help you work through successes and challenges and strategically design next instructional steps. Think about how to schedule time to reflect alone and with trusted colleagues. Some teachers plan regular reflection time during professional learning meetings.

## Describe What Worked

Reflect on what worked during the lesson, and describe what you and the students were doing that contributed to the success. When you ask yourself these questions, you heighten your awareness and positive potential for change (Cooperrider & Whitney, 2005). By focusing on what has worked and dissecting those elements that contributed to success, you can identify what aspects to repeat (Hammond, 1998).

Some teachers like to chart these ideas in two columns to help them discover connections (see example in Figure 14.2). This process is a key component for moving forward. Often, your inspiration about tackling challenges will come from your understanding of why a particular teaching practice was successful.

**Figure 14.2**

| What Worked | Why |
|---|---|
| Numberless word problem | • Students were relaxed. |
| | • Students were curious. |
| | • Students immediately started putting numbers into the word problem to make sense of the problem. |
| | • Students were not encumbered with a right or wrong answer. |
| | • Students were allowed to collaborate and work together. |

## Describe the Challenge

By describing a challenge that you experienced in the lesson, you can begin to imagine how you can leverage your success to tackle your challenge. This could be something that is significant to this particular lesson, or it could be something that you have noticed as a pattern in your daily lessons. As the example in Figure 14.3 shows, it can be helpful to unpack the challenge by considering potential reasons why it exists (Figure 14.3).

**Figure 14.3**

| Challenge | Why |
|---|---|
| Supporting students' productive struggle | • I am worried about pushing students too hard, and I think they know this. |
| | • I need to be better prepared with scaffolding questions. |
| | • I need to make sure that I am providing an environment that helps the students feel safe. |
| | • Some students are exhibiting learned helplessness. |
| | • Students are worried about being right and/or getting wrong answers. |

## Leverage the Success to Address the Challenge

By examining the elements of the success alongside the challenge, you can often uncover contributing elements of the success that you can leverage to help you with the challenge. For example, if you note your success with a numberless word problem but also your challenge with supporting productive struggle with some of your students, the details might prompt you to recognize that the numberless word problem was so successful because the students knew that there was not a correct answer. Based on this reflection, you might decide to use more open-ended problems with multiple solutions. This approach would also help you focus your students more on the process of solving, rather than on the answers.

## Conduct Your Teaching Experiment

You conduct **teaching experiments** all the time! A teaching experiment occurs when you pose a question, try out an idea, reflect, and adjust based on the results (Tschannen-Moran & Tschannen-Moran, 2010). Teachers who share challenges often enjoy collaborating on teaching experiments and celebrating the results.

The first step in conducting your teaching experiment is to think about how to design your experiment. Consider the following questions:

- What would you like to pay more attention to in your mathematics classroom?

- What changes do you think your students would really appreciate?

- What changes would increase achievement?

- What things can you imagine doing differently?

- How might your mathematics teaching be different a few months from now?

- What changes would you like to experiment with in your mathematics teaching?

The next step is to describe your experiment and make a design plan for implementation. Consider the timeline, materials, and resources you will need to conduct your teaching experiment.

- Will you need to talk with other teachers, gain permission from your principal, or read new information to conduct your teaching experiment?

- What activities will you implement?

- What kinds of evidence will you collect?

Finally, you will need to reflect on your experiment.

- How will you know if your teaching experiment is successful?

- How will you revise your experiment?

- How will you integrate your experiment into your daily practice?

- How will you share the results of your experiment with your colleagues and leadership?

> **How can you use your reflection to design a teaching experiment through lesson planning? Record your responses here.**
>
> _____
> _____
> _____
> _____
> _____
> _____
> _____
> _____
> _____
> _____
> _____
> _____

# Epilogue

You began this lesson-planning process by thinking about and examining your students' needs and considering the important ideas of coherence, rigor, and purpose. By now, we hope you have come to see the many important facets of building purposeful and cohesive mathematics lessons and maybe even fully engaged in the lesson-planning process, using the sections of this book as your guide, and filling in the lesson-planning template! Likewise, we hope you and your students are reaping the benefits of thorough planning, or at the very least getting a taste of the success yet to come. Whether you have designed a lesson fully from scratch, adapted a lesson, or even just read a few sections of this book, you have likely thought about the lesson-planning process with a new perspective that has deepened your knowledge about your own choices and decisions. The teachers we work with tell us that when they study and engage in the lesson-planning process, they

- become more confident and intentional in their teaching;
- are able to listen and respond to their students more authentically and react to their students' understandings with clarity and purpose;
- find greater meaning in the lessons because they have made sense of large and small teaching decisions, including task selection or adaptation; lesson purpose; lesson format; and lesson launch, facilitation, and closure; and
- report a renewed confidence and find they are energized and excited by the lesson-planning and implementation cycle.

As you have hopefully experienced, lesson planning builds cohesion for both students and yourself (Jensen, 2001). Thorough lessons, strategically planned, support students' ability to build connections among and between mathematical ideas (Panasuk, Stone, & Todd, 2002). This is, after all, our goal. Teachers and students see and understand how today's learning connects to yesterday's, last week's, even last year's learning *and* forecasts future learning.

You may have also noticed that the lesson-planning process can help you clarify your own understanding of the mathematics content, standard, and potential student misconceptions. This is perhaps one of the most powerful teacher benefits of lesson planning—a benefit that will extend beyond any one lesson you teach. The teachers we work with report that they experience new insight about the mathematics they are teaching, which, in turn, helps them to strategically facilitate their students' learning.

As you continue this journey, we recommend that you do the following:

*Start slowly.* Select a few pieces of the lesson-planning process to focus on, and then build from there. Start with what is most comfortable for you, and then extend or add new pieces to your planning repertoire. Before you know it, you will be able to spend your time on the parts of the lesson that need your attention the most.

*Find planning partners.* Search for other teachers to plan with regularly. They don't necessarily have to be in your school or grade level. Online platforms support co-creation and sharing across the country. Simply having an opportunity to share your planning decisions with others can be immensely rewarding and satisfying. Make sure you share your successes as well as your challenges.

*Determine how you will organize and store your lessons.* Many teachers store the lessons for each grade level by using online formats. This organization will support you in the future and reduce planning time in subsequent years. Storing lessons will also help you track revisions as you respond to the particular needs of your students. Be sure to record reflections or thoughts about the lesson!

*Communicate with leaders.* As you know, planning lessons takes time and perseverance. Invite school and district leaders to participate in your planning sessions. Engage them in your process as you plan, implement, and reflect on your teaching successes and challenges.

*Celebrate and showcase your success.* So much of teaching is privately shared between students and teachers. Publicly sharing your lessons with teammates and school leaders can inspire others to plan and innovate powerful lessons. Organize opportunities for colleagues to share successful lessons that affected student learning.

Always remember that you are the architect of your classroom. You have the fortune to design and implement lessons that help children learn mathematics. You get to establish the learning environment you want to foster, and you have not only the opportunity but also the responsibility to build the best foundation and best structure for your learners as possible. We wish you every success.

# Appendix A

*Complete Lesson Plans*

### Big Idea(s):

Use numbers to represent quantities.

### Essential Question(s):

How can numbers help us in everyday life?

### Content Standard(s):

Write numbers from 0 to 20. Represent a number of objects with a written numeral 0 to 20 (with 0 representing a count of no objects).

### Mathematical Practice and/or Process Standards:

Construct viable arguments and critique the reasoning of others.

Attend to precision.

### Learning Intention(s):

#### Mathematics Learning Intentions

We are learning to
- Understand that a written number represents how many are in a group of objects by
  - Recording or writing numbers after we count groups of objects
  - Making a group of objects to match a number we see

#### Language Learning Intentions

- Write or record numbers 0 to 20 after hearing the number called by our teacher or classmate.
- Use mathematical words like *subitize*, *group*, *set*, *match*, and *record*.

#### Social Learning Intentions

- Listen to each other count.
- Ask questions about each other's counting.
- Explain how we know that a group of objects matches a number we see or hear.

### Success Criteria (written in student voice):

I know that I am successful when I can:
- Write a number I hear (even when not counted in order).
- Count a group of objects and record or write the number I counted.
- Write the number 0 for when there is no group of objects.
- Match a collection of objects with a subitized set.
- See a number and make a group of objects that matches that number.
- Match a group of objects to a number.

### Standards for Mathematical Practice Success Criteria:

- Stick with a problem even when I am not sure at first how to solve it.
- Listen to my classmates' explanations about place value and ask questions that show I understand place value.

## Purpose:

☑ Conceptual Understanding ☐ Procedural Fluency ☐ Transfer

## Task:

**How Many Insects?**

The insects are crawling all over the leaves! We need to find out how many insects are on each leaf. How can we find out?

Note: The downloadable student worksheets contain 11 leaves representing numbers 10 to 20.

## Materials (representations, manipulatives, other):

Two-color counters

## Misconceptions or Common Errors:

Students may count every dot without subitizing.

Students cannot decompose teen numbers.

Students may struggle with one-to-one correspondence.

Students read teen numbers like 11 as onety-one or one-one.

## Format:

☐ Four-Part Lesson ☐ Game Format ☐ Small-Group Instruction

☑ Pairs ☐ Other_____

## Formative Assessment:

Use observation checklist to observe the following:

- One-to-one correspondence
- Grouping of tens and some ones
- Counting technique
- Conservation

(Continued)

## Launch:

*Number Talk:*

First, "flash" the ten-frame cards to the students in a series. Ask the students to show how many dots they see using their fingers or numeral cards. Then post all the ten-frame cards on the board. Pose these questions:

- What do you see?
- What do you notice about the ten-frame cards?

*Anticipate:*

Some students will still need extra time to mentally count the dots on the cards.

Some students will instantly see how many dots are on the cards.

Some students may need to see how the dots can fill in the spaces.

Questions to help the students make the connection:

- Do you notice anything about the arrangement of the dots that will help you find out how many dots are on the ten-frame card?
- Is there a way you can figure out how many dots are there without counting all the dots?

## Facilitate:

Include plans for mathematical discourse and questions.

Present students with the *How Many Insects?* problem and visual.

1. Conduct a Notice and Wonder (see lesson launch chapter) with the students, and record their notices and wonders.
2. Connect the notices and wonders and ask, "How can we find out how many insects are on the leaves?"
3. Ask the students to write an estimate on a sticky note and post the estimates in order from least to greatest.
4. Elicit from the students that they can count the insects on the leaves.
5. Ask the students,
   - What tools might be helpful to keep track of your counting?
   - How can we find out if there is a group of ten insects on the leaves?
6. Explain that this lesson will include the following success criteria:
   - Count a group of objects and record or write the number I counted.
   - Stick with a problem even when I am not sure at first how to solve it.
   - Listen to my classmates' explanations about counting and ask questions that show I understand counting.

7.  Arrange the students in pairs to use counters, ten-frames cards, and the recording sheet to decompose the number of insects on the leaves (give pairs different amounts). Monitor the students as they work, and ask questions like, "How did you figure out how many tens? How many leftovers? How did you organize your counting? Did you and your partner count the same way? How did you keep track of the insects you counted on the leaf?"

8.  Encourage the students to explain their thinking by asking questions.

9.  Have the students record the number of ten ones and some more ones on the recording sheet and explain how they figured it out.

10. Have student pairs post their work and conduct a gallery walk. Give students a sticky dot and ask them to post a sticky dot on students' work that is interesting.

11. Select three student pairs to share how they counted, decomposed, and used the blank ten-frame card to find out how many insects were on the leaf. Have student pairs share based on clarity of examples. As the pairs share, encourage them to comment on each other's ideas. Ask, "How was your strategy alike or different than _____?"

12. Ask, "What do you notice about all the leaves?" Elicit from the students that every leaf has ten ones and some more ones.

13. Use students' work to highlight the pattern. For example, begin with ten. Each time, highlight student work to reveal the pattern. Ask students to Turn and Talk about the patterns they are noticing.

    10 = 1 group of ten insects and 0 more

    11 = 1 group of ten insects and 1 more

    12 = 1 group of ten insects and 2 more

    13 = 1 group of ten insects and 3 more

    14 = 1 group of ten insects and 4 more

    15 = 1 group of ten insects and 5 more

    16 = 1 group of ten insects and 6 more

    17 = 1 group of ten insects and 7 more

    18 = 1 group of ten insects and 8 more

    19 = 1 group of ten insects and 9 more

14. Ask the students, "What do you notice about the teen numbers? How many groups of ten are in all the teen numbers? What do you notice about the *some more* part?"

15. Close by asking the students to Turn and Talk about the patterns in the teen numbers. "What do you notice about all the numbers that had a ten and some more ones?"

16. Connect back to the sticky-note estimates. Ask the students to Turn and Talk. "What do you notice about your estimates and the actual number of insects?"

*(Continued)*

Anticipating student responses:

Some students will need organizational help. Encourage them to use a ten-frame organizer and other tools to help them keep track.

Some students will want to work independently rather than collaboratively. Give pairs one sheet of large chart paper to encourage them to work together. Call attention to pairs and groups that work together and remind them what working together means. Connect their struggle to the success criteria.

Pairs and groups will work at different rates. Organize the pairs and small groups to reflect differing learning needs to support each other's learning.

Monitoring the students' productive struggle:

Scaffold as needed by identifying mini-goals for some students. For example, ask students to find one leaf first and then check in with the teacher. Reward the students' "stick with it" behavior by calling attention to their perseverance.

## Closure:

Exit task: Give each student a baggie that contains 17 cubes. Students write down the number of ten cubes and leftover cubes:

_____ group of tens

_____ leftover

 Download the complete Kindergarten Snapshot from resources.corwin.com/mathlessonplanning/k-2

**Big Idea(s):**

Group with tens and ones for place value.

**Essential Question(s):**

How can a number be represented with tens and ones in more than one way?

**Content Standard(s):**

Understand that the two digits of a two-digit number represent amounts of tens and ones.

**Mathematical Practice and/or Process Standards:**

Construct viable arguments and critique the reasoning of others.

Attend to precision.

**Learning Intention(s):**

**Mathematics Learning Intention**

We are learning to
- Understand that a written number represents how many are in a group of objects by
  - Recording or writing numbers after we count groups of objects
  - Making a group of objects to match a number we see

**Language Learning Intentions**

- Write or record numbers 0 to 20 after hearing the number called by our teacher or classmate.
- Use mathematical words like *subitize*, *group*, *set*, *match*, and *record*.

**Social Learning Intentions**

- Listen to each other count.
- Ask questions about each other's counting.
- Work with a partner to count out how many tens and ones are in a group of objects.
- Explain how we know that a group of objects matches a number we see or hear.

**Success Criteria (written in student voice):**

- Write a number I hear (even when not counted in order).
- Count a group of objects and record or write the number I counted.
- Write the number 0 for when there is no group of objects.
- Match a collection of objects with a subitized set.
- See a number and make a group of objects that matches that number.
- Match a group of objects to a number.

**Purpose:**

☐ Conceptual Understanding    ☐ Procedural Fluency    ☑ Transfer

## Task:

**Aunt Jasmine and Uncle Ronnie's Cupcakes**

Aunt Jasmine has a new cupcake business. Uncle Ronnie is helping Aunt Jasmine keep track of how many she sells. He wants to know how many cupcakes she sold last week, but she doesn't know! She is so busy making cupcakes that she cannot keep track of her orders!

Aunt Jasmine needs your help sorting the cupcake orders. Uncle Ronnie needs to know how many groups of ten are in each order and how many leftovers are in each order. Can you help find the number of groups of tens and ones? You must be able to show and explain all of your thinking. The orders they received today are 47, 56, 39, 87, and 62.

| Aunt Jasmine's Cupcakes Order Form | Aunt Jasmine's Cupcakes Order Form | Aunt Jasmine's Cupcakes Order Form | Aunt Jasmine's Cupcakes Order Form | Aunt Jasmine's Cupcakes Order Form |
| --- | --- | --- | --- | --- |
| 47 | 56 | 39 | 87 | 62 |

## Materials (representations, manipulatives, other):

Counters, base-ten blocks, blank ten frames, order form, chart paper

## Misconceptions or Common Errors:

Difficulty decomposing numbers into tens and ones

Difficulty counting

## Format:

☑ Four-Part Lesson ☐ Game format ☐ Small-Group Instruction

☐ Pairs ☐ Other_____

## Formative Assessment:

Show Me prompt: Show me 34 using base-ten blocks. How many tens and ones?

Interview prompt: How did you figure out how many tens and ones are in 34?

## Launch:

(This is the *before* part of the four-part lesson format.)

Pose the first part of the problem and tell the story to the students.

Aunt Jasmine has a new cupcake business. Uncle Ronnie is helping Aunt Jasmine keep track of how many she sells. He wants to know how many cupcakes she sold last week, but she doesn't know! She is so busy making cupcakes that she cannot keep track of her orders!

Record students' notices and wonders on a chart for all the students to see. Then, introduce the second part of the problem and ask students if they have more notices and wonders they would like to add to the chart.

Aunt Jasmine needs your help sorting the cupcake orders. Uncle Ronnie needs to know how many groups of ten are in each order and how many leftovers are in each order. Can you help find the number of groups of tens and ones? You must be able to show and explain all of your thinking. The orders they received today are 47, 56, 39, 87, and 62.

| Aunt Jasmine's Cupcakes Order Form | Aunt Jasmine's Cupcakes Order Form | Aunt Jasmine's Cupcakes Order Form | Aunt Jasmine's Cupcakes Order Form | Aunt Jasmine's Cupcakes Order Form |
|---|---|---|---|---|
| 47 | 56 | 39 | 87 | 62 |

Anticipate student responses for Part I Notice:

Lots of cupcakes

They don't know how many they sold

Very busy business

Anticipate student responses for Part I Wonder:

How many cupcakes?

What are the kinds of cupcakes?

How many cupcakes are in an order?

Anticipate student responses for Part 2 Notice:

Cupcakes will need to be in groups of ten

Leftover cupcakes

Find the groups of tens and ones

Students explain their thinking

Anticipate student responses for Part 2 Wonder:

How big will the order be?

What does left over mean?

How will we organize the cupcakes?

(Continued)

**Facilitate:**

*During*

1. Connect the students' notices and wonders to the task by explaining to the students that they are going to have a chance to help Uncle Ronnie find out the number of groups of tens and ones.

2. Explain that this lesson will include the following success criteria:

   - Group objects by their place value and record.
   - Show a two-digit number using base-ten blocks or by drawing.
   - See a number and represent that number using place value.
   - Stick with a problem even when I am not sure at first how to solve it.
   - Listen to my classmates' explanations about counting groups, and ask questions that show I understand how they counted.

3. Arrange the students in pairs or groups of three. Say to the students, "You will receive a cupcake order form with the number of cupcakes, chart paper to record all of your thinking, counters, and blank ten frames. Your task is to find out how many groups of tens and ones are in the cupcake order."

4. As the pairs and groups work together, monitor their work by asking questions such as these:

   - How can you represent the tens and ones on the chart paper?
   - How will you show your thinking?
   - How will you keep track of your work?
   - How will you get started?
   - What ideas did your partner have?
   - How can you use the ten frame as a tool to show your thinking?
   - How are you working with your partner?
   - What are you noticing?

5. Conduct a group gallery walk: Have the students hang their posters around the room. Have the students do a gallery walk to view everyone else's work. Give the students a sticky note or a sticker and ask them to post a sticker or a comment on another group's work they have a question about or on one that is different from their own.

*After*

6. Conduct a group Notice: As students finish looking at others' work, bring them back together as a group. Ask them to Turn and Talk with their partners to discuss what they noticed or had a question about.

7. Highlight strategies the students used by selecting three posters for students to share. Look for evidence of use of ten frames to find groups of ten, accuracy, and explanation.

8. Record the students' work from each poster on a chart like the following, moving in order from least to greatest:

| Cupcake Order | Groups of Ten | Ones |
|---|---|---|
| 27 | 2 | 7 |
| 35 | 3 | 5 |

9. Have the students Turn and Talk to a partner and ask, "What do you notice?" Elicit from the students that there is a pattern. The number of the groups of ten is the same as the digit in the tens place.

Anticipating student responses:

Some students will need organizational help. Encourage them to count out the total using counters and then organize the total on the ten frames. Have plenty of extra ten frames if students want to draw a dot on the ten frame and then glue the ten frame to the poster.

Some first graders will want to work independently rather than collaboratively. Give them one sheet of large chart paper to encourage them to work together. Call attention to pairs and groups that work together and remind the first graders what working together means.

Pairs and groups will work at different rates. Differentiate the numbers of the order forms for groups that might need more time. Have extra order forms for groups that would like to work on another order form.

Monitoring students' productive struggle:

Monitor the students carefully, encourage students to solve their own problems, and collaborate with each other. Scaffold the questions if students need more time to work on the problem.

## Closure:

Journal prompt: Represent the number 29 two different ways using pictures, words, and/or numbers.

(Teddy bear counters provided for students not at the abstract level.)

 Download the complete First-Grade Snapshot from resources.corwin.com/mathlessonplanning/k-2

**Big Idea(s):**

Extend the base-ten system to relationship among the unit.

**Essential Question(s):**

How is the number 10 used in our number system with ones and hundreds?

**Content Standard(s):**

Demonstrate that each digit of a three-digit number represents amounts of hundreds, tens, and ones (e.g., 387 is 3 hundreds, 8 tens, 7 ones).

**Mathematical Practice and/or Process Standards:**

Construct viable arguments and critique the reasoning of others.

Attend to precision.

**Learning Intention(s):**

**Mathematics Learning Intentions**

- Show three-digit numbers using base-ten blocks or other materials.
- Break apart three-digit numbers into the place values of hundreds, tens, and ones using manipulatives and drawings.
- Represent three-digit numbers using base-ten materials and pictures.

**Social Learning Intentions**

- Make sense of base-ten problems in collaboration with others.
- Productively struggle while solving them.

**Language Learning Intentions**

- Explain our reasoning about place value to our classmates.
- Ask and answer questions about our place value understanding to our classmates.

**Success Criteria (written in student voice):**

- Explain the place value and value of each number in a one-, two-, and three-digit number.
- Explain and construct the place value and value of numbers when presented in varying orders (e.g., 3 tens, 4 hundreds, and 5 ones).
- Show the place value of three-digit numbers using base-ten blocks or pictures when presented with the number.
- Stick with a problem even when I am not sure at first how to solve it.
- Listen to my classmates' explanations about place value and ask questions that show I understand place value.

**Purpose:**

☑ Conceptual Understanding      ☐ Procedural Fluency      ☐ Transfer

## Task:

### Bucket of Blocks!

Elaine, Roberto, and Janine all grabbed a bucket of base-ten blocks. Elaine's bucket has 2 hundreds, 9 tens, and 2 ones. Roberto's bucket has 8 ones, 6 hundreds, and 5 tens. Janine's bucket has 50 ones and 20 tens. Elaine, Roberto, and Janine each think they have the greatest value. Help them figure out who has the greatest value. Represent and explain your thinking to prove who is right!

## Materials (representations, manipulatives, other):

Base-ten blocks

## Misconceptions or Common Errors:

Some students will think of a three-digit number as three separate digits and not hundreds, tens, and ones.

## Format:

☑ Four-Part Lesson      ☐ Game format      ☐ Small-Group Instruction

☐ Pairs      ☐ Other_____

## Formative Assessment:

Brief formative Interview

How did you decide to represent the number?

Which value is greatest? How do you know?

## Launch:

This is the before part of the four-part lesson.

Present the following numberless word problem to the students:

Elaine, Roberto, and Janine all grabbed a bucket of base-ten blocks. Elaine's bucket has hundreds, tens, and ones. Roberto's bucket has ones, hundreds, and tens. Janine's bucket has ones and tens. Elaine, Roberto, and Janine each think they have the greatest value. Help them figure out who has the greatest value. Represent and explain your thinking to prove who is right!

Ask the students to talk with a partner about what is happening in the word problem. Next ask the students to share their ideas.

Anticipate student responses:

* Notice that Janine's bucket has only ones and tens
* Notice that Roberto's bucket information is presented in a different order
* Want to know the exact numbers
* Assume that Elaine's bucket has more
* Need manipulatives to determine the actual value

## Facilitate:

*During*

1. After ideas have been shared from the launch, transition to the problem to reveal the actual problem.

2. Elaine, Roberto, and Janine all grabbed a bucket of base-ten blocks. Elaine's bucket has 2 hundreds, 9 tens, and 2 ones. Roberto's bucket has 8 ones, 6 hundreds, and 5 tens. Janine's bucket has 50 ones and 20 tens. Elaine, Roberto, and Janine each think they have the greatest value. Help them figure out who has the greatest value. Represent and explain your thinking to prove who is right!

3. Ask the students to discuss with a partner what they are noticing. Elicit ideas from the students, but make sure that they do not give any answers away!

4. Arrange the students in pairs or groups of three. Say to the students, "You will solve this problem with your partner or group of three. Each group will receive a piece of chart paper to show all of your work. You may also use, but are not required to use, base-ten blocks, hundreds charts, and blank ten frames. Your task is to determine and prove who has the greatest value. You must show all of your thinking on the chart paper. Here are your success criteria for this lesson:

   - Explain and construct the place value and value of numbers when presented in varying orders, such as 3 tens, 4 hundreds, and 5 ones.

   - Show the place value of three-digit numbers using base-ten blocks or pictures when presented with the number.

   - Stick with a problem even when I am not sure at first how to solve it.

   - Listen to my classmates' explanations about place value and ask questions that show I understand place value.

5. How can you represent the hundreds, tens, and ones on the chart paper?

   - How will you show your thinking?

   - How will you keep track of your work?

   - How will you get started?

   - What ideas did your partner have?

   - How can you use the manipulatives and tools to show your thinking?

   - How are you working with your partner?

   - What are you noticing?

*After*

6. Conduct a group gallery walk: Have the students hang their posters around the room. Have the students do a gallery walk to view everyone else's work. Give the students a sticky note or a sticker and ask them to post a sticker or a comment on another group's work they have a question about or on one that is different from their own.

7. Conduct a group Notice: As students finish looking at others' work, bring them back together as a group. Ask them to Turn and Talk with their partners to discuss what they noticed or had a question about.

8. Highlight strategies the students used by selecting three posters for students to share. Look for evidence of use of place value to prove the values. Note if students were able to notice the values even when the order was different. Select groups based on understanding of place value, accuracy, and explanation.

*Reflect*

Ask the students to work individually to determine which of these numbers has the greatest value:

9 ones, 5 hundreds, 7 tens OR 6 hundreds, 4 ones, 9 tens

*Anticipating student responses:*

Some students will need organizational help. Encourage them to use a place value organizer and other tools to help them keep track.

Some students will want to work independently rather than collaboratively. Give them one sheet of large chart paper to encourage them to work together. Call attention to pairs and groups that work together and remind them what working together means. Connect their struggle to the success criteria. Pairs and groups will work at different rates. Organize the pairs and small groups to reflect differing learning needs to support each other's learning.

*Monitoring students' productive struggle:*

Scaffold as needed by identifying mini-goals for some students.

## Closure:

Text: On a phone text template, students write a text to their parents telling them what 629 means.

 Download the complete Second-Grade Snapshot from resources.corwin.com/mathlessonplanning/k-2

# Appendix B

*Lesson-Planning Template*

**Big Idea(s):**

**Essential Question(s):**

**Content Standard(s):**

**Mathematical Practice or Process Standards:**

**Learning Intention(s):**
**(mathematical/language/social)**

**Success Criteria:**
**(written in student voice)**

**Purpose:**

☐ Conceptual Understanding      ☐ Procedural Fluency      ☐ Transfer

**Task:**

**Materials (representations, manipulatives, other):**




**Misconceptions or Common Errors:**




**Format:**

☐ Four-Part Lesson          ☐ Game Format          ☐ Small-Group Instruction

☐ Pairs                     ☐ Other_____

**Formative Assessment:**




**Launch:**




**Facilitate:**




**Closure:**

# Appendix C

## *Further Reading/Resources*

### Online

___

#### Mathematics Content, Standards, and Virtual Manipulatives

http://www.achievethecore.org

A nonprofit organization dedicated to helping teachers and school leaders implement high-quality, college- and career-ready standards. The site includes planning materials, professional development resources, assessment information, and implementation support.

http://illustrativemathematics.org

A variety of videos, tasks, and suggestions for professional development accessible to all teachers.

http://ime.math.arizona.edu/progressions

The series of progressions documents written by leading researchers in the field summarizing the standards progressions for specific mathematical content domains.

http://nlvm.usu.edu

The National Library of Virtual Manipulatives offers a library of uniquely interactive, web-based virtual manipulatives or concept tutorials for mathematics instruction.

#### Sources for Problems, Tasks, and Lesson Protocols

https://bstockus.wordpress.com/numberless-word-problems

Numberless word problems designed to provide scaffolding that allows students the opportunity to develop a better understanding of the underlying structure of word problems.

https://gfletchy.com

Three-Act Lessons and Mathematical Progressions videos for Grades K–7.

http://illuminations.nctm.org

A collection of high-quality tasks, lessons, and activities that align with the Common Core standards and include the standards for mathematical practice.

http://mathforum.org

The Math Forum at NCTM provides a plethora of online resources, including Problem of the Week and the Notice and Wonder protocol.

http://mathpickle.com

A free online resource of original mathematical puzzles, games, and unsolved problems for K–12 teachers. It is supported by the American Institute of Mathematics.

http://nrich.maths.org

Free enrichment materials, curriculum maps, and professional development for mathematics teachers.

http://www.openmiddle.com

A crowd-sourced collection of challenging problems for Grades K–12. Open middle problems all begin with the same initial problem and end with the same answer, but they include multiple paths for problem solving and require a higher depth of knowledge than most problems that assess procedural and conceptual understanding.

http://robertkaplinsky.com/lessons

A collection of free real-world, problem-based lessons for Grades K–12.

## Books

Caldwell, J. H., Karp, K., Bay-Williams, J., & Zbiek, R. M. (2011). *Developing essential understanding of addition and subtraction for teaching mathematics in pre-K–Grade 2*. Reston, VA: NCTM.

Dougherty, B. J., Karp, K., Caldwell, J., & Kobett, B. (2014). *Putting essential understanding of addition and subtraction into practice pre-K–2*. Reston, VA: NCTM.

Fennell, F., Kobett, B. M., & Wray, J. A.(2017). *The formative 5: Everyday assessment techniques for every math classroom*. Thousand Oaks, CA: Corwin.

Gojak, L., & Harbin Miles, R. (2015). *The common core mathematics companion: The standards decoded, Grades K–2*. Thousand Oaks, CA: Corwin. [For Common Core states]

Gojak, L., & Harbin Miles, R. (2017). *Your mathematics standards companion: What they mean and how to teach them, Grades K–2*. Thousand Oaks, CA: Corwin [For Non–Common Core states]

Hattie, J., Fisher, D., Frey, N., Gojak, L. M., Moore, S. D., & Mellman, W. (2016). *Visible learning for mathematics, Grades K–12: What works best to optimize student learning*. Thousand Oaks, CA: Corwin.

Hull, T., Harbin Miles, R., & Balka, D. S. (2014). *Realizing rigor in the mathematics classroom*. Thousand Oaks, CA: Corwin.

Huniker, D., & Bill, V. (2017). *Taking action: Implementing effective mathematics teaching practices in K–Grade 5*. Reston, VA: NCTM.

National Council of Teachers of Mathematics. (2014). *Principles to actions: Ensuring mathematical success for all*. Reston, VA: Author.

O'Connell, S., & SanGiovanni, J. (2013). *Putting the practices into action: Implementing the common core standards for mathematical practice, K–8*. Portsmouth, NH: Heinemann.

Ray-Reik, M. (2013). *Powerful problem solving: Activities for sense making with the mathematical practices*. Portsmouth, NH: Heinemann.

Schrock, C., Norris, K., Pugalee, D., Seitz, R., & Hollingshead, F. (2013). *NCSM great tasks for mathematics K–5*. Reston, VA: NCTM.

Smith, M. S., & Stein, M. K. (2011). *Five practices for orchestrating productive mathematics discussions*. Reston, VA: National Council of Teachers of Mathematics and Corwin.

Van de Walle, J., Karp, K., & Bay-Williams, J. (2016). *Elementary and middle school mathematics: Teaching developmentally*. New York, NY: Pearson.

Van de Walle, J. A., Lovin, L. A. H., Karp, K. S., & Bay-Williams, J. M. (2017). *Teaching student-centered mathematics: Developmentally appropriate instruction for grades pre-K–2* (3rd ed.). Upper Saddle River, NJ: Pearson Education.

# Appendix D

## Glossary

**academic language.** The vocabulary used in schools, textbooks, and other school resources.

**access to high-quality education.** Phrase refers to the National Council of Teachers of Mathematics (NCTM) position statement on equal opportunity to a quality K–12 education for all students. Related to the NCTM position on equitable learning opportunities.

**agency.** The power to act. Students exercise agency in mathematics when they initiate discussions and actively engage in high-level thinking tasks. When students exercise agency, they reason, critique the reasoning of others, and engage in productive struggle.

**algorithm.** In mathematics, it is a series of steps or procedures that, when followed accurately, will produce a correct answer.

**big ideas.** Statements that encompass main concepts in mathematics that cross grade levels, such as place value.

**classroom discourse.** Conversation that occurs in a classroom. Can be teacher to student(s), student(s) to teacher, or student(s) to student(s).

**closed-ended questions.** Questions with only one correct answer.

**closure.** The final activity in a lesson with two purposes: (1) helps the teacher determine what students have learned and gives direction to next steps and (2) provides students the opportunity to reorganize and summarize the information from a lesson in a meaningful way.

**coherence.** Logical sequencing of mathematical ideas. Can be vertical, as in across the grades (e.g., K–2), or can be horizontal, as in across a grade level (e.g., first-grade lessons from September through December).

**common errors.** Mistakes made by students that occur frequently; usually these mistakes are anticipated by the teacher due to their frequency.

**computation.** Using an operation such as addition, subtraction, multiplication, or division to find an answer.

**conceptual understanding.** Comprehension of mathematical concepts, operations, and relationships.

**content standards.** See *standards*.

**decompose.** To break a number down into addends. A number may be decomposed in more than one way (e.g., 12 can be decomposed as $10 + 2$, $9 + 3$, and $5 + 5 + 2$).

**discourse.** See *classroom discourse*.

**distributed practice.** See *spaced practice*.

**district-wide curriculum.** A K–12 document outlining the curriculum for a school system.

**drill.** Repetitive exercises on a specific math skill or procedure.

**English Language Learner (ELL).** A person whose first language is not English but who is learning to speak English.

**essential question.** A question that unifies all of the lessons on a given topic to bring the coherence and purpose to a unit. Essential questions are purposefully linked to the big idea to frame student inquiry, promote critical thinking, and assist in learning transfer.

**exit task.** A task given at the end of a lesson or group of lessons that provides a sampling of student performance. An exit task is more in depth than an *exit slip.*

**exit ticket/exit slip.** A form of lesson closure where students answer a question related to the main idea of the lesson on a slip of paper. Teachers collect these slips of paper.

*formative assessment.* Also called *formative evaluation.* The ongoing collection of information about student learning as it is happening and the process of responding to that information by adapting instruction to improve learning.

*formative evaluation.* See *formative assessment.*

*habits of mind.* Ways of thinking about mathematics as mathematicians do (e.g., always choosing solution methods, asking questions, and having productive attitudes). These habits help us understand mathematics and solve problems, and they are linked to process standards. Habits of mind include (but are not limited to) perseverance in problem solving, comparing, finding patterns, and asking "what if…" questions.

*hands-on learning.* Learning that takes place while students are using manipulatives.

*high cognitive demand.* Characteristic of a problem or task that requires using higher-order thinking skills as defined by Bloom's Taxonomy. Also see *higher-order thinking skills.*

*higher-order thinking skills.* The more complex thinking skills as defined by Bloom's Taxonomy. Examples include predicting, creating, synthesizing, and analyzing.

*hinge question.* A classroom-based assessment technique where the teacher delivers a question at a pivotal point in a lesson. Student responses to the question determine the path the teacher takes on the next part of the lesson.

*horizontal coherence.* See *coherence.*

*hundred chart.* A table with 10 rows and 10 columns with one number per cell in numerical order from 1 to 100.

*identity.* How individuals know and see themselves, such as *student, teacher, good at sports,* and how others know and see us, such as *short, smart, shy.* Defined broadly, it is a concept that brings together all the interrelated elements that teachers and students bring to the classroom, including beliefs, attitudes, and emotions.

*Individualized Education Plan (IEP).* A roadmap for a particular student's learning. Usually written for students in a special education program, it includes goals and accommodations needed for the child to be successful.

*instructional decisions.* Decisions made that affect classroom teaching and learning.

*interleaving.* The practice of cycling back to a previous skill, concept, or big idea to help children build their understanding of that topic.

*interview.* A classroom-based assessment technique where the teacher has a brief talk with a student to collect more information on the student's thinking.

*learning community.* A group of teachers (usually at the same grade level)—and sometimes other professionals—who work together to plan lessons, discuss student concerns, and support one another's teaching.

*learning intention.* Statement of what a student is expected to learn from a lesson. Also known as the lesson goal. There are three types: mathematical, social, and language goals.

*learning progressions.* Specific sequence of mathematical knowledge and skills that students are expected to learn as they progress from kindergarten through high school and beyond.

*lesson format.* The manner in which students are organized for a lesson. Whole-group lessons and small-group lessons are two examples.

*lesson launch.* How the teacher introduces a lesson.

*manipulative.* Any concrete material that can be used by students to further their mathematical understanding. Examples include counters, blocks, coins, and fraction circles.

*math anxiety.* A feeling of stress, fear, or worry about one's ability to do mathematics, which may interfere with one's mathematical performance.

*math talk.* See *number talk.*

*mathematical discourse.* See *classroom discourse.*

*metacognitive.* Adjective for *metacognition,* the process of thinking about one's thinking. One type of metacognition includes knowing about using certain strategies for problem solving.

*misconception.* An incorrect understanding or belief about a mathematical topic or concept.

*multiple entry points.* The many different methods one can use to attack a problem. Methods can range from simple approaches to more complex approaches.

*number routine.* A mathematics activity that takes place on a regular basis (e.g., daily, every Friday, etc.).

*number talk.* Also known as *math talk.* A number routine that focuses on building student number sense through scaffolded problem-solving experiences where students verbalize and justify their solutions to one another and the teacher.

*numberless word problem.* A word problem with the numbers blocked out encouraging students to make sense of the problem before they work with the numbers.

*observation.* A classroom-based formative assessment technique where the teacher informally watches students and documents what is seen in order to inform instruction.

*one-to-one correspondence.* In general, it is a one-to-one relationship between two sets. It occurs when there are two sets and each element of the first set is paired with one and only one element of the second set. In counting, one set consists of the number words, and the other set consists of the objects being counted.

*open-ended questions.* Description for mathematical problems that have more than one acceptable answer and multiple solution strategies.

*pacing guide.* Grade-level document for district-wide implementation that determines the order of the standards to be taught and the amount of time to be spent on each topic. The level of specificity of these documents varies.

*practice.* Brief, engaging, and purposeful exercises, tasks, or experiences on the same idea spread out over time.

*precise use of vocabulary.* Using exact mathematical language as a strategy to build a shared understanding of important mathematical terms. Some common mathematics terms have nonmathematical meanings. Precise use of vocabulary refers to using the mathematical definition.

*prior knowledge.* Mathematical knowledge students know before they begin a topic or task.

*problem solving.* The process of finding a solution to a situation for which no immediate answer is available. What may be a problem for one student may not be a problem for another.

*procedural fluency.* The ability to carry out procedures/algorithms flexibly, accurately, efficiently, and appropriately.

*process standards.* See *standards.*

*productive struggle.* Students wrestle with ideas to make sense of mathematics; this phrase describes the effort involved in solving a problem when an immediate solution is not available.

*reflecting in action.* See *reflection.*

*reflecting on action.* See *reflection.*

*reflection.* The process of thinking about one's learning. For teachers there is *reflecting in action,* which occurs during teaching so that the teacher can monitor and adjust instruction as it occurs. *Reflecting on action* occurs when teacher looks back on a lesson and the students after instruction takes place.

*representations.* Any concrete, pictorial, or symbolic model that can stand for a mathematical idea.

*resources.* For a primary mathematics teacher, anything that can be used to assist in the design and implementation of lessons (e.g., textbooks, curriculum guides, manipulatives, and supplemental materials).

*rigor.* Results from active participation in rich mathematical problem-solving tasks. The two types of rigor are *content* and *instructional.* *Content rigor* results from a deep connection among the concepts and the breadth of supporting skills that students are expected to master. *Instructional rigor* is the continuous interaction between the instruction and students' reasoning about concepts, skills, and challenging tasks.

*scaffold.* Name for a variety of teaching strategies that support student learning; techniques that help students bridge from what they know to something new.

*Show Me.* A classroom-based assessment technique where the teacher asks students to demonstrate what they have learned. Students may use any materials such as manipulatives or drawings.

*spaced practice.* Also called *distributed practice.* A learning strategy where practice is broken up into a number of short sessions over a period of time.

*standard form.* The traditional way of writing numbers in the base-ten system. For example, one hundred twenty-five in standard form is 125.

*standards.* Concise, written descriptions of what students are expected to know and be able to do at a specific grade level, age, or stage of development. In mathematics, there are *content standards* (what student are expected to know) and *process standards* (how students are expected to do the mathematics). Process standards are closely linked to mathematical habits of mind. The *Standards for Mathematical Practice* define the processes for the *Common Core State Standards for Mathematics* (*CCSS-M*).

*Standards for Mathematical Practice.* See *standards*.

*strategy.* A plan for solving a problem. Some common problem-solving strategies in primary mathematics are counting down, drawing a picture, and using a model.

*subitizing.* The ability to immediately identify a quantity without counting.

*success criteria.* Defines what learning looks like when achieved.

*summative assessment.* Testing used to determine students' achievement levels at specific points in time, such as at the end of teaching units, semesters, and grade level.

*task.* A mathematical problem. Rich tasks or worthwhile tasks are problems with several characteristics, such as accessibility, authenticity, and being active with a focus on significant mathematics for the grade level.

*teaching experiments.* Research in education conducted through three components: modeling, teaching episodes, and individual or group interviews where student thinking is the focus of the experiment.

*textbook.* In mathematics, textbooks are one of the many types of resources teachers use; contents follow a logical teaching order and usually match the curriculum being taught.

*timed tests.* In mathematics, assessments to be completed within a specific period of time; often associated with basic fact practice.

*transfer.* One of the three main types of math lessons that prompt students to demonstrate their ability to use content knowledge and skill in a problem situation.

*unintended consequences.* Unforeseen outcomes from a purposeful action.

*unit plan.* Several coherent lessons on a given topic that flow logically from one another.

*unpack.* Using one's knowledge to extract the main ideas and knowledge embedded in the standard; to break down a standard into its main ideas.

*vertical coherence.* See *coherence*.

*whole group.* A type of classroom grouping where the entire class is instructed as one large group. This contrasts with small groups, where the whole class is divided into small groups of students for instruction.

*word problem.* Any mathematical exercise where significant background information on the problem is presented as text rather than in mathematical notation.

# References

Annenberg Learner Foundation. (2003). *Teaching math, Grades 3–5*. Retrieved from https://learner.org/courses/teachingmath/grades3_5/session_05/index.html

Bamberger, H. J., Oberdorf, C., Schultz-Ferrell, K., & Leinwand, S. (2011). *Math misconceptions, preK–Grade 5: From misunderstanding to deep understanding*. Portsmouth, NH: Heinemann.

Banse, H. W., Palacios, N. A. G., Merritt, E. G., & Rimm-Kaufman, S. (2016). 5 strategies for scaffolding math discourse with ELLs. *Teaching Children Mathematics, 23*(2), 100–108.

Barousa, M. (2017). Which one doesn't belong? Retrieved from http://wodb.ca

Boaler, J. (2012, July). Timed tests and the development of math anxiety. *Education Week*. Retrieved from www.edweek.org/ew/articles/2012/07/03/36boaler.h31.html

Boaler, J. (2015). *Mathematical mindsets: Unleashing students' potential through creative math, inspiring messages and innovative teaching*. San Francisco, CA: Jossey-Bass.

Boaler, J. (2017). Brains grow and change. Retrieved from www.youcubed.org/resources/many-ways-see-mathematics-video/

Boaler, J., & Staples, M. (2008). Creating mathematical futures through an equitable teaching approach: The case of Railside school. *Teacher College Record, 110*(3), 608–645.

Bransford, J. D., Brown, A., & Cocking, R. (1999). *How people learn: Mind, brain, experience, and school*. Washington, DC: National Research Council.

Braswell, J. S., Dion, G. S., Daane, M. C., & Jin, Y. (2005). *The nation's report card: Mathematics 2003* (NCES 2005–451). U.S. Department of Education, Institute of Education Sciences, National Center for Education Statistics. Washington, DC: U.S. Government Printing Office.

Bushart, B. (2017). Numberless word problems. Retrieved from https://bstockus.wordpress.com/numberless-word-problems/

Calmenson, S. (1991). *The principal's new clothes*. New York, NY: Scholastic.

Cavanaugh, R. A., Heward, W. L., & Donelson, F. (1996). Effects of response cards during lesson closure on the academic performance of secondary students in an earth science course. *Journal of Applied Behavior Analysis, 29*(3), 403–406.

Committee on Early Childhood Mathematics National Research Council. (2009). *Mathematics learning in early childhood: Paths toward excellence and equity*. Washington, DC: National Academies Press.

Constantino, P. M., & De Lorenzo, M. N. (2001). *Developing a professional teaching portfolio: A guide for success*. Boston: Allyn & Bacon.

Cooperrider, D. L., & Whitney, D. (2005). Appreciative inquiry: A positive revolution in change. In P. Holman & T. Devane (Eds.), *The change handbook* (pp. 245–263). Oakland, CA: Berrett-Koehler.

Danielson, C. (2016). Which one doesn't belong? Retrieved from http://wodb.ca

Danielson, L. M. (2008). Making reflective practice more concrete through reflective decision making. *The Educational Forum, 72*, 129–137.

Day, C. (1999). Researching teaching through reflective practice. In J. J. Loughran (Ed.), *Researching teaching: Methodologies and practices for understanding pedagogy* (pp. 215–232). London, UK: Falmer Press.

Dewey, J. (1933). *How we think: A restatement of the relation of reflective thinking to the educative process*. New York, NY: D.C. Heath.

Dewey, J. (1944). *Democracy in education*. New York, NY: Free Press. (Original work published 1916)

Dolezal, S. E., Welsh, L. M., Pressley, M., & Vincent, M. M. (2003). How nine third-grade teachers motivate student academic engagement. *The Elementary School Journal, 103*(3), 239–267.

Dougherty, B. J., Karp, K., Caldwell, J., & Kobett, B. (2014). *Putting essential understanding of addition and subtraction into practice, pre-K–2*, Reston. VA: NCTM.

Erickson, K., Drevets, W., & Schulkin, J. (2003). Glucocorticoid regulation of diverse cognitive functions in normal and pathological emotional states. *Neuroscience & Biobehavioral Reviews, 27*(3), 233–246.

Farah, M. J., Shera, D. M., Savage, J. H., Betancourt, L., Giannetta, J. M., Brodsky, N. L., Malmud, E. K., & Hurt, H. (2006). Childhood poverty: Specific associations with neurocognitive development. *Brain Research, 1110*(1), 166–174.

Fennell, F. (2006, December). Go ahead! Teach to the test! *NCTM News Bulletin*. Retrieved from www.nctm.org/News-and-Calendar/Messages-from-the-President/Archive/Skip-Fennell/Go-Ahead,-Teach-to-the-Test!/

Fennell, F., Kobett, B. M., & Wray, J. A. (2017). *The formative 5: Everyday assessment techniques for every math classroom.* Thousand Oaks, CA: Corwin.

Fletcher, G. (2017). 3-act lessons. Retrieved from https://gfletchy.com/3-act-lessons/

Ganske, K. (2017). Lesson closure: An important piece of the student learning puzzle. *The Reading Teacher, 71*(1), 95–100.

Gelman, R., & Lucariello, J. (2002). Role of learning in cognitive development. In H. Pashler (Series Ed.) & C. R. Gallistel (Vol. Ed.), *Stevens' handbook of experimental psychology: Vol. 3. Learning, motivation, and emotion.* (3rd ed., pp. 395–443). New York, NY: John Wiley.

Grootenboer, P., Lowrie, T., & Smith, T. (2006). Researching identity in mathematics education: The lay of the land. In P. Grootenboer, R. Zevenbergen, & M. Chinnappan (Eds.), *Identities, cultures and learning spaces* (Proceedings of the 29th annual conference of Mathematics Education Research Group of Australasia, Vol. 2, pp. 612–615). Canberra, Australia: MERGA.

Hammond, S. (1998). *The thin book of appreciative inquiry.* Plano, TX: Thin Book Publishing.

Harris, A. S., Bruster, B., Peterson, B., & Shutt, T. (2010). *Examining and facilitating reflection to improve professional practice.* Lanham, MD: Rowman & Littlefield Publishers.

Harvard Center for the Developing Child. (2007). The impact of poverty on early development. Retrieved from http://46y5eh11fhgw3ve3ytpwxt9r.wpengine.netdna-cdn.com/wp-content/uploads/2015/05/inbrief-adversity-1.pdf

Hattie, J., (2009). *Visible learning: A synthesis of over 800 meta-analyses relating to achievement.* New York, NY: Routledge.

Hattie, J., Fisher, D., Frey, N., Gojak, L. M., Moore, S. D., & Mellman, W. (2016). *Visible learning for mathematics, Grades K–12: What works best to optimize student learning.* Thousand Oaks, CA: Corwin.

Hattie, J., & Yates, G. C. (2013). *Visible learning and the science of how we learn.* New York, NY: Routledge.

Herbel-Eisenmann, B. (2010). Beyond tacit language choice to purposeful discourse practices. In L. Knott (Ed.), *The role of mathematics discourse in producing leaders of discourse* (pp. 451–485). Charlotte, NC: Information Age Publishing.

Herbel-Eisenmann, B., & Breyfogle, M. (2005). Questioning our patterns of questioning. *Mathematics Teaching in the Middle School, 10*(9), 484–489.

Hiebert, J. (1999). Relationships between research and the NCTM standards. *Journal for Research in Mathematics Education, 30*(1), 3–19.

Hiebert, J., & Morris, A. (2012). Teaching, rather than teachers, as a path toward improving classroom instruction. *Journal of Teacher Education, 63*(2), 92–102.

Huinker, D., & Bill, V. (2017). *Taking action: Implementing effective mathematics teaching practices in K–Grade 5.* Reston, VA: NCTM.

Hull, T., Harbin Miles, R., & Balka, D. S. (2014). *Realizing rigor in the mathematics classroom.* Thousand Oaks, CA: Corwin.

Illustrative Mathematics. (2017). Content standards. Retrieved from www.illustrativemathematics.org/content-standards.

Inside Mathematics. (2017). Problem of the month. Retrieved from www.insidemathematics.org/problems-of-the-month/download-problems-of-the-month

Institute of Educational Sciences (IES). (2009). Assisting students struggling with mathematics: Response to intervention (RtI) for elementary and middle schools. Retrieved from https://ies.ed.gov/ncee/wwc/PracticeGuide/2

Isaacs, A. C., & Carroll, W. M. (1999). Strategies for basic-facts instruction. *Teaching Children Mathematics, 5*(9), 508–515.

Jensen, L. (2001). Planning lessons. In M. Celce-Murcia (Ed.), *Teaching English as a second or foreign language* (pp. 403–408). Boston, MA: Heinle & Heinle.

Kaplinsky, R. (2017). Lessons. Retrieved from http://robertkaplinsky.com/lessons/

Kapur, M. (2010). Productive failure in mathematical problem solving. *Instructional Science*, 38(6), 523–550.

Karp, K. S., Bush, S. B., & Dougherty, B. J. (2014). 13 rules that expire. *Teaching Children Mathematics*, 21(1), 18–25.

Kazemi, E., & Hintz, A. (2014). *Intentional talk: How to structure and lead productive mathematical discussions*. Portland, ME: Stenhouse Publishers.

Lager, C. A. (2006). Types of mathematics-language reading interactions that unnecessarily hinder algebra learning and assessment. *Reading Psychology*, 27(2–3), 165–204.

Lappan, L., & Briars, D. (1995). How should mathematics be taught? In I. M. Carl (Ed.), *75 years of progress: Prospects for school mathematics* (pp. 131–156). Reston, VA: NCTM.

Larson, J. (2002). Packaging process: Consequences of commodified pedagogy on students' participation in literacy events. *Journal of Early Childhood Literacy*, 2(1), 65–95.

Leinwand, S. (2009). *Accessible mathematics: 10 instructional shifts that raise student achievement*. Portsmouth, NH: Heinemann.

Leinwand, S. (2014, July). *Math misconceptions*. Paper presented at the Summer Utah Academy, Salt Lake City, UT.

Lucariello, J. (2012). How my students think: Diagnosing student thinking. Retrieved from www.apa.org/education/k12/student-thinking.aspx

Lupien, S. J., King, S., Meaney, M. J., & McEwen, B. S. (2001). Can poverty get under your skin? Basal cortisol levels and cognitive function in children from low and high socioeconomic status. *Development and Psychopathology*, 13(3), 653–676.

Markworth, K., McCool, J., & Kosiak, J. (2015). *Problem solving in all seasons*. Reston, VA: NCTM.

Math Forum. (2015). Beginning to problem solve with "I notice, I wonder." Retrieved from http://mathforum.org/pow/noticewonder/intro.pdf

Math Forum. (2017). Primary problems of the week. Retrieved from http://mathforum.org/library/problems/primary.html

Math Learning Center. (2017). Free math apps. Retrieved from www.mathlearningcenter.org/resources/apps

Math Pickle. (2017). Puzzles, games and mini-competitions organized by grade. Retrieved from http://mathpickle.com/organized-by-grade/

Mohyuddin, R. G., & Khalil, U. (2016). Misconceptions of students in learning mathematics at primary level. *Bulletin of Education and Research*, 38(1), 133–162.

Morris, A., & Hiebert, J. (2017). Effects of teacher preparation courses: Do graduates use what they learned to plan mathematics lessons? *American Educational Research Journal*, 54(3), 524–567.

Moyer, P. S., Bolyard, J. J., & Spikell, M. A. (2002). What are virtual manipulatives? *Teaching Children Mathematics*, 8(6), 372–377.

Moyer-Packenham, P. S., & Milewicz, E. (2002). Learning to question: Categories of questioning used by preservice teachers during diagnostic mathematics interviews. *Journal of Mathematics Teacher Education*, 5(4), 293–315.

National Center for Children in Poverty. (2017). Child poverty. Retrieved from www.nccp.org/topics/childpoverty.html

National Council of Supervisors of Mathematics. (2009, Fall). Improving student achievement in mathematics by addressing the needs of English language learners. *NSCM Student Achievement Series*, (6).

National Council of Teachers of English (NCTE). (2008). English language learners: A policy research brief produced by the National Council of Teachers of English. Retrieved from www.ncte.org/library/NCTEFiles/Resources/PolicyResearch/ELLResearchBrief.pdf

National Council of Teachers of Mathematics (NCTM). (1991). *Professional standards for teaching mathematics*. Reston, VA: Author.

National Council of Teachers of Mathematics (NCTM). (2000). *Principles and standards for school mathematics*. Reston, VA: Author.

National Council of Teachers of Mathematics (NCTM). (2014a). Access and equity in mathematics education. Retrieved from www.nctm.org/uploadedFiles/Standards_and_Positions/Position_Statements/Access_and_Equity.pdf

National Council of Teachers of Mathematics (NCTM). (2014b). *Principles to actions: Ensuring mathematical success for all*. Reston, VA: Author.

National Council of Teachers of Mathematics (NCTM). (2014c). Procedural fluency in mathematics: A position of the National Council of Teachers of Mathematics. Retrieved from http://www.nctm.org/uploadedFiles/Standards_and_Positions/Position_Statements/Procedural%20Fluency.pdf

National Council of Teachers of Mathematics (NCTM). (2017). *Taking action: Implementing effective teaching practices*. Reston, VA: Author.

National Governors Association Center for Best Practices & Council of Chief State School Officers. (2010). *Common core state standards for mathematics*. Washington, DC: Author.

National Institute of Child Health and Human Development Early Child Care Research Network. (2005). Duration and developmental timing of poverty and children's cognitive and social development from birth through third grade. *Child Development*, 4(76), 795–810.

National Library of Virtual Manipulatives. (2017). All topics, grades pre-k–2. Retrieved from http://nlvm.usu.edu/en/nav/grade_g_1.html

National Research Council. (2001). *Adding it up: Helping children learn mathematics* (J. Kilpatrick, J. Swafford, & B. Findell, Eds.). Washington, DC: National Academies Press.

Nrich. (2011). Primary curriculum. Retrieved from http://nrich.maths.org/12632

Open Middle. (2017). Open middle: Challenging problems worth solving [Kindergarten, Grade 1, Grade 2]. Retrieved from http://www.openmiddle.com

Panasuk, R., Stone, W., & Todd, J. (2002). Lesson planning strategy for effective mathematics teaching. *Education*, 122(4), 808–829.

Parrish, S. (2011). Number talks build numerical reasoning. *Teaching Children Mathematics*, 18(3), 198–206.

Piaget, J. (1964). Part I: Cognitive development in children: Piaget development and learning. *Journal of Research in Science Teaching*, 2(3), 176–186.

Piaget, J., & Inhelder, B. (1969). *The psychology of the child*. New York, NY: Basic Books.

Pollock, J. E. (2007). *Improving student learning one teacher at a time*. Alexandria, VA: Association for Supervision and Curriculum Development.

Powell, A. (2004). The diversity backlash and the mathematical agency of students of color. In M. J. Høines & A. B. Fuglestad (Eds.), *Proceedings of the twenty-eighth conference of the International Group for the Psychology of Mathematics Education* (Vol. 1, pp. 37–54). Bergen, Norway: Bergen University.

Protheroe, N. (2007). What does good math instruction look like? *Principal*, 87(1), 51–54.

Raposo, J., & Stone, J. (1972). One of these things is not like the other [Song lyrics]. Retrieved from www.metrolyrics.com/one-of-these-things-is-not-like-the-others-lyrics-sesame-street.html

Rasmussen, C., Yackel, E., & King, K. (2003). Social and sociomathematical norms in the mathematics classroom. In R. Charles (Ed.), *Teaching mathematics through problem solving: It's about learning mathematics* (pp. 143–154). Reston, VA: NCTM.

Ray-Reik, M. (2013). *Powerful problem solving: Activities for sense making with the mathematical practices*. Portsmouth, NH: Heinemann.

Reimer, K., & Moyer, P. S. (2005). Third-graders learn about fractions using virtual manipulatives: A classroom study. *Journal of Computers in Mathematics and Science Teaching*, 24(1), 5–10.

Resnick, L. B. (1982). Syntax and semantics in learning to subtract. In T. Carpenter, J. Moser, & T. A. Romberg (Eds.), *Addition and subtraction: A cognitive perspective* (pp. 136–156). Hillsdale, NJ: Lawrence Erlbaum.

Resnick, L. B. (1983). A developmental theory of number understanding. In H. P. Ginsburg (Ed.), *The development of mathematical thinking* (pp. 109–151). New York, NY: Academic Press.

Resnick, L. B., & Omanson, S. F. (1987). Learning to understand arithmetic. In R. Glaser (Ed.), *Advances in instructional psychology* (Vol. 3, pp. 41–95). Hillsdale, NJ: Lawrence Erlbaum.

Ritchhart, R., Church, M., & Morrison, K. (2011). *Making thinking visible: How to promote engagement, understanding, and independence for all learners*. New York, NY: John Wiley.

Rodgers, C. (2002). Defining reflection: Another look at John Dewey and reflective thinking. *Teachers College Record*, 104(4), 842–866.

Rohrer, D. (2012). Interleaving helps students distinguish among similar concepts. *Educational Psychology Review, 24,* 355–367.

Rolli, J. H. (2014). *Just one more.* New York, NY: Viking Books for Young Readers.

Schmidt, W. H., Wang, H. C., & McKnight, C. (2005). Curriculum coherence: An examination of US mathematics and science content standards from an international perspective. *Journal of Curriculum Studies, 37*(5), 525–559.

Schön, D. A. (1983). *The reflective practitioner: How professionals think in action.* New York, NY: Basic Books.

Schrock, C., Norris, K., Pugalee, D., Seitz, R., & Hollingshead, F. (2013). *Great tasks for mathematics, K–5.* Denver, CO: National Council of Supervisors of Mathematics.

Sealander, K. A., Johnson, G. R., Lockwood, A. B., & Medina, C. M. (2012). Concrete-semiconcrete-abstract (CSA) instruction: A decision rule for improving instructional efficacy. *Assessment for Effective Intervention, 30,* 53–65.

Smith, M. S., & Stein, M. K. (1998). Mathematical tasks as a framework for reflection: From research to practice. *Mathematics Teaching in the Middle School, 3*(4), 268–275.

Smith, M. S., & Stein, M. K. (2011). *Five practices for orchestrating productive mathematics discussions.* Reston, VA: NCTM.

Smyth, J. (1992). Teachers' work and the politics of reflection. *American Educational Research Journal, 29*(2), 267–300.

Sousa, D. (2014). *How the brain learns mathematics.* Thousand Oaks, CA: Corwin.

Steen, K., Brooks, D., & Lyon, T. (2006). The impact of virtual manipulatives on first-grade geometry instruction and learning. *Journal of Computers in Mathematics and Science Teaching, 25*(4), 373–391.

Stein, M. K., Engle, R. A., Smith, M. S., & Hughes, E. K. (2008). Orchestrating productive mathematical discussions: Five practices for helping teachers move beyond show and tell. *Mathematical Thinking and Learning, 10*(4), 313–340.

Trocki, A., Taylor, C., Starling, T., Sztajn, P., & Heck, D. (2015). Launching a discourse-rich mathematics lesson. *Teaching Children Mathematics, 21*(5), 276–281.

Troiano, J. (2001). *Spookley the square pumpkin.* Wilton, CT: Holiday Hill Enterprises, LLC.

Tschannen-Moran, B., & Tschannen-Moran, M. (2010). *Evocative coaching: Transforming schools one conversation at a time.* Hoboken, NJ: John Wiley.

Van de Walle, J., Karp, K., & Bay-Williams, J. (2016). *Elementary and middle school mathematics: Teaching developmentally.* New York, NY: Pearson.

Vogler, K. E. (2008, Summer). Asking good questions. *Educational Leadership, 65*(9). Retrieved from www.ascd.org/publications/educational-leadership/summer08/vol65/num09/Asking-Good-Questions.aspx

Vygotsky, L. S. (1962). *Thought and language.* Cambridge, MA: MIT Press.

Vygotsky, L. S. (1978). *Mind in society: The development of higher mental processes* (M. Cole, V. John-Steiner, S. Scribner, & E. Souberman, Eds. & Trans.). Cambridge, MA: Harvard University Press.

Wagganer, E. L. (2015). Creating math talk communities. *Teaching Children Mathematics, 22*(4), 248–254.

Walsh, J. A., & Sattes, B. D. (2005). *Quality questioning: Research-based practice to engage every learner.* Thousand Oaks, CA: Corwin.

Walshaw, M., & Anthony, G. (2008). The role of pedagogy in classroom discourse: A review of recent research into mathematics. *Review of Educational Research, 78,* 516–551.

Wenmoth, D. (2014). Ten trends 2014: Agency [Video file]. Retrieved from https://vimeo.com/85218303

Wiliam, D. (2011). *Embedded formative assessment.* Bloomington, IN: Solution Tree Press.

Wiliam, D., & Thompson, M. (2008). Integrating assessment with instruction: What will it take to make it work? In C. A. Dwyer (Ed.), *The future of assessment: Shaping teaching and learning* (pp. 53–82). Mahwah, NJ: Lawrence Erlbaum.

Wood, T., Williams, G., & McNeal, B. (2006). Children's mathematical thinking in different classroom cultures. *Journal for Research in Mathematics Education, 37,* 222–255.

Yackel, E., & Cobb, P. (1996). Sociomathematical norms, argumentation, and autonomy in mathematics. *Journal for Research in Mathematics Education, 27,* 458–477.

Young, C. B., Wu, S. S., & Menon, V. (2012). The neurodevelopmental basis of math anxiety. *Psychological Science, 23*(5), 492–501.

# Index

Rigor, 16
    active student participation and, 16, 17
    content rigor, 16
    instructional rigor, 16
    one-to-one correspondence lesson and, 16–17, 16–17 (figure)
    reasoning skills and, 17
    *See also* Lesson-planning process
Rodgers, C., 172
Rolli, J. H., 118

Scaffolded learning, 3, 8, 8 (figures), 11, 12 (figure), 37, 147, 152
Schön, D. A., 172
Second grade:
    big ideas in, 27, 34
    compose/decompose numbers lesson and, 54, 54–57 (figure)
    content standards for, 34
    essential questions for, 34, 62 (figure)
    formative assessment techniques and, 124
    interview technique and, 124
    learning intentions for, 39–40, 39 (figure), 46
    lesson plan examples and, 34, 46, 66, 76, 90, 100, 110, 124, 142, 158–159, 169, 188–191
    manipulatives, selection of, 90
    mathematical discourse, facilitation of, 158–159
    misconceptions and, 100
    numeric relationship, base-ten number system and, 82 (figure)
    pair lesson format and, 110
    place value concept and, 100
    process standards for, 34
    purpose of lessons and, 66
    representations and, 82 (figure), 90
    See/Think/Wonder lesson launch and, 142
    success criteria for, 46
    task selection and, 76
    text message activity, lesson closure and, 169
    three-digit numbers lesson and, 54, 54–57 (figure), 100
    transfer tasks for, 62 (figure)
    *See also* Big ideas; Common Core State Standards for Mathematics (CCSS-M); Essential questions; First grade; Kindergarten; Lesson plan examples; Standards; *Standards for Mathematical Practice* (SMPs)
See/Think/Wonder (STW) lesson launch, 129–131, 130–131 (figures)
Sentence stems, 146
Show Me technique, 95, 112, 118, 123
Small-group instruction, 103 (figure), 104, 105–107, 106 (figures), 112, 114
Smith, M. S., 69
Snap cubes, 84, 88
Social learning intentions, 43
    first-grade curriculum and, 39–40, 39 (figure), 45
    kindergarten curriculum and, 44
    second-grade curriculum and, 39–40, 39 (figure), 46

    *See also* Learning intentions; Success criteria
Social norms, 6
Socioeconomic status, 9–10
Spaced practice, 134
    *See also* Distributed practice; Learning process; Practice opportunities
Standard number form, 134
Standards, 26–27
    classroom discourse technique and, 29–30
    content standards, 22, 27, 29–30, 194
    habits of mind and, 29
    implementation, flexibility in, 27
    pacing guides and, 30
    process standards, 22, 27, 29, 194
    standards resources and, 197
    unit coherence, building of, 31, 31 (figure)
    *See also* Big ideas; Common Core State Standards for Mathematics (CCSS-M); Content standards; Essential questions; First grade; Kindergarten; Learning intentions; Process standards; Second grade; *Standards for Mathematical Practice* (SMPs); Success criteria
*Standards for Mathematical Practice* (SMPs), 29
    enumeration of, 29
    habits of mind and, 29
    instructional decisions, learning intentions/success criteria and, 46
    language learning intentions and, 38, 38 (figure)
    lesson launch and, 129
    mathematics learning intentions and, 46
    social learning intentions and, 39–40, 39 (figures)
    *See also* Common Core State Standards for Mathematics (CCSS-M); Standards
Steen, K., 82
Stein, M. K., 69
Strategic competence, 49
Structure. *See* Lesson format/structure
Student needs, 2
    agency and, 5–6
    engaged learners and, 5, 6, 16, 17, 20, 37
    equitable learning opportunities and, 5
    high-quality math instruction, access to, 5
    identity and, 5–6
    knowing the students, importance of, 2–3, 12
    knowledge gaps, instructional gaps and, 5
    learning needs, recognition of, 3, 10, 12
    learning profile of strengths/needs and, 10, 11 (figure)
    lesson-planning process and, 3, 103
    personal/cultural preferences and, 3
    prior mathematics knowledge, engagement of, 4
    representation opportunities, use of, 11, 12 (figure)
    scaffolded learning and, 3, 8, 8 (figure), 11, 12 (figure)
    social-emotional needs and, 12
    social nature of learning and, 5–6
    socioeconomic status disadvantage, instructional strategies and, 9–10
    student-centered learning and, 6

student preparation, varying levels of, 3

*See also* English Language Learners (ELLs); Instructional decisions; Learning process; Lesson format/structure; Lesson plan examples; Lesson-planning process; Lesson-planning templates; Mathematics lessons; Misconceptions

Subitizing, 98, 135, 136, 139, 179

Success criteria, 22, 36, 41, 194

clarity in, 41

components of, 41

deep learning, encouragement of, 41

definition of, 41

first-grade curriculum and, 45

formative assessment and, 113

kindergarten curriculum and, 44

learning intentions, linkage with, 41

lesson plan construction template and, 47

second-grade curriculum and, 46

sharing success criteria with students and, 42

student-friendly language, use of, 41

unit coherence, building of, 43, 43 (figure)

*See also* Instructional decisions; Learning intentions; Learning process; Student needs

Summative assessment, 20, 113

*See also* Assessment; Formative assessment

*Taking Action: Implementing Effective Teaching Practices,* 147

Talk. *See* Classroom discourse; Discourse; Mathematical communication; Number talk lesson launch

Task selection, 68

adaptation process and, 72–73, 72–73 (figures)

first-grade curriculum and, 75

higher-order thinking skills and, 69

kindergarten curriculum and, 74

lesson plan construction template and, 77

multiple entry points and, 70, 72

second-grade curriculum and, 76

standards, lesson seeds and, 68, 68 (figures)

tasks, importance of, 69

unit coherence, building of, 73

worthwhile tasks, characteristics of, 69–71, 71 (figure)

worthwhile tasks, sources of, 73, 197–198

*See also* Lesson launch; Lesson-planning process; Tasks

Tasks, 194

active tasks and, 70, 71 (figure)

agency and, 6

authentic/interesting tasks and, 70, 71 (figure)

concentration, difficulties in, 9

conceptual learning tasks and, 20

equitable tasks and, 70, 71 (figure)

exit tasks and, 95, 119–121, 120 (figures)

grade-level significance of, 69, 71 (figure)

high cognitive demand tasks and, 69, 70, 71 (figure)

importance of, 69

learning intentions and, 20

low threshold/high ceiling tasks and, 70

multiple entry points and, 20, 61, 70, 72

problem-solving tasks, productive struggle and, 70, 71 (figure)

process standards-focused tasks and, 70, 71 (figure)

rich tasks and, 69, 71 (figure)

safe learning environment and, 6

transfer tasks and, 20, 61

unit-end assessment and, 20

worthwhile tasks, characteristics of, 69–71, 71 (figure)

*See also* Lesson-planning process; Lesson-planning templates; Task selection

Teaching experiments, 175

Teaching practices. *See* Big ideas; Essential questions; Exemplary Teaching Practice; Instructional decisions; Learning intentions; Learning process; Lesson facilitation planning; Lesson-planning process; Lesson-planning templates; Purpose of lessons; Reflective practice; Standards; Success criteria

Templates. *See* Lesson-planning templates

Textbook lessons, 86

*See also* Resources

Think Aloud technique, 146

"13 Rules That Expire," 94

Thompson, M., 113

Timed tests, 59

Transfer lessons, 20, 61, 194

definition of, 61

essential questions, foundational role of, 61, 61–62 (figures)

first-grade essential questions and, 62 (figure)

kindergarten essential questions and, 62 (figure)

metacognitive processes and, 20

multiple entry points and, 20, 61

procedural fluency and, 19

proficiency strands and, 49

second-grade essential questions and, 62 (figure)

transfer tasks, definition/description of, 61, 62 (figure)

*See also* Conceptual understanding lessons; Lesson-planning process; Lesson-planning templates; Mathematics lessons; Procedural fluency lessons; Purpose of lessons

Troiano, J., 93

Understanding. *See* Conceptual understanding; Procedural fluency

Unintended consequences of teaching, 93, 94

Unit coherence:

big ideas/essential questions/standards and, 31, 31 (figure)

formative assessment and, 121

learning intentions/success criteria and, 43, 43 (figure)

lesson closure activities and, 166

lesson facilitation planning and, 153

lesson format/structure and, 107

lesson launch protocols and, 138

misconceptions and, 97, 97 (figure)

# About the Authors

**Beth McCord Kobett, EdD,** is an associate professor in the School of Education at Stevenson University, where she works with preservice teachers and leads professional learning efforts in mathematics education both regionally and nationally. She is also the lead consultant for the Elementary Mathematics and Specialist and Teacher Leadership Project. She is a former classroom teacher, elementary mathematics specialist, adjunct professor, and university supervisor. She is the current president of the Association of Maryland Mathematics Teacher Educators (AMMTE) and former chair of the Professional Development Services Committee of the National Council of Teachers of Mathematics (NCTM). Dr. Kobett is a recipient of the Mathematics Educator of the Year Award from the Maryland Council of Teachers of Mathematics (MCTM). She has also received Stevenson University's Excellence in Teaching Award as both an adjunct and full-time member of the Stevenson faculty.

**Ruth Harbin Miles** coaches rural, suburban, and inner-city school mathematics teachers. Her professional experience includes coordinating the K–12 Mathematics Teaching and Learning Program for the Olathe, Kansas, public schools for more than 25 years, teaching mathematics methods courses at Virginia's Mary Baldwin University, and serving on the Board of Directors for the National Council of Supervisors of Mathematics, The National Council of Teachers of Mathematics, and the Kansas Association of Teachers of Mathematics. Ruth is a coauthor of 37 books, including 11 Corwin publications. As an International Fellow with the Charles A. Dana Center, Ruth works with classroom teachers in Department of Defense Schools, helping them implement College and Career Ready Standards. Developing teachers' content knowledge and strategies for engaging students to achieve high standards in mathematics is Ruth's specialty.

**Lois A. Williams, EdD,** has worked in mathematics education (K–Algebra I) teaching, supervising, coaching, and doing international consulting for more than 35 years. She is a retired mathematics specialist for the Virginia Department of Education. Currently, Lois is an adjunct professor at Mary Baldwin University and The College of William and Mary. She is an International Fellow with the Charles A. Dana Center helping teachers in Department of Defense Schools implement College and Career Ready Standards. She is a recipient of a Fulbright Teacher Exchange and honored as a Virginia Middle School Mathematics Teacher of the Year.

# ALL students should have the opportunity to be successful in math!

Trusted experts in math education such as Linda M. Gojak, Ruth Harbin Miles, John SanGiovanni, Francis (Skip) Fennell, and many more offer clear and practical guidance to help students move from surface to deep mathematical understanding, from procedural to conceptual learning, and from rote memorization to true comprehension. Through books, videos, consulting, and online tools, we offer a truly blended learning experience that helps you demystify math for students.

Our forward-thinking and practical offerings help you enable all students to realize the power and beauty of math and its connection to everything they do.

## Your whole-school solution to mathematics standards

### When it comes to math, standards-aligned is achievement-aligned...

**Linda M. Gojak and Ruth Harbin Miles**
Grades K–2
ISBN: 978-1-4833-8156-5

**Linda M. Gojak and Ruth Harbin Miles**
Grades 3–5
ISBN: 978-1-4833-8160-2

**Ruth Harbin Miles and Lois A. Williams**
Grades 6–8
ISBN: 978-1-5063-3219-2

**Frederick L. Dillon, W. Gary Martin, Basil M. Conway IV, and Marilyn E. Strutchens**
High School
ISBN: 978-1-5063-3226-0

### New series for states with state-specific mathematics standards

Grades K–2, ISBN: 978-1-5063-8223-4

Grades 3–5, ISBN: 978-1-5063-8224-1

Grades 6–8, ISBN: 978-1-5063-8225-8

High School, ISBN: 978-1-5443-1740-3

## www.corwin.com/math

# Supporting Teachers, Empowering Learners

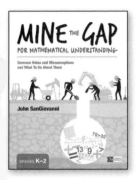 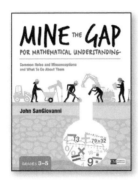 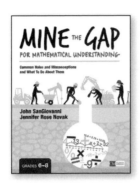

**See what's going on in your students' minds, plus get access to hundreds of rich tasks to use in instruction or assessment**

**John SanGiovanni, Jennifer Rose Novak**

Grades K–2, ISBN: 978-1-5063-3768-5
Grades 3–5, ISBN: 978-1-5063-3767-8
Grades 6–8, ISBN: 978-1-5063-7982-1

**The what, when, and how of teaching practices that evidence shows work best for student learning in mathematics**

**John Hattie, Douglas Fisher, Nancy Frey, Linda M. Gojak, Sara Delano Moore, William Mellman**

Grades K–12, ISBN: 978-1-5063-6294-6

**Move the needle on math instruction with these 5 assessment techniques**

**Francis (Skip) Fennell, Beth McCord Kobett, Jonathan A. Wray**

Grades K–8, ISBN: 978-1-5063-3750-0

**Differentiation that shifts your instruction and boosts ALL student learning**

**Nanci N. Smith**

Grades K–5, ISBN: 978-1-5063-4073-9
Grades 6–12, ISBN: 978-1-5063-4074-6

**Everything you need to promote mathematical thinking and learning**

**Page Keeley, Cheryl Rose Tobey**

Grades K–12
Volume 1, ISBN: 978-1-4129-6812-6
Volume 2, ISBN: 978-1-5063-1139-5

Corwin educator discount
★★★
**20% OFF**
**EVERY DAY!**
★★★

CM CORWIN MATHEMATICS

N17C43

# CORWIN
A SAGE Publishing Company

**Helping educators make the greatest impact**

**CORWIN HAS ONE MISSION:** to enhance education through intentional professional learning.

We build long-term relationships with our authors, educators, clients, and associations who partner with us to develop and continuously improve the best evidence-based practices that establish and support lifelong learning.

NATIONAL COUNCIL OF TEACHERS OF MATHEMATICS

The National Council of Teachers of Mathematics supports and advocates for the highest-quality mathematics teaching and learning for each and every student.